West Indian Business History

West Indian Business History

Enterprise and Entrepreneurship

EDITED BY

B. W. Higman and Kathleen E. A. Monteith

UNIVERSITY OF THE WEST INDIES PRESS
Jamaica • Barbados • Trinidad and Tobago

University of the West Indies Press
7A Gibraltar Hall Road   Mona
Kingston 7   Jamaica
www.uwipress.com

© 2010 by B.W. Higman and Kathleen E.A. Monteith

All rights reserved. Published 2010

CATALOGUING-IN-PUBLICATION DATA

West Indian business history: enterprise and entrepreneurship /
edited by B.W. Higman and Kathleen E.A. Monteith.

p. cm.

Includes bibliographical references.

ISBN 978-976-640-240-2

1. Business – Caribbean, English-speaking – History. 2. Business enterprises – Caribbean, English-speaking – History. 3. Entrepreneurship – Caribbean, English-speaking – History. 4. Caribbean, English-speaking – Economic conditions. I. Higman, B.W., 1943–. II. Monteith, Kathleen E.A.

HC151.W487 2010   338.9

Cover illustration: Cargo vessels at piers 1–3, Kingston Harbour, Jamaica, 1963. Courtesy of the National Library of Jamaica.

Book and cover design by Robert Harris.
Set in Adobe Garamond 11/14.5 x 27
Printed in the United States of America.

Contents

Preface and Acknowledgements / *vii*

1   West Indian Business History: Scale and Scope / *1*
B.W. HIGMAN and KATHLEEN E.A. MONTEITH

SECTION 1   MERCHANTS, PRIVATEERS AND PLANTERS

2   "A Frugal, Prudential and Hopeful Trade": Privateering in Jamaica, 1655–1689 / *11*
NUALA ZAHEDIEH

3   Planters and Merchants: The Oliver Family of Antigua and London 1716–1784 / *42*
RICHARD B. SHERIDAN

4   Incalculability as a Feature of Sugar Production during the Eighteenth Century / *55*
DOUGLAS HALL

5   Women in the Trinidad Cocoa Industry, 1870–1945 / *73*
KATHLEEN PHILLIPS LEWIS

Section 2 Bankers and Financiers

6 Patterns of Investment and Sources of Credit in the
British West Indian Sugar Industry, 1838–1897 / *101*
RICHARD A. LOBDELL

7 Financing Agriculture and Trade:
Barclays Bank (DCO) in the West Indies, 1926–1945 / *125*
KATHLEEN E.A. MONTEITH

8 Black Economic Empowerment in Barbados, 1937–1970:
The Role of the Non-Bank Financial Intermediaries / *151*
AVISTON DOWNES

Section 3 Traders, Transporters and Retailers

9 Joseph Rachell and Rachael Pringle-Polgreen:
Petty Entrepreneurs / *179*
JEROME S. HANDLER

10 The Economic Role of the Chinese in Jamaica:
The Grocery Retail Trade / *193*
JACQUELINE LEVY

11 The Rise of Black Businesses in Barbados, 1900–1966 / *214*
HENDERSON CARTER

Suggested further readings / *225*

Index / *231*

Preface and Acknowledgements

The study of business history as a distinct discipline is well established in many places but relatively neglected in the West Indies. *West Indian Business History: Enterprise and Entrepreneurship* has as its objective that of locating West Indian business history within the scope of Caribbean/Atlantic world economic history and placing it within the broader context of business history. As well as providing the foundation text for courses in West Indian business history, it is expected that the volume will be valued by students of other areas of Caribbean history, wherever they may be enrolled, and also by Caribbean business studies students.

The editors and publisher of this volume are grateful to Taylor and Francis Group, United Kingdom; the University of California Press, United States; the Departments of History, University of the West Indies; the Sir Arthur Lewis Institute of Social and Economic Studies, University of the West Indies, Mona, Jamaica; the Jamaica Historical Society; Sharon Levy-Callen; Peter and David Hall; Audrey Sheridan; and the authors who gave their kind permission for the reproduction of their essays.

CHAPTER I

West Indian Business History
Scale and Scope

B.W. HIGMAN AND KATHLEEN E.A. MONTEITH

Business enterprise has played a central role in the economic, social and political history of the modern West Indies. It constitutes one of the most important mechanisms connecting the territories to the wider world. However, in spite of its centrality in the experience of the region, the history of business has been relatively neglected. Monographs have been published on the histories of particular enterprises, including plantations, merchant houses, banks and manufacturing industries, but these have generally been located within the broader stream of economic and social history rather within the conceptual frame of business history. Works in this tradition have an uneasy relationship with histories commissioned by companies and corporations, most of the latter designed to celebrate anniversaries and achievements.

As a systematic scholarly pursuit, business history had its origins not in academic history but rather in the business schools of the United States in the 1930s, when big business and financial capitalism seemed to need defenders. Emerging from this process was the Center for Research on Entrepreneurial History, established at Harvard in 1948, which led ultimately to the comparative study of enterprise – small as well as large – placed in a social and political context, linked through a dynamic analysis of capitalist evolution to models of economic growth.

As a distinct discipline, business history is concerned with the history of individual and collective (private) enterprise, the structure, organization and decision-making behaviour of such concerns, the managing (regulation) of enterprise by government, and the impact of business on the larger economy. A "business" is taken to be an enterprise or a firm organized to provide goods and services to consumers, with the objective of making a profit from such exchange. The "business" of business enterprise is to be engaged in some activity or occupation to this end. A business can be conducted by an individual, a partnership or a corporation. Differences in scale can be dramatic, from the higgler as sole trader to the vast modern multinational corporation with a turnover larger than the whole economy of a nation state.

Business history has as its major tasks analysis of the origins, development and collapse of business enterprises; of their role in the production, distribution and exchange of material goods and services; of their systems of management; of the profitability of enterprises; of the structure and scale of business; and of the internal organization of enterprises. In doing this, the role of the entrepreneur and of entrepreneurship have central roles, but the relationship of business enterprise to the state and to the broader society and economy are equally important.

How does business history relate to other types of history? Generally, business history is understood as a branch of economic history concerned with the organization, structure and profitability of enterprises rather than focused on the macroeconomic history of states or geographical regions or concerned with the progress of particular industries or trades. In this way, business history can be seen as contributing elements to the larger interpretation of national, regional and global economic performance. However, business history also has the capacity to transcend boundaries, not only in the case of the modern multinational corporation but, equally importantly, in early modern partnerships and joint stock companies. In addition to its central place in economic history, the study of business history intersects with social and political history. In an often confrontational manner, business history is also separated from labour history and from the history of institutions such as slavery or indentureship. A further problematic relationship can be found in the connection between business history and histories of technology and innovation.

The complex relationship between business history and other branches of historical study is paralleled by its relations with the modern concept of "business studies". The disciplinary study of business is directed at an analysis of the structure and conduct of enterprises, with a particular emphasis on management (meaning the internal manipulation of existing firms) but also concerned with notions of entrepreneurship. The Master of Business Administration (MBA), a popular option among West Indian students since the 1980s, emphasizes the centrality of management to business studies. A tension exists between the writing of business history within the broader discipline of history (with an emphasis on the biographical approach) and seeing business history as an analytical study (with an emphasis on the intrinsic qualities of business and attempts to generalize about the structure and functioning of business as a system). The study of business as a system poses significant challenges to the historian, since it is well known that most enterprises fail in their infancy and even the more healthy units rarely prosper sufficiently strongly to leave behind a substantial archive of evidence. Almost by definition, the firms with the greatest longevity and visibility are the least representative. The creation of electronic rather than paper archives poses a fresh challenge to business historians.

West Indian business history is particularly significant because, on the one hand, the region was the site of some of the world's first large-scale production units in terms of both capital and labour force (sugar plantations), while on the other it was equally the site of vibrant and subversive small business enterprise (the internal marketing system), both of which have had long-term visibility. In order to understand the business history of the West Indies, it is necessary have an appreciation of all of these elements and their articulation over time.

Surveys of the scope of business history for the Caribbean region are scarce. The overall emphasis is on Europe, North America and Asia.[1] Latin America has received a fair amount of attention, but the focus has been largely on the South American continent, and the existence of a West Indian business history is generally unrecognized.[2]

The essays included in this collection bring together a selection of work in West Indian business history, some of it first published several decades ago. The essays are intended to provide an introduction to the state of the field and illustrate the ways in which business history connects with other themes in Caribbean history. They offer examples of the varieties of ways in which business history can be researched and written, and examples of the range of subjects that can be studied.

Much business history has been cast in a biographical mould. The great attraction of this method is that the enterprise of an individual entrepreneur can be tracked over the span of a career or life. It also has the advantage of locating the business person within his or her context and thus providing immediate clues to the sources of their success or failure and to the character of their activities. In the history of the West Indies, the method has been applied effectively to the study of leading figures among the planter and merchant classes, such as Richard Sheridan's studies of Samuel Martin of Antigua and Simon Taylor of Jamaica during the period of slavery, and for the twentieth century Clem Seecharan's account of Jock Campbell of Guyana.[3] An obvious disadvantage of treating business history biographically is the lack of a substantial archival record for all but the most wealthy and successful of entrepreneurs. Jerome Handler's studies of Joseph Rachell and Rachael Pringle-Polgreen of Barbados, included in this volume, push the limits of the documentary record, illustrating what can be achieved from scattered and scanty references for such "petty entrepreneurs".

As well as studying the individual entrepreneur, business history is also often written as a family story over a series of generations. Examples of this type are Richard Pares' study of the Pinney family in *A West-India Fortune*[4] and Sheridan's account of the Olivers, which is included in this volume. Both of these studies bridge the ocean as well as the generations, tracking the "transnational" experience of merchant and planter networks in Bristol and London as well as Antigua and Nevis.

A development of the biographical approach to business history is writing that traces the origins, development and perhaps decline of a particular enterprise, matching the role of "case studies" in management studies. Thus the history of the Jamaican sugar plantation Worthy Park, written by Michael Craton and James Walvin, follows the trajectory of that property from 1670 to 1970.[5] Although ownership changed hands several times over the centuries, the plantation as an enterprise persisted strongly as a family business, never changing its name or its staple crop. Examples of the application of the approach to public companies are equally common, particularly for the period after slavery. Manufacturing companies, marketing firms and banks, for instance, have been studied in this way, often emphasizing the transnational organization of these enterprises.

Alternative ways of writing business history include studies that follow the experience of a particular class or group. This can work well in those cases where there is a close connection between a group of entrepreneurs and particular types of enterprise. Jacqueline Levy's account of the role of Chinese people in the grocery trade of Jamaica, included in this volume, is a good example of this method. A similar approach is found in Henderson Carter's tracking of the development of black business in Barbados, and Kathleen Phillips-Lewis' study of the role of women in the cocoa industry of Trinidad. Both of these essays are included in this volume.

Overlapping more obviously with economic and financial history are studies that connect units of enterprise along particular channels. The provision of capital and credit to agriculturists and merchants by banks and non-bank financial institutions illustrates this kind of association, as studied in this volume in the essays of Aviston Downes, Richard A. Lobdell and Kathleen E.A. Monteith. Here the emphasis is on the provider of credit and capital, because it was the provider who held the purse strings, but such a study selects a particular aspect of the institutional history for analysis and equally requires an understanding of the situation of the borrower. The role of insurance companies is similarly extensive. Why banks appeared only after slavery remains an important question, as is the reason for the restricted role of insurance companies – confined largely to maritime and fire insurance – until the nineteenth century.

Finally, business history can be written in its own terms. Here the objective is not to interpret relationships between particular entrepreneurs and enterprises and their broader familial and economic contexts, but rather to attempt to find a key to the changing structure and organization of businesses. This is an approach little used in the West Indies and long neglected elsewhere as well. Probably the most influential example of business history in this vein is Alfred Chandler's analysis of the managerial structure of modern American enterprise, which is characterized by multiple separate operating units and controlled by a hierarchy of salaried executive managers.[6] It is hard to identify a West Indian counterpart to this style of conceptual analysis, though modern enterprise in the Caribbean and elsewhere shares many of these structural and managerial features. At the macroeconomic level, however, the "plantation economy" models developed in the 1960s by Lloyd Best and associates provides the basis for an interpretation of the most characteristic West Indian business enterprise – the plantation – that could be adapted to the building of a business history of this sort.[7]

Of the essays included in this volume, perhaps Nuala Zahedieh's study comes closest to the analytic-managerial approach. In dissecting the abnormal though effective system that constituted seventeenth-century privateering enterprise, Zahedieh identifies the distinctive characteristics that derived from activities conducted, at best, on the edge of legality. Privateering had very specific capital and personnel requirements and created unique hierarchical-democratic models of redistribution. Although this specific form of plunder could not persist in the long term, the business model did not die with the privateers, as seen in the global persistence of piracy. Enterprise outside the law continues to develop its own distinctive modes of organization, whether associated or not with alternative modes sanctioned by the state.

Whatever the approach taken to the writing of business history, a number of common threads and themes can be identified in the subject. These include the origins of enterprises, the relationship between business and government, the role of family, kinship and group-identity (including ethnic minorities), the sources of capital, the structure of management and changes in the scale of operation. More broadly, any attempt to measure the success or failure of business is hampered by the inescapable fact that the evidentiary record of success is always greater than that of failure, even though spectacular examples of the collapse of big business may be prominent in the history. The failure of an enterprise, particularly in its early life, is often the trigger for the destruction of its archive.

The relationship between business and the state has always been intimate in the modern West Indies. Imperial government made the rules encouraging and controlling enterprise, offering both protected markets and security based on military force, while limiting exchange with colonial competitors and, particularly through slavery, denying the full participation of the majority of the people in capitalist development. In this way, the business history of the West Indies can be understood as the internal history of capitalism and the taproot of imperialism. Classical theories of the economic origins of imperialism saw capitalist business enterprise as the principal tool of colonial expansion and the management of the system has been justly called "the business of empire".

Without business, the Caribbean would be a very different place, as would the First World without imperialism. In the period since political independence, beginning in the 1960s, the national governments of the West Indies have attempted a variety of modes of economic organization, from laissez-faire capitalism to versions of socialism, with fundamentally different implications for the regulation and prosperity of business. Although business may often have been a tool of political policy it is equally clear that, when it comes to the crunch, politics trumps business. For the greater part of modern West Indian history, however, business success has gone together with the exploitation of human and physical resources, the concentration of wealth, and stunted economic growth.

Notes

1. Franco Amatori and Geoffrey Jones, eds., *Business History around the World* (Cambridge: Cambridge University Press, 2003).
2. Carlos Davila and Rory Miller, eds., *Business History in Latin America: The Experience of Seven Countries* (Liverpool: Liverpool University Press, 1999). An earlier publication, H.V. Nelles' "Latin American Business History since 1965: A View from North of the Border", *Business History Review* 59 (1985): 543–62, was less restrictive in its focus, with a few references being made to studies on West Indian territories.
3. Clem Seecharan, *Sweetening Bitter Sugar: Jock Campbell, the Booker Reformer in British Guiana, 1934–1966* (Kingston: Ian Randle, 2005).
4. Richard Pares, *A West India Fortune* (London: Longmans, 1950).
5. Michael Craton and James Walvin, *A Jamaican Plantation: The History of Worthy Park 1670–1970* (London: W.H. Allen, 1970).
6. Alfred D. Chandler, Jnr., *Strategy and Structure: Chapters in the History of the American Industrial Enterprise* (Cambridge, Mass.: MIT Press, 1962); *Visible Hand: The Managerial Revolution in American Business* (Cambridge, Mass.: Harvard University Press, 1977); *Scale and Scope* (Cambridge, Mass.: Harvard University Press, 1990).
7. Lloyd Best, "Outlines of a Model of Pure Plantation Economy", *Social and Economic Studies* 17 (1968): 283–326; and George L. Beckford, *Persistent Poverty: Underdevelopment in Plantation Economies of the Third World* (New York: Oxford University Press, 1972).

SECTION 1

Merchants, Privateers and Planters

CHAPTER 2

"A Frugal, Prudential and Hopeful Trade"

Privateering in Jamaica, 1655–1689*

NUALA ZAHEDIEH

Most accounts of English activity in the Caribbean in the sixteenth and seventeenth centuries make some reference to the depredations of privateers and pirates. However, the emphasis has been on the "glamour and excitement" of their exploits.[1] This article looks at the more neglected and more prosaic business aspects of the privateering trade which led Sir Thomas Modyford, the governor of Jamaica, to claim that no course could be "more frugall, more prudentiall, more hopeful in laying a good foundation . . . for the great increase of His Majesties dominions in these parts".[2] These sentiments make him far removed from the world described by a neo-classical economist; a world where property rights are assigned, enforced without cost and, in Alfred Marshall's words, "inseparable from human progress", and perhaps this why the role of plunder in financing colonization has been underplayed.[3] But this examination of privateering in one early English colony, Jamaica, shows that Modyford's claims had ample justification. All colonies faced funding problems in the first years of settlement before agricultural production

---

*Originally published in the *Journal of Imperial and Commonwealth History*, 18 (1990): 145–68. Reprinted by permission of Taylor and Francis Ltd.

was under way; and privateering was an ideal start-up trade since it required a small capital outlay and offered a quick return which could be used to finance the expensive work of settlement.[4] But it was not a strategy for long-term growth. Just as fishermen must take care not to overfish, freebooters must take care not to overplunder if their prey is to survive and provide further sustenance.[5] This is why the level of privateering, which reached a peak in Jamaica in 1671, fell a little and subsequently stabilized at a lower rate. It had reached the practical limit of growth. Privateering did not dwindle away, nor was there a whole-hearted change in islanders' attitudes which would have enabled governors to suppress the plunderers entirely. But, while privateering remained an important part of the economy throughout the seventeenth century, it was increasingly outstripped in value by planting and merchandizing.[6]

I

The prime target for marauders in early modern America was the Spanish Empire and the prominence of privateering in Early English Jamaica derived first and foremost from the island's geographic location in the heart of the Spanish Indies convenient for the major ports and straddling the principal trade routes. Although Spanish wealth and power was seen by other Europeans to be in decline by the late seventeenth century, the "dead carcass" still provided rich pickings.[7] Even at a low point in Spanish American trade, between 1671 and 1700, unofficial estimates indicate that quinquennial totals varied between 40 and 67.5 million pesos (£10 and 16.8 million) with precious metals forming between 85 and 90 per cent of the returns.[8] The Spaniards, well aware that this rich commerce aroused general covetousness, devoted the bulk of the resources earmarked for the defence of America to the protection of the treasure. The trade was organized into official fleets, sailing between well fortified ports, and was effectively protected with armed convoys.[9] But the priorities meant that the long, thinly populated coastlines outside the bullion routes were neglected by the metropolitan authorities. In the seventeenth century new plantation economies brought modest prosperity to some of these areas, notably the eastern coast of Venezuela, but they sold their produce directly to foreigners or to other colonies and remained largely outside imperial concerns. Their towns and commerce fell easy prey to marauders.[10]

The marauders of the late seventeenth century drew on a tradition which dated from soon after the first discoveries. Spain tried to reserve the wealth of the Indies for itself by declaring a monopoly of trade and navigation in the area. Other nations responded with force and claimed that a colonial monopoly was impermissible unless based on effective possession and occupation. The treaties of 1604 and 1630, which regulated Anglo-Spanish relations, dealt with mutual intransigence by excluding any reference to affairs "Beyond the Line".[11] Spain continued to claim that any Englishman found in the Indies should be treated as a pirate. England, disputing the Spaniards' right to monopoly, asserted that if the treaties applied beyond the line, then they had been broken by Spain in the Indies and it was fair to seek reparation; but if there was no peace in the Indies, then the English were doing nothing against the treaties with Spain and, furthermore, force alone would persuade the Spaniards to abandon their pretension to monopoly.[12] It was this rhetoric, encapsulated in the slogan "No Peace Beyond the Line", that was used to justify Cromwell's "Western Design" of 1654–55 which culminated in the seizure of Jamaica.[13] The same slogan justified continuation of Jamaica's war with the Spaniards after the Restoration brought peace with Spain in Europe.[14] Charles II appears to have shared Cromwell's view that only force would persuade the Spaniards to open the door to trade in the Indies.[15] Although the king did not give the Jamaican privateers official blessing in the 1660s, he did (apart from brief intervals when he hoped to gain concessions through diplomacy) turn a blind eye to a whole-hearted demonstration that they did not wish to implement "peace beyond the line".[16]

II

Given Jamaica's strategic location and the rhetoric underpinning Cromwell's "Western Design" and the island's capture, it is not surprising that the first settlers, many from the conquering army, enthusiastically took to plunder. The English inherited little from the Spaniards in Jamaica and sufficient evidence survives about the economics of privateering to indicate its attractions as a start-up business in a new colony. The trade required a small investment of, at most, a few hundred pounds and offered the prospect of a quick, substantial profit. The largest item of capital expenditure for promoters of plunder

Table 2.1: Privateers' Fleets at Jamaica 1663, 1665, 1670

	No. of Ships	Tonnage		Men		Guns	
		Total	Ave.	Total	Ave.	Total	Ave.
1663	11	629.0*	57.18	740	67.27	81	7.36
1665	9	552.5*	61.38	650	75.22	71	7.88
1670	28	1120.0	40.00	1326	47.35	180	6.42

*The lists for 1663 and 1665 do not include tonnage. The man to ton ratio found in 1670 has been assumed to apply to the earlier years.

Source: BL Add. MS 11,410, fo. 10, "An Account of the Private Ships of War Belonging to Jamaica and Tortudos in 1663"; CO 1/19, fo. 278, "A True and Perfect Narrative by Col. Theodore Cary Declaring the Proceedings in the Late Expedition from this Island of Jamaica Against the Dutch", 17 Nov. 1665; CO 138/1, fo. 105, "A List of the Ships Under the Command of Admiral Morgan", 1670.

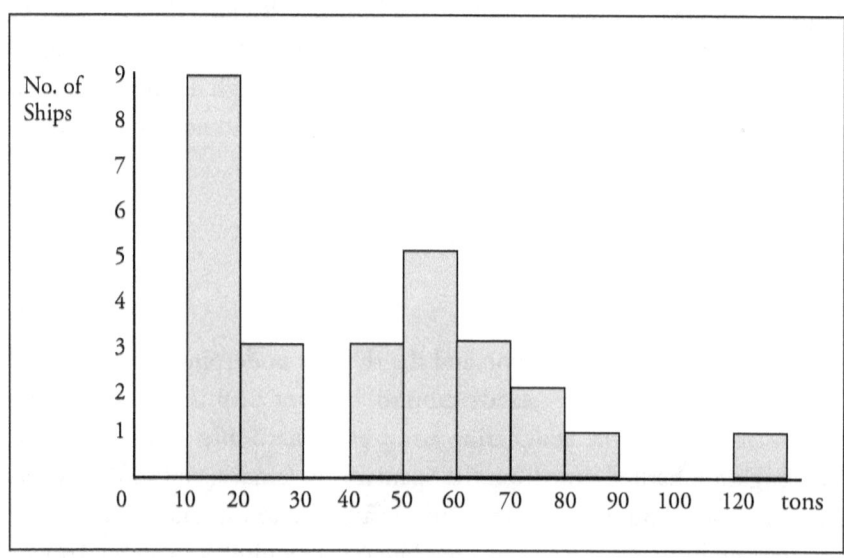

Figure 2.1: Size of ships in Morgan's fleet, 1670

Source: CO 138/1, fo.105, "A List of the Ships Under the Command of Admiral Morgan, 1670".

("which generally live on shore") was the ship. Most of the vessels were small, 60 tons or less, and often island built (table 2.1). Deeds of sale in the Jamaica Island Record Office indicate that these changed hands for less than £100.[17] Fitting out was usually done on credit and cost between £100 and £200.[18]

The privateers did have some larger ships (figure 2.1). But even these represented a surprisingly small capital outlay on the part of their Jamaican promoters. The first ships of the conquering fleet were provided by the state which maintained a small squadron at the island until 1660.[19] After the Restoration the navy supplied flagships for major expeditions, like the *Centurion* for Christopher Myngs' raids on Cuba and Campeché in 1662 and 1663, or the *Oxford* which was blown up in 1668.[20] A more common source of large vessels for privateering was seizure. Prizes were bought at a knock-down price. There was no island admiralty court under martial law but Edward D'Oyley, the acting commander-in-chief in 1656 and 1657–61, felt entitled to dispose of prize vessels in Jamaica rather than despatch them to be condemned and sold in England.[21] Some ships were retained for "the State's service against the Spaniards"; others were sold publicly by inch of candle and certificates of purchase issued.[22] When Lord Windsor arrived as governor of Jamaica in 1662 he formalized the system and set up an admiralty court. A precedent book compiled by a Jamaican lawyer in the early 1660s records the activities of this court and shows that prize vessels were sold well below their true value. On Myngs' return from Campeche in 1663, nine ships were sold for a total of £797. Size was recorded for seven vessels, giving an average of 127 tons and an average prize of £85.[23] Between 1666 and 1668 fourteen ships were condemned and sold for an average price of £113.[24] A prize of 200 tons burden fetched £180.[25] According to Ralph Davis it cost about £2,000 to buy and fit out a ship of this size in England.[26] In 1664 Morris Williams captured the patache of the galleons, the *Santo Christo*, when it was separated from the fleet by a hurricane. The owner, Ximenes de Bohorques, was indignant that a ship which he claimed was worth several thousand pounds was sold in a Jamaican court for £50. The vessel was renamed the *Speaker* and, commanded by Morris Williams, provided the flagship for an expedition against Curacao in 1665.[27] Similarly Morgan's flagship for his famous attacks on Portobello and Panama was a Spanish prize.[28]

Privateers frequently retained prizes without any reference to the authorities. Tropical waters were hard on wooden hulls. It was tempting to abandon old ships and seize new ones to continue the voyage.[29] Scant observation of legal formalities reflects the opportunistic nature of the privateering trade. In 1670 George Home put Humphrey Thurston in command of his ship the *Port Royal* (30 tons) with instructions to load logwood in the Bay of Campeche. Thurston "did make of the said shipp a man of warr" and seized a Spanish ship of 40 tons laden with silk, wine, new Spanish cloth and other goods. Thurston fitted and rigged the prize out of the *Port Royal* which he then abandoned as a wreck although the "said ship was really worth £300 sterling". Thurston took his new ship, renamed the *Jamaica,* to join Morgan's expedition to Panama and George Home retained the rights of an owner.[30]

The enemy provided the privateers with victuals as well as ships. Thomas Modyford reported that the men of war "never victual or careen in our harbours". Large tracts of sparsely populated Spanish territory were "infinitely stored with cattle and hogs". The rovers often carried a gang of dogs and soon supplied themselves with meat which they salted to last for several months' cruising.[31] Meat was supplemented with turtle, fish and abundant fruit. The Port Royal promoter had only to provide bread and liquor – even this was often seized in raids. While Henry Morgan assembled his fleet for the raid on Panama in 1670 he despatched Edward Collier with six ships to the Main to get victuals "for the whole fleet". The captain returned after two months with plentiful provisions and two enemy vessels.[32]

Having fitted and victualled a ship as a private man-of-war the captain generally obtained a commission to "take, seize, apprehend and possess or otherwise destroy all [Spanish] ships and vessels together with their men, ladeing, goods, wares or merchandize".[33] Papers made no difference when their holders were captured by the Spaniards who treated all unauthorized ships in the Indies as pirates. But a commission did prevent interference by other nations.[34] There was also an incentive for the governors to insist on commissions and, if possible, to issue them as it provided them with a means to increase their control over privateering and secure a substantial share of the profits for themselves – a strong temptation as other remuneration was uncertain. D'Oyley, who was in command for most of the period of martial law, received no pay as commander but profited substantially from his authority to issue commissions and William Beeston, who arrived in the island in 1660, ruefully remarked on the acting governor's vice-like grip on the trade.[35] Those who were discovered attempting to evade his control were dealt with severely. George Freebourne, who landed a prize cargo secretly in 1661, was arrested and sent back to England to be tried for piracy. His crew was distributed in plantations around the island to serve as slaves.[36] Subsequent governors were equally tempted to try to control the privateers with commissions because they were ordered to take their salary out of the proceeds of prize goods.[37] Windsor's admiralty court charged a flat fee of £50 for a commission, although their validity ranged from six to 23 months. Modyford claimed he charged £20 for a commission. The court also required that two gentlemen should give bond that the privateer would "observe, perform, fulfill" his commission and instructions to enter all prize in the admiralty court and pay the expenses, fifteenths to the King and tenths to the admiralty. Under Windsor's government the security varied between £200 and £2,000.[38]

Privateers' ships, bought, fitted, commissioned and victualled for a few hundred pounds, were heavily manned. The man to ton ratio in Morgan's fleet of 1670 was 1 to 0.84. Crews were particularly numerous in the smallest ships, being one man to 0.49 tons in the nine ships of 10 to 20 tons burden.[39] This compares with Davis' estimated ratio of about 1 to 8 on a typical merchant ship sailing in waters inhabited by corsairs.[40] The privateers' aim was to capture a ship and cargo with as little damage as possible – cunning and surprise were preferred tactics to bloody confrontation. This was easier with a large crew. Most captains would surrender when they saw heavy odds against them, particularly as their men had no economic stake in the cargo and no incentive to risk their lives to defend it. The crew of nine aboard the *Blue Dove* anchored in Blewfields Bay in 1664, for example, surrendered immediately when a small bark carrying three times their number sneaked up beside them after dark and opened attack. All thought of resistance crumbled when their captain was shot in the arm. The assailant John Douglas and his crew came aboard, shut their prisoners in the hold, cut the cables and sailed away.[41]

The heavy manning did not erode the shipowners' profits as much as might be expected. A practice had emerged which ensured that the costs of large crews were borne by the men themselves. The crews were not paid wages but were taken on the basis of "No Purchase, No Pay".[42] Having deducted expenses like the court fees, tenths for the admiralty and fifteenths for the King, any plunder was divided between owners and crew in a fixed proportion agreed before the voyage. Surviving examples of articles of association show that it was usual to halve the net proceeds, although there were exceptions.[43] Peter

Earle quotes the agreement drawn up by Henry Morgan before his expedition of 1668 which allowed the owners only a quarter share of the plunder taken at sea.[44] The privateers divided their booty according to strict regulations based on long-standing tradition. Boys got half shares, specialists such as carpenters rather more than one share, captains and the admiral still more. There were agreed bonus payments both for those who showed especial bravery and for those who lost a limb, with a fixed scale of benefits. In 1663 the admiralty court records payment of £10 to Edward King "whose leg was shot off".[45] The court directed that "such reasonable and just articles as shall generally be appointed unto all . . . are to be fairly written and affixed to the main mast that noe officer, mariner or souldier be surprised or ignorant of the same".[46]

Despite the fairness of the division, dreams of great riches were largely disappointed. The prize was often small and, even when large, the division was among very many claimants. Nine ships taken at Campeche in 1663 yielded £1,341 together with their cargoes. After deduction of tenths and other expenses there remained £782 4s 0d to be divided among the owners and survivors of 1,500 men who participated in the expedition (table 2.2).[47] The most successful cruise recorded during Windsor's government was John Harmenson's which yielded £5,210 for two Spanish ships brought into Port Royal in October 1663. After deduction of the tenths and fifteenths £4,342 remained. If this had been divided equally between owners and crew, each of the 70 men would have received a relatively satisfying £30. In fact, as the Campeche accounts show, there would have been further deductions for court fees and expenses as well as payments to fitters and victuallers (table 2.2). The least successful cruise cited in these records produced a negligible return. Richard Guy's prize Flemish ship with its cargo of cocoa, salt and skins was condemned and sold for £60. There was little profit for his crew of 90 men.[48]

Land expeditions were generally more profitable for the men than those at sea. Since the risks were higher and more men were needed, the privateers usually organized in fleets for land action. But the prize was generally larger and the privateers were not liable to pay tenths, fifteenths or the accompanying court fees as they were on prize taken at sea. Furthermore, owners were often excluded from sharing booty from land.[49] Morgan's raid of Portobello in 1668 gave each man a share of about £120.[50] The raid on Maracaibo in 1669 gave each man a share of about £30.[51] Prince's expedition to Granada in 1670 was regarded as disappointing even though it yielded about £26 per man.[52]

Table 2.2: Account of Campeche Prizes, 1663

	£	s	d
Gratuities for 3 captains	100	00	00
Gratuities for surgeons for wounded men	70	00	00
Payment to Edward King whose leg was shot off	10	00	00
To pilotage of ships up and other charges laid Out to feed them for voyage	32	02	06
Charges of waiters on board and unloading The prizes and Marshall's fees with court Charges and other fees	192	16	00
Contingent charges allowed Capt Myngs	20	00	00
	424	19	04
For Duke of York's 1/10s on £1341	134	02	00
	559	01	04
Balance to be divided	782	04	00
	1341	05	04

Source: HCA 49/59, fo. 43b.

Clearly the prospect of "great booty" which drew men to serve on a privateer was largely a chimera, and the risks were high. A privateer's life was a lottery with few winning the jackpot and injury, death or imprisonment in Spain as the loser's draw. The great risks and frequently disappointing returns were reflected in a high turnover of crews and captains. It is possible to trace the fate of 12 of the 26 privateer captains commissioned between September 1662 and July 1663.[53] By 1670, six had been killed (one more was killed in 1673), one was a prisoner, two were planters and two were cutting logwood. None was still privateering.[54]

Yet there was no difficulty in raising men for privateering. The English conquerors of Jamaica drew willing recruits from a large pool of marauders who infested the Caribbean long before 1655. Governor D'Oyley invited 250 buccaneers from Hispaniola and, as one commentator remarked, it could not be supposed that they expected to be "protected in all those insolencies which they should commit" or that D'Oyley intended anything but "connivance at least of such miscarriage among them as did tend to the prejudice of others".[55] The number of freebooters was constantly replenished because, in the Caribbean, the alternative occupations available for those with few resources were bleak, quite apart from the rovers' reputed "temptingly alluring boldness and success".[56] To clear and farm land in Jamaica required hard work and cash with a slow return.[57] Work on a naval ship was under strict discipline for £15–£20 per year.[58] Worst of all was the life of an indentured servant – often grinding toil with little prospect of advancement.[59] By contrast the life of a privateer, as described in a journal by one of the men who crossed the isthmus of Panama in 1680, was one of adventure, variety, comradeship, with an ever-present hope of great and wonderful riches.[60] The power of the temptation was reflected in the ease with which Captain Myngs raised 1,300 men for an attack on Cuba in 1662 (at a time when Jamaica's total population of white men was 2,500).

While the returns to those serving aboard the privateers were often relatively paltry, men in port made great gains. Not only investors and creditors benefited. The influxes of men with money were so great that repercussions rippled right through the Port Royal economy. The notoriously spendthrift habits of the privateers increased the impact of their large purchasing power. A few, such as Henry Morgan, saved their loot and bought plantations, but these were definitely the exceptions.[61] Most spent their gains in a few days settling debts then buying food, arms, other necessaries and "giving themselves up to all sorts of debauchery with strumpets and wine".[62] Attempts to limit the credit given by vintners or the number of ale-houses were to no avail.[63] Consumption of liquor doubled in the 1660s and it was generally assumed by both their friends and enemies that this was due to the privateers.[64]

The free-spending habits of the privateers on their return to port created gluts of the prize commodities they disposed of. Cocoa, indigo, sugar, dyewoods, precious stones, plate, bullion, and other commodities could be bought "dogge cheape" after a successful cruise and resold later at a large profit.[65] In August 1667 Captain Dempster brought in a Spanish prize laden with logwood. The large supply caused the price to fall to £10 per ton but by December it recovered its usual price of £20 per ton.[66] Spanish slaves captured on the coasts were unpopular in the island, being responsible for "many mischiefs" but could be bought cheap and re-exported with considerable gain.[67] As Sir

James Modyford explained in 1668, privateers' exploits presented anyone in Port Royal who had cash with excellent opportunities. He thanked his London agent, Sir Andrew King, for putting out his money to interest, "which I know you did for the best". However, he pointed out that the privateers presented far better opportunities for profit in Port Royal than there were in England for "we often . . . double nay treble our money without any hazard".[68]

III

Unfortunately little information survives about the total value of the privateers' plunder even in the early years when their trade had semi-official sanction. Admiralty records are available for only two short periods. The records from Windsor's government indicate that 31 commissions to private men-of-war were issued between September 1662 and July 1663. Twenty-one vessels were condemned in the court between November 1662 and December 1663. The twenty for which an account of sale survives produced a total of £7,533 15s 2d with their cargoes.[69] An account of fifteenths deducted in the years 1666 to 1668 indicates that fourteen prizes and their cargoes were brought in and sold for a total sum of £12,908 15s 9d.[70] These are surprisingly small figures, even allowing for low prices paid for prize goods. However, admiralty records tell a very partial story as fifteenths were payable only on prizes taken at sea and not on land.[71] Furthermore, there is ample evidence that, despite elaborate preventative measures, embezzlement was common. It was a simple matter to land a cargo secretly before coming into port where the governor's officers came on board.[72] The information about prize taken on land is even more sketchy. All we have are scattered estimates. Myngs, for example, reputedly seized plunder worth £40,000 from Coro and Comina in 1659.[73] At the end of the decade Henry Morgan seized an estimated £75,000 at Portobello, £30,000 from Maracaibo and £30,000 from Panama.[74]

While the proceeds of plunder cannot be measured with precision, literary references to the pervasiveness of privateering are abundant. By 1662 there were about 1,500 full-time privateers based at the island[75] and all commentators, including a strong opponent of privateering like the planter John Style, agreed that in the 1660s the island's trade consisted almost entirely of "plate, money, jewels and other things brought in [by the privateers] and sold cheap to the merchants".[76] The economic dominance of privateering is reflected in the fact that the prosperity of Port Royal preceded the establishment of planting in the island or peaceful commerce. Port Royal's population grew from 670 in 1662 to almost 2,000 in 1670 and the port attracted 178 ships in 1668–70. Sir Thomas Lynch remarked that they were drawn by the prospect of privateering loot.[77] The busy commerce as yet owed little to the island's produce for although clearing and planting the land progressed in the 1660s, production was still very small in 1670. Cocoa, the island's main crop, was entirely destroyed by blight in 1669–71, and while sugar works increased from 18 in 1664 to 57 in 1671, exports were worth less than £10,000 in 1670. This is a small figure beside plunder brought in by Morgan from Portobello or Panama.[78] Records documenting the business life of Port Royal in the 1660s illustrate clearly the pervasiveness of privateering in the economy. All the individuals who played a prominent role in the island's history, including those who later became vigorously opposed to privateering like Lynch and Molesworth, were involved in privateering in the early years. Lynch gave bond for three privateers, including the well-known George Brimacain, during 1662–63.[79] Lynch's later disenchantment with the trade derived from his interest in the peaceful smuggling trade, but in the early years contraband and plunder were overlapping activities. Lynch, for example, was involved with contraband traders Nicholas Rion and Francis Peron who also carried a privateering commission with Lynch providing their security.[80] Peter Quadman, a Dutch merchant of Port Royal, was known to be "very practiced in [peaceful] trade with the Spaniards" but he also bought a small privateer in Morgan's Panama fleet.[81] By 1670 the prosperity of Port Royal was enabling the townspeople to make an investment in the agricultural hinterland and it is possible to show some connection with privateering for ten of those twelve residents who had patented over two thousand acres by 1670.[82] Privateering, with its quick returns, had proved an ideal trade for a strategically placed island whose colonists had little capital and needed to accumulate funds to begin the expensive work of settlement.

IV

But by the end of the 1660s there signs that the Jamaica privateers were "overfishing". Between 1655 and 1671 the buccaneers had sacked eighteen cities, four towns and more than 35 villages. They had raided Tolu eight times, Rio de la Hacha five times, Granada and Santa Marta three times, Santa Catalina and Cumanagoto twice, Campeche, Chagres, Portobello, Panama, Maracaibo, Merida, Cumana and Santiago de Cuba. Smaller towns and villages in Cuba and Hispaniola were plundered over and over and again.[83] Returns on these repeated raids were falling. When Prince, Lubborough and Harris captured Granada with 200 men in 1670 they were bitterly disappointed. The plunder amounted to about about £26 per head which was "nothing to what they had five years since". The town had already been raided by Morgan, Morris and Fackman in 1664 and by another group of privateers in 1665 which had caused a general decline in prosperity; many of the principal inhabitants had moved to the greater security of Guatemala. By 1671 William Beeston noted the impoverishment in the less populous Spanish territories: "They in these latter years having been so infested in the dayly allarum of the privateers are kept much in armes by which planting is neglected."[84]

As returns fell in the privateers' traditional hunting grounds on the periphery of the Spanish colonial economy, the predators became more daring, stepping nearer to the treasure trade. Morgan captured Portobello in 1668 (which was almost deserted as no fleet was expected but still of symbolic importance to the Spaniards) and Panama in 1671. This audacity increased the cost and risk of privateering. Since more men were needed to attack the better fortified targets, they received smaller returns. The raid on Panama produced a prize worth £30,000 according to Morgan, which gave each of the 1,500 men who survived about £16. This was regarded as pitiful remuneration and led to accusations that Morgan had cheated the men. But the main problem was that the division was among so many. Even had the plunder been twice as much and each man's share been £32, it would not have seemed a great return for the risks of the six-month expedition. Furthermore, many creditors were not satisfied and there was some discontent in Port Royal.[85]

The increasing boldness and moves towards breaching the defence of the treasure trade also alarmed the Spaniards into stepping up protection. The *Armada de Barlovento* designed to patrol the Caribbean had long lapsed[86] but, despite the Spanish crown's mounting financial difficulties,[87] the squadron was reformed in 1665. The five ships which arrived in America in 1667 achieved little, as three were burned by Morgan soon after arrival and the other two were ordered to accompany the treasure fleets back to Spain.[88] The squadron was not reformed until 1676, but meanwhile the local Spanish governors were taking measures to compensate for metropolitan inaction. In 1666 the President of Panama launched a brutal but successful expedition to recapture Providence which had been seized by Jamaican privateers.[89] The island lay too close to Portobello and Cartegena to be allowed to remain in foreign hands. The President also improved the fortifications in his jurisdiction.

In 1669 the Spanish government sent letters to the colonial governors authorizing them to issue commissions against the English[90] (also giving Modyford an excuse to abandon Jamaica's recently declared peace and renew war on the Spaniards).[91] The Spanish action did not eradicate privateering but it did enhance the costs and risks of "the course". The fate of the one long-standing Jamaican privateer, Captain Bart Nicholas, demonstrated the heightened danger. In 1669 he was killed in a fight with a Spanish commissioned captain, Manuel Rivero Pardal, returning from a peaceful trade mission to Cuba. This caused consternation in Jamaica.[92]

Information about falling marginal profits and rising risks encouraged the privateers to diversify their activities and seek new hunting grounds. A brief decline in traditional privateering activity occurred after 1670 with no major land raids in the early part of the decade. Many took to logwood cutting which, taking place on neglected edges of the Spanish colonial economy, had attracted much the same men as privateering since the early 1660s. The wood grew in "morose and swampish grounds" along coasts where it was "impossible to plant", so that vessels could put in undisturbed, take in a full loading, and then return within three months to Port Royal to sell the wood at £25–30 per ton.[93] In October 1670 Modyford reported that 12 Jamaican vessels were plying the trade, including one commanded by John Coxon whose career as a privateer was to be one of the most enduring. By July 1671 there were said to be 40 such vessels – many of Morgan's Panama fleet having repaired to the logwood coasts.[94] Thomas Lynch claimed that 2,000 tons of logwood were cut in 1671 which, valued at £20 per ton, amounted to £40,000 worth, four times the value of sugar exports. The English hoped that, as the logwood coasts were uninhabited, the Spaniards would turn a blind eye to the trade. In fact, the

Spaniards had no intention of doing so. They maintained that logwood in an English ship was contraband and that Englishmen cutting it on Spanish shores, whether inhabited or not, were pirates. The Spaniards seized any ships bearing logwood and hired buccaneers to police the seas, Yhallahs and Fitz-Gerald being the most notorious. In 1672 Lynch claimed that "we have lost this year of peace by these kind of seizures twice as much as in Thomas Modyford's seven years of war". The Spanish activities did not halt the trade but merely fuelled hatred between the two nations and encouraged mutual brutalities.[95]

V

Disquiet over the falling profitability of privateering in 1670–71 coincided with growing doubts about the desirability of the trade among all those in England with some interest in the island. Little of the profit of plunder returned directly to the mother country. The fifteenths and tenths for the king and Admiralty yielded the relatively insignificant sums described above despite the high level of privateering activity in the 1660s and, furthermore, these sums were generally retained in the island to cover expenses of administration. Attempts to secure a more direct share of the profits of plunder foundered through ill-luck and the difficulties of overseeing absentee investments. The *Oxford*, despatched by the king as a privateer flagship, was destroyed in an explosion. The *Lilly*, which accompanied Morgan to Panama, was abandoned and taken into the state's service in 1671, having brought no profits to the "gentlemen at court" who owned it.[96] In England statesmen and traders became convinced that more might be gained by promoting planting and peaceful contraband trade than plunder which drained away the island's labour and fostered Spanish hostility. This latter animosity was a particular problem because the Royal African Company was being reformed with hopes of its being allowed to supply slaves to the Spanish colonies.[97] These hopes crystallized in 1670 when the Treaty of Madrid was concluded to considerable English satisfaction. The treaty promised an end to hostilities between the two nations in America with both sides' commissions for war to be called in at once. Spain at last agreed to recognize England's right to retain territories which its "King and subjects at present hold and possess". Jamaica was not named, but the English assumed it was included. The treaty did not grant trade concessions but a clause allowed the ships of each nation to enter the others' ports when under stress of weather or to repair, refit and revictual, which would ease illicit trading. The English had high hopes for a growth of friendship in America and expected that, if they could observe the peace, further concessions might be granted.[98]

This mood of optimism made Jamaica's whole-hearted patronage of the buccaneers appear a liability. The governor, Sir Thomas Modyford, and the leading privateer, Henry Morgan, were both recalled to England and placed under arrest to placate the Spaniards. The former soldier and Jamaican landowner, Sir Thomas Lynch, was appointed governor with directions to implement the Treaty of Madrid.[99] As his arrival in the Caribbean in 1671 coincided with the adjustment in the privateering trade following the over-expansion of the late 1660s, Lynch was, fortuitously, able to claim some success for his proclamations against plunder.[100] His boastful claims have caused some historians to see the 1670 treaty as a watershed in attitudes to privateering at Jamaica after which it was regarded as a nuisance.[101] But this is an over-simplification. After a brief fall in privateering activity in the early 1670s it stabilized at an earlier lower level. In December 1675 Lord Vaughn, the governor between 1674 and 1678, reported that Jamaica had eleven privateering ships.[102] In 1678 Carlisle estimated that there were about 1,200 privateers based at the island – much the same number as in 1662.[103] Land raids were resumed. For example, there were large-scale raids on Maracaibo in 1676, Santa Marta in 1677, Campeche in 1678, Portobello in 1679 and a spectacular raid on Vera Cruz in 1683 which produced plunder of about £200 per man.[104] In the 1680s the Caribbean privateers also pushed forward the geographical frontier of operations when they crossed the Panama isthmus to the South Seas and caused havoc up and down the Pacific coast.[105] Jamaican views after 1670 were reflected far more accurately in the enthusiastic welcome given to Henry Morgan when he returned as deputy governor in 1674 than in Lynch's boastful claims that he had eradicated piracy.[106]

VI

In fact no governor could have hoped to control the unruly mob of "wild, dissolute and tattered fellows" who used Port Royal as a base for privateering. They were "tyed to noe rules but some of their own by tradition". They were "all nations and languages", English, Dutch, French and many more.[107] A quarter of Morgan's Panama fleet of 36 ships was French.[108] Crews were also very mixed; Captain Duglas who took the *Blue Dove* in 1664 had a crew of 27, only 13 of whom were English.[109] Many of the privateers had no loyalty to the king of England and took little heed of proclamations like Lynch's which promised nothing more than 35 acres of uncleared land in return for a change in their chosen way of life. A privateer down on his luck did occasionally change his ways willingly[110] but, like John Coxon, who gave security for good behaviour in the 1680s, they often found it a "dull way of living and not answerable to ... expectation" returned to their former trade.[111] If privateers did reform there were always others to replace them. Lynch likened them to "weeds or hydras" of the Caribbean that "sprung up as fast as we can cut them down".[112]

The marauders preferred to operate with a commission because it did give them some protection in law if they were arrested. However most did not greatly care which government authorized it or even whether the date was still valid.[113] When papers could not be obtained in Jamaica, a privateer would get them elsewhere. The French governor at Tortuga was the most common source and issued commissions until the late 1680s.[114] During the 1670s co-operation was so close that Robert Bindloss, Morgan's brother-in-law, received a deputation to collect tenths on the French governor's behalf from privateers putting into Jamaica.[115] There were also Danish, Brandenburger and even, for a brief period, English, commissions (the latter from the Bahamas). In 1675 Governor Vaughn was ordered to issue a proclamation forbidding Englishmen to serve under a foreign prince or state. Neither this nor subsequent and repeated exhortations had a noticeable impact on the privateers, particularly as many were not English.[116] Whatever their papers or nationality the rovers spent much of their money in Port Royal which had the most convenient harbour, best supplies and best market for prize goods in the Caribbean.[117]

In the 1660s the trade in prize goods had dominated Port Royal's economy and, although it became relatively less important as planting and contraband trade developed strength in 1670s and 1680s, it would have been surprising if there had been a sudden whole-hearted conversion away from plunder. Some islanders did advance arguments against privateering. Some claimed, for example, that the influxes of prize commodities drove prices down to levels which forced the island's planters to sell their own produce at a loss, as when Coxon brought in a vast quantity of indigo in 1679.[118] But since many planters participated in the trade in prize goods themselves and shared the gains, their complaints were muted.[119] As Henry Morgan remarked, the loss of scarce white servants was seen as a major problem, but an answer was to try to ensure that recruitment was from other groups rather than to abandon privateering.[120] Another objection was that the freebooters might provoke retaliation against Jamaica's own ships. But, in fact, after the reaction to Morgan's exploits, Spanish retaliation was restrained. The Spanish government could not sustain strong measures against privateering – as activity stabilized in the 1670s losses were at a level which it was cheaper to tolerate than to eliminate. Defence outside the treasure trade was largely left to local interests and action against Jamaica was limited. A report to the Council of Jamaica indicated that the island's losses to the Spaniards between October 1684 and July 1687 were valued at £7,530 (a further £320 was lost to the French). The Spaniards took 17 vessels (12 sloops and five other ships) in the entire period lasting almost three years.[121] This was a very small proportion of the island's trade – in 1686 alone 151 ships traded at Jamaica.[122] None of the arguments was sufficiently weighty to tip the balance of advantage entirely away from privateering. Even Port Royal merchants primarily concerned with contraband trade in the Spanish colonies, like William and Francis Hall, were also prepared to do business with "pirates" despite the apparent contradiction between peaceful and forced trade.[123] The governors Thomas Lynch and Hender Molesworth, who were actively involved in Spanish colonial trade, were also selective in their anti-privateering sentiments. They encouraged attacks on their main rivals, Dutch ships trading with the Spaniards, "which will be of advantage to our traders here to have them discouraged".[124] The effect must have been to raise Dutch defence costs and prices which assisted Jamaican penetration of Spanish colonial markets.

There were, of course, unpleasant incidents, as in 1688 when a large group of French privateers fell into rowdy dispute with some Spanish traders in a Port Royal tavern. Insults abounded: "Damme ye cowardly doggs are you here while wee have beene looking for you in the South Seas?"[125] But on the whole raiders and traders managed to co-exist remarkably peacefully. In December 1680 four Brandernburger privateers came into port to sell two prizes and refit at the same as a Spanish ship was loading slaves.[126] An even starker reflection of the dichotomy in the Jamaican economy was Lynch's entrusting of John Coxon to convoy a Spanish ship carrying slaves to Cuba in 1682 and collect the bullion payment due.[127]

Thus Port Royal's townspeople continued to act as promoters of privateering and receivers of the loot even after the Treaty of Madrid. Jamaica's long indented coastline was thinly populated, particularly to the west which was scarcely settled. Lord Vaughn described the ease with which a privateer could put into a quiet bay and send word to correspondents in Port Royal for help in unloading the plunder and bringing necessities.[128] Extensive details of these clandestine exchanges appear in letters and documents relating to Morgan and his brother-in-law Robert Bindloss' involvement in privateering during Vaughn's governorship. A typical arrangement was that of John Coxon whose ship was jointly owned by himself, Robert Bindloss and Roger Pemberton, a Port Royal merchant. Coxon sailed with a French commission, in company with French privateers, but supplied his ship and sold his prize in Jamaica.[129] While Carlisle and Morgan were in authority (1678–81), the privateers were able to come into Port Royal openly, though both governors made a vigorous pretence of anti-privateering sentiment in letters home. Lord Carlisle devised subtle ploys to avoid charges of collusion with the rovers. In 1678 Coxon and his fellows requested permission to bring in booty taken in a raid on Honduras. Carlisle instructed them to unload the plunder on to small island sloops which brought it into port and paid customs. The governor could thus claim that all plunder was brought into the island "in lawful ships and by lawful men, no privateer ever bringing any such thing hither". Meanwhile, the customs revenue replenished the island coffers from which the governor drew his salary.[130] Had the marauders been denied entry into Port Royal they would not have abandoned their trade; they would have taken their prize elsewhere. Furthermore, if denied Jamaican patronage the privateers would have preyed on the island's own trade. The Jamaicans would have had the worst of all worlds – less profit and more danger. As Henry Morgan said, "orders be they ever so strict will never do" for there "never wants evasion of orders when profit is to be had".[131]

As neither rovers nor receivers would abandon their well-established and lucrative business voluntarily, the Jamaican governors would have needed strong and effective naval support to force the privateers to obedience. But the governors never had more than two naval ships at their disposal, and frequently none at all.[132] As in the 1660s, the English government's enthusiasm for peace after the 1670 Treaty was short-lived. The Spaniards did not make further concessions on trade in the Indies; in fact they continued to treat English ships in the Caribbean as pirates. Although not publicly admitted, arguments for using force regained some popularity in England, as reflected in the appointment of Henry Morgan as deputy governor in 1674 and the failure of the home authorities to do more than issue reprimands even when presented with firm evidence of the old privateer's sponsorship of his former colleagues. Carlisle's governorship coincided with the strong anti-Spanish sentiment prevailing after the Popish plot.[133] The reduction of privateering in the Caribbean never received priority in the allocation of naval resources in those years. Lynch (governor 1671–74 and 1681–84) supplemented scant naval support by hiring other ships for the state's service, and this became common practice with his successors.[134] He also organized the building of a galley to patrol shoal waters. But all action was concentrated against those preying on English trade, such as one Joseph Bannister who turned pirate and took several English vessels in the first four months of 1686. After a long chase he was captured and brought into Port Royal hanging on the yardarm of HMS *Drake*, much to Governor Molesworth's satisfaction.[135] None of the anti-privateering measures had more than minimal success. There were hordes of "little rogues" lurking in small barques and canoes in the shallow waters of the multitude of bays, creeks and cays in the Caribbean as well as "great ones" in fast-sailing, heavily manned and armed ships.[136] William Beeston described in his journal his difficulties on two pirate-hunting missions as captain of the *Assistance* in 1672. Repeatedly out-sailed and out-manoeuvred by the rogues, he was finally thwarted by the foulness of his ship.[137]

If a privateer was arrested and brought to trial it was almost impossible to secure a conviction in a Port Royal court. When Beeston brought in the "two small rogues" du Mangles and Weatherborne in 1672, Lynch tried them by court martial. They were convicted and condemned to die but Lynch wavered because of public petitions. The governor decided to send Weatherborne back to England but released du Mangles and all the two men's followers.[138] In 1672 Peter Johnson was wrecked on the coast of Jamaica, arrested and brought to trial.[139] Johnson openly confessed to a string of murders and depredations but the Chief Justice, Thomas Modyford (the former governor's son), told the jury that they could not find against him and he was acquitted. The judge and the privateer then went drinking in the tavern together. Lynch was enraged. He dismissed Modyford and arranged a retrial in which the judgement was reversed and Johnson was executed. The popular unrest which followed disconcerted Lynch and he reported that this self-confessed murderer was mourned in Port Royal "as if he had been as pious and innocent as one of the primitive martyrs". To make matters worse, the king reprimanded the governor for the irregular conduct of the legal proceedings.[140] Lynch took heed and did not take the law into his own hands again. Lord Vaughn later remarked that Johnson was the only privateer who suffered for "all the murders, rapine and violence these privateers had committed on the Spaniards".[141] Partial judges could usually find some devious way of acquitting a privateer – for example, a residence qualification or insufficient evidence. When Coxon was arrested in 1686, Molesworth declared that the only hope of securing a conviction for this popular rogue, who never attacked the island's own ships, was to hold the trial in Spanish Town where the jury would consist of country people, "who are more sensible of the dangers we suffer by privateering than the generality of people at Port Royal".[142] The plan was abortive as Coxon's friends arranged his escape.

In 1687 James II renewed a general proclamation against pirates and privateers and commissioned Sir Robert Holmes to take steps to enforce it.[143] Holmes' agent, Stephen Lynch, met a hostile reception when he arrived in Jamaica in 1688. He immediately arrested 56 "pirates or privateers" with French commissions (some of whom had served under an Englishman, Captain Townley, in the South Seas), who were enjoying themselves in Port Royal's taverns. Instead of applying for pardon and offering security for future good behaviour, as required in the king's proclamation, Lynch claimed that they "intended off on their wanted depredations". The privateers were heavily chained and thrown into gaol. Their petitions reflect how surprised they were at receiving this treatment, "little differing from slaves under the Turks", instead of that "mercy and protection they expected here". The governor, the Duke of Albemarle, was sympathetic to the privateers and soon found a pretext to release the prisoners. They immediately sued Stephen Lynch for damages and, when he refused to pay, took out a warrant for his arrest. Lynch continued to meet obstructions and after repeated public threats he finally "stole privately away".[144] Many planters deplored him as a "very troublesome, unsatisfied man" whose "ill and too severe management" of affairs had generally disrupted trade.[145] Stephen Lynch's experience in Jamaica reflects the fact that even in the late 1680s, almost 20 years after the Treaty of Madrid officially ended hostilities with Spain in the Indies, privateering continued to play a significant role in the economy of Port Royal.

By 1689 Jamaica was settled as a sugar colony and poised to overtake Barbados as England's leading producer in the eighteenth century. But the men listed by John Taylor as the island's "principal gentlemen and planters" were mainly men who had come to Jamaica looking to make a fortune in the years before 1670.[146] They owed much to the profits of plunder. While a twentieth century economist might claim that property rights are "inseparable from human progress", a seventeenth century observer does not share his view.

> If a number of men . . . having neither any fortunes of their owne, nor yet any capacity of the raising of a fortune themselves, regularly by the ordinary course of planting and husbandry or by that of trade and manufacture . . . the consequence is plaine that they must . . . of necessity resolve to make themselves a fortune upon the goods of others, for as such men cannot propound a fortune any other way to themselves than by a course of plunder and of violence.[147]

Privateering required a small capital investment and offered a quick return which made it an ideal start-up trade for a new colony situated in the midst of a traditional enemy. "Frugal, prudential and hopeful" it did indeed prove to be. But plunder could not provide a base for long-term growth because it was constrained by the size of the host economy and, by about 1670, privateering had reached the limits of expansion. By this time planting and merchandizing were established at Jamaica and quickly overtook plunder in value. But privateering did not dwindle away and, though it became relatively less significant, Port Royal was still in 1689 the privateering capital of the Caribbean, "a sodom filled with all manner of debauchery",[148] welcoming the privateers' large purchasing power as ever before.

Notes

1. Richard S. Dunn, *Sugar and Slaves: The Rise of the Planter Class in the English West Indies, 1624–1713* (Chapel Hill, NC: University of North Carolina Press, 1972), 10, 11, 149–50.
2. Public Record Office, Colonial Office (hereafter CO) 138/1, fo. 50, Sir Thomas Modyford to Lord Ashley, 6 July 1670.
3. Alfred Marshall, *Principles of Economics*, 8th ed. (London, 1920), 48. Only limited work has been done on the economics of privateering and piracy. John J. McCusker

and Russell R. Menard, *The Economy of British America, 1607–1789* (Chapel Hill, NC: University of North Carolina Press, 1985), 147–49. An exception is Kenneth R. Andrews, *Elizabethan Privateering: English Privateering during the Spanish War, 1585–1603* (Cambridge: Cambridge University Press, 1964) and *Drake's Voyages: A Re-assessment of their Place in Elizabethan Maritime Expansion* (New York: Charles Scribners Sons, 1967). Also see Violet Barbour, "Privateers and Pirates of the West Indies", *American Historical Review* 16 (1911): 529–66; Robert C. Richie, *Captain Kidd and the War against the Pirates* (London: Harvard University Press, 1986); C.H. Haring, *The Buccaneers in the West Indies in the Seventeenth Century* (London: Metheun, 1910), 197–229.

4. Nuala Zahedieh, "Trade, Plunder and Economic Development in early English Jamaica, 1655–89", *Economic History Review*, 2nd ser., 39, no. 2 (1986): 205–22.

5. H. Scott Gordon, "The Economic Theory of a Common Property Resource: The Fishery", *Journal of Political Economy* 62 (1954): 124–42; Anthony Scott, "The Fishery: The Objectives of Sole Ownership", *Journal of Political Economy* 62 (1955): 116–24. Fishing literature has similarly been applied to American street crime. Philip A. Neher, "The Pure Theory of the Muggery", *American Economic Review* 68 (1978): 437–45.

6. Nuala Zahedieh, "The Merchants of Port Royal, Jamaica, and the Spanish Contraband Trade, 1655–1692", *William and Mary Quarterly*, 3rd ser., 43, no. 3 (1986): 570–93.

7. Institute of Jamaica, Kingston (hereafter IJ) MS 390, Letter to Nottingham, March 1689.

8. John Lynch, *Spain under the Habsburgs*, 2nd ed. (Oxford: Basil Blackwell, 1981), 2: 209.

9. P.E. Hoffman, *The Spanish Crown and the Defense of the Caribbean, 1535–1589* (Baton Rouge, Louisiana: Louisiana State University Press, 1980); Roland D. Hussey, "Spanish Reaction to Foreign Aggression in the Caribbean to about 1680", *Hispanic American Historical Review* 9 (1929): 286–302; C.H. Haring, *Trade and Navigation between Spain and the Indies in the Time of the Hapsburgs* (Cambridge, Mass: Harvard University Press, 1918); Cornelius H. Goslinga, *The Dutch in the Caribbean, 1580–1680* (Gainesville, Florida: University of Florida Press, 1971), 173–98.

10. Murdo J. Macleod, *Spanish Central America. A Socioeconomic History, 1520–1720* (London, Berkeley: University of California Press, 1973), 235–373.

11. A. MacFayden, "Anglo-Spanish Relations, 1625–60" (PhD thesis, University of Liverpool, 1967). The line was the prime meridian passing through the Azores and the Tropic of Cancer. G. Mattingly, "No Peace Beyond What Line", *Transactions of the Royal Historical Society*, 5th ser., 13 (1963): 145–62.

12. *Calendar of State Papers, Domestic, 1636–37*, 503–4, Thomas Roe to Elizabeth of Bohemia, 17 March 1637.

13. Frank Strong, "The Causes of Cromwell's West Indian Expedition", *American Historical Review* 4 (1898): 224–45; British Library (hereafter BL) Add. MS 11,410, fo. 97, "Commission to Venables, Penn, Winslow, Searle, Butler"; Thomas Gage, *The English American; A New Survey of the West Indies*, ed. A.P. Newton (London: G. Routledge and Sons, 1928); Karen Ordahl Kupperman, "Errand to the Indies: Puritan Colonization from Providence Island through the Western Design", *William and Mary Quarterly*, 3rd ser., 45 (1988): 70–99.
14. BL Add. MS 12,423, fo. 97b, "D'Oyley's Journal"; CO 1/15, fo. 75, D'Oyley to Nicholas, March 1661; BL Add. MS 12,430, fo. 45, "Beeston's Journal".
15. This belief was reflected in the instructions given to the first royal governor, Lord Windsor, appointed in 1662. "If the governors of the King of Spain shall refuse to admit our subjects to trade with them you shall in such case endeavour to procure and settle a trade with his subjects in those parts by force." CO 138/1 fo. 20, 3 May 1662.
16. A.P. Thornton, *West India Policy Under the Restoration* (Oxford: Clarendon Press, 1956), 67–123.
17. Island Record Office, Spanish Town, Jamaica (hereafter IRO), Deeds, OS I, fos. 22, 27b, 40, 43b, 68, 87, 90b.
18. CO 138/3, fos. 468–Q9, Morgan to Committee, 27 January 1681.
19. *Calendar State Papers Colonial, Addenda, 1574–1674* (hereafter *CSP Col*), no. 231, "Instructions to Capt. William Goodson". CO 1/32, fo. 194, "Disposal of the Fleet at Jamaica". CO 1/33, fo. 3, fo. 18, Vice Admiral Goodson to Commissioners of the Admiralty, 14 July 1656; Goodson to Admiralty, 23 Aug. 1656. Thurloe State Papers, vol. 5, 771, 778, Goodson to Thurloe, 10 January 1657; Brayne to Thurloe, 10 January 1657. CO 1/33, fo. 74, Order of the Council of State, 23 July 1657. D'Oyley's orders and instructions to the ships are in his journal, BL Add. MS 12,423.
20. *CSP Col 1661–8*, no. 364, Minutes of Council of Jamaica, 5–30 September 1662; BL Add. MS 12,430, fo. 49, 61, "Beeston's Journal".
21. BL Add. MS 12,423, fo. 61b, D'Oyley's Instructions to Captain Povey, 5 April 1659. For a full description of the development of the admiralty courts in Jamaica see H.J. Crump, *Colonial Admiralty Jurisdiction in the Seventeenth Century* (London, New York: Longmans, Green, 1931), 91–116.
22. CO 1/33, fos. 74–75, Order of the Council of State, 23 July 1657. BL Add. MS 12,423, fo. 61b, 91, "D'Oyley's Journal", 2 May 1659, 14 June 1660.
23. PRO, High Court of Admiralty (hereafter HCA) 49/51, fos. 29–44.
24. CO 138/1, fo. 161, "Fifteenths of Prizes for Accompt of His Majestie". The date 1665 appears at the head of the page. However, other records show the real dates of the account.
25. CO 1/23, fo. 149, Richard Browne to Joseph Williamson, 9 November 1668; by courtesy of the Dean and Chapter of Westminster, Westminster Abbey Muniments (here-

after WAM) 11,921, Sir James Modyford to Sir Andrew King, 4 November 1668. This document and others in the collection are printed in A.P. Thornton, "The Modyfords and Morgan", *Jamaican Historical Review* 2 (1952): 36–60.
26. Ralph Davis, *The Rise of the English Shipping Industry in the Seventeenth and Eighteenth Centuries* (London: Macmillan, 1962), 86.
27. CO 1/19, fos. 60–61, "Several Goods Seized on ye account of Spanish Interests and sold by inch of candle 27", 15 March 1665.
28. Peter Earle, *The Sack of Panama* (London: Norman and Hobhouse, 1981), 108–9, 156.
29. BL Add. MS 11,410, fos. 675–84, "An Accompt of our Intended Voyage from Jamaica with a party of ships, departing from the aforesaid island to Bartanell".
30. CO 140/1, fos. 233–35, Minutes of Council of Jamaica, 21 September 1671.
31. CO 138/1, fo. 38, Sir Thomas Modyford to the Privy Council.
32. BL Add. MS 11,410, fos. 332–33, Morgan's "Relation".
33. HCA 49/59, fo. 83b–92b. Letters of marque, which legally authorized the holder to seize enemy ships and goods, were issued freely by belligerent powers to almost anyone who applied for them. In peace, letters of marque were an instrument of private redress, whereby a state authorized subjects who had received injury at the hands of foreigners to obtain compensation at the expense of the subjects of the offending state. F.R. Stark, *The Abolition of Privateering and the Declaration of Paris* (New York: Columbia University, 1897) 53.
34. The importance of holding a commission is reflected in instructions to Jamaican pirate hunting missions in 1672 and 1682 not to meddle with anyone with papers. BL Add. MS 12,424, fo. 7. CO 138/4, fo. 111. Henry Morgan set great store by possession of a commission. When two English translations of A.O. Exquemelin's *History of the Bucaniers* appeared in 1684, Morgan objected to being called pirate and buccaneer and sued both publishers for libel claiming that, "In the West Indies there are such thieves and pirates called buccaneers who subsist by piracy, depredation and evil deeds of all kinds without lawful authority, that of these people Henry Morgan always had and still has hatred". The suit was settled by consent and the publishers printed apologies prefaced to new editions.
35. CO 1/14, fo. 22, D'Oyley to Commissioners of Navy, 1 June 1660; BL Add. MS 12,430, fo. 46, "Beeston's Journal".
36. HCA 49/59, fos. 21–25b. George Freebourne was acquitted of piracy in England and returned to Jamaica where he obtained a Commission on 15 November 1662.
37. CO 1/17, fos. 175, 177, "Statement of Sir Charles Littleton's Case", 1663; CO 138/1, fo. 134, "An Abstract or Accompt of the Profits accrued to Sir Thomas Modyford by being Governor of Jamaica".
38. HCA 49/59, fos. 120b, 83b–92b, CO 1/20, fo. 49b, Modyford to Arlington, 5 June 1665.

39. CO 138/1, fo. 105, "List of the Ships under Admiral Morgan".
40. Davis, *Rise of the English Shipping Industry*, 59.
41. Massachusetts State House, Boston, Archives of Massachusetts, 1622–1799 (hereafter A.Mass), 60, fos. 73–76, 217–35a, 256–74, 289, "Papers Relating to the Blue Dove".
42. CO 138/1, fos. 49–51, Modyford to Ashley, 6 July 1670.
43. BL Add. MS 12,423, fo. 86b, "D'Oyley's Journal".
44. Earle, *Sack of Panama*, 186.
45. HCA 49/59, fo. 43b.
46. Ibid., fo. 109b.
47. Ibid., fo. 43b.
48. Ibid., fos. 46–49b, 55b, 56, 59, 64.
49. CO 1/25, fo. 144b, "Narrative of Sir Thomas Modyford", 23 August 1669.
50. WAM 11,920, Sir James Modyford to Sir Andrew King, 4 Oct. 1668; CO 1/24, fo. 1, "Spanish Ambassador's Memorial", 17 January 1669.
51. WAM 11,925, Sir James Modyford to Sir Andrew King, 24 May 1669.
52. CO 1/25, fo. 123, Modyford to Arlington, 31 October 1670.
53. HCA 49/59, fos. 83b–92b.
54. John Morris, William James, John Moreau, Nicholas Bart, Nicholas Rion and Adrian Swart were killed, John Harmanson was killed in 1673; Morris Williams was a prisoner; George Brimacain and Richard Guy were planters; David Martin and Adrian Mitchell were cutting logwood.
55. BL Egerton MS 2395, fo. 145, "Letter from Col. D'Oyley upon the death of Col. Brayne", 1657. BL Add. MS 11,410, fo. 636, "Mr Worsley's Discourse of the Privateers of Jamaica".
56. CO 138/3, fos. 417–18, Morgan to Sunderland, 5 July 1680.
57. Zahedieh, "Trade, Plunder and Economic Development", 206–10.
58. *CSP Col 1677–80*, no. 988, "Estimate for Monthly Charges for Maintaining at Sea three Fourth and three Fifth Rate Men-Of-War for the Security of the Leeward Islands", 12 May 1679; Davis, *Rise of the English Shipping Industry*, 133–37. There were complaints to the Council of Jamaica that seamen were tempted to "frequently desert" naval and merchant ships to join the privateers. CO 140/1, fos. 253–54, Minutes of Council of Jamaica, 26 Oct. 1671.
59. IJ MS 105, II, fos. 536–37, "Taylor's History".
60. BL Add. MS 11,410, fos. 685–743, "The Journal of our Intended Voyage into the South Seas".
61. Jamaica Archives, Spanish Town (hereafter JA), Inv.IB/11/3, III, fos. 259–67, "Inventory of Henry Morgan", 1688. Other examples of privateers turned planter include Richard Guy, CO 138/1, fo. 70, "Survey of Jamaica", 1670; Lawrence Prince IRO Deeds OSI, fo. 129.
62. Exquemelin, *History of the Bucaniers*, 1: 106–7.

63. BL Add. MS 12,423, fo. 62, "D'Oyley's Journal". BL Add. MS 11,410, fo. 20, "The Relation of Col. D'Oyley". CO 140/1, fo. 8, Minutes of Council, 3 July 1661. CO 1/25, fo. 2, John Style to Principal Secretary of State, 4 January 1670.
64. BL Add. MS 11,410, fos. 395–430, Lynch to Clifford, 20 August 1671, Lynch to Slingsby, 29 November 1671.
65. WAM 11,913, Sir James Modyford to Sir Andrew King, 27 December 1667. The wide variety of prize goods is reflected in the inventories of the Blue Dove: 40 hogsheads of sugar, some cocoa, ebony, granadilla, brasiletta, oaken storkfish, 30 chests of quicksilver, 2 gold crowns "with divers other jewels", 1 barrel of knives, some swords, 60 jars of oil, 9 cases of spirits, 8 packs of white wax, and lignum vitae. A.Mass, 60, fo. 223.
66. WAM 11,913, Sir James Modyford to Sir Andrew King, 27 December 1667; CO 1/22, fo. 56, "Copy of Condemnation of Ship Nostra Senora de la Conception de San Joseph", 28 August 1667; CO 138/1, fo. 161, "Accompt of fifteenths".
67. CO 140/1, fos. 170, 261, Minutes of Council of Jamaica, 26 November 1667, November 1668.
68. WAM 11,920, 11,921, Sir James Modyford to Sir Andrew King, 4 October 1667, 4 November 1668.
69. HCA 49/59, fos. 29–44.
70. CO 1/24, fo. 161, "Fifteenths of Prizes".
71. CO 1/24, fo. 145, "Narrative of Sir Thomas Modyford", 23 Aug. 1669. HCA 49/59, fo. 36.
72. The master of the *Santo Christo* taken in 1664 claimed his ship and cargo were worth 13,450 pieces of eight (£3,500). However, all that was left by the time the officers came on board to list the goods were 13 packs of silvester and one small box of cloth and vanillas which, with £50 for the ship produced a total of £127 3s. CO 1/19, fos. 60–61, "Severall goods seized on for ye account of Spanish interests and sold by inch of candle", 15 March 1665; CO 1/20, fos. 52, 244–45, "Complaint of Don Juan Ximenes de Bohorques", "Modyford to Privy Council", 21 August 1666.
73. Massachusetts Historical Society, Boston, Gay Papers, Box 1, D'Oyley to Commissioners of Army and Navy, 25 April 1659.
74. WAM 11,920, 11,925, Sir James Modyford to Sir Andrew King, 4 October 1668, 24 May 1669; BL Add. MS 11,410, fo. 338, "Morgan's Relation", 20 April 1671.
75. BL Add. MS 11,410, fos. 26–31, "Littleton's Account of the State of Jamaica".
76. CO 1/24, fo. 19, John Style to William Morice, 14 January 1669.
77. CO 1/15, fo. 192, "A Briefe Accompt of the Severall Inhabitants in the Island of Jamaica"; *Journal of House of Assembly of Jamaica, 1663–1826* (Jamaica, 1811–29), 1, 28. CO 138/1, fos. 107–11, "A List of What Shipps and Vessells have arrived in Port Royall Harbour from the 1st of January 1668 untill the 1st of January 1670".
78. Zahedieh, "Trade, Plunder and Economic Development", 207.
79. HCA 49/59, fos. 84b, 85, 88, 90.

80. CO 1/18, fos. 22–23, "Deposition of John Haines", 25 January 1664; HCA 49/59, fo. 52.
81. BL Add. MS 11,410, fo. 406, Lynch to Williamson, 7 September 1671; IRO Deeds OS1, fo. 90b.
82. Zahedieh, "Trade, Plunder and Economic Development", 213.
83. Haring, *Buccaneers in the West Indies*, 267; CO 138/1, fo. 100, "The Governor of Jamaica's Answer to the Inquiries of His Majestie's Commissioners".
84. BL Add. MS 12,424, fo. 6, "Journal of Sir William Beeston, 1671–1702".
85. BL Add. MS 11,410, fo. 338, "Morgan's Relation", 20 April 1671; Ibid., fos. 377–78, Thomas Lynch to Arlington, 27 June 1671.
86. The King of Spain despatched a small squadron of six frigates and other craft, the Armada de Barlovento, to patrol the Caribbean in 1598. However, it soon began to be used for convoy duties instead of remaining in the Indies. No one questioned the desirability of an Armada de Barlovento, finances were the problem. The American provinces paid special taxes for the fleet for most of the century but it proved almost impossible to withhold these moneys from the general Spanish needs. Hussey, "Spanish Reaction", 292–93, 296–97.
87. Hoffman, *Spanish Crown*, 224–28; H. Chaunu and P. Chaunu, *Seville et l'Atlantique, 1504–1650*, 8 vols. (Paris: A. Colin, 1955–59), 1: 169–237; 5: 415–16; 6: tables, 183–84.
88. Earle, *Sack of Panama*, 115–30.
89. A.P. Newton, *The European Nations in the West Indies, 1493–1688* (London: A. and C. Black, 1933), 259–61.
90. CO 138/1, fos. 43, 46, Modyford to Arlington, 6 July 1670; "Copy of a Commission of War by the Spaniard against the English in the West Indies being the translation of the original in Spanish".
91. CO 138/1, fo. 136, "Considerations from Sir Thomas Modyford which moved him to give his consent for fitting the privateers of Jamaica against the Spaniards".
92. HCA 49/59, fo. 98b, "Commission to Capt. Barnard Nicholas", 23 May 1663; CO 1/25, fo. 34, Modyford to Arlington, 18 March 1670; WAM 11,937, James Modyford to King, 2 May 1670.
93. CO 1/28, fo. 122, Godolphin to Arlington, 10 May 1672. On the logwood trade see Arthur M. Wilson, "The Logwood Trade in the Seventeenth and Eighteenth Centuries", in *Essays in the History of Modern Europe*, ed. Douglas McKay (New York: Harper and Bros., 1936), 1–15.
94. CO 1/25, fos. 123, 225, Modyford to Arlington, 31 Oct. 1670, 18 December 1670; CO 138/1, fo. 112, "Account of Ships that trade for logwood at Campeche and belong to Port Royal", March 1671; CO 1/27, fo. 11, Browne to Williamson, 6 July 1671.
95. CO 1/27, fo. 193, Lynch to Arlington, 25 December 1671; CO 1/28, fo. 122, Godolphin to Arlington, 10 May 1672; CO 1/31, fo. 213b, Lynch to Williamson, 20 November 1674.

96. CO 1/28, fos. 15–15b, Lynch to Joseph Williamson, 27 January 1672.
97. K.G. Davies, *The Royal African Company* (London: Longmans, Green, 1957), 59–60.
98. F.G. Davenport, *European Treaties Bearing on the History of the United States* (Washington, DC: Carnegie Institution of Washington, 1929), 2: 176–87; Thornton, *West India Policy*, 98–123.
99. CO 138/1, fos. 92–93, "Instructions for Sir Thomas Lynch our Lieutenant Governor of Jamaica", 24 February 1671.
100. BL Add. MS 11,410, fos. 390–92, 402–3, Lynch to Sandwich, 20 Aug. 1671, Lynch to Williamson, 7 September 1671.
101. A.P. Thornton describes the Treaty of Madrid as bringing the Law of Nations beyond the line. He sees it as part of an emerging "Imperial Scheme", Thornton, *West India Policy*, 67–123. Also see Barbour, "Privateers and Pirates", 563–66; Hussey, "Spanish Reaction", 301. Some historians describe a lag between colonial attitudes and official policy, but claim that by the 1680s piracy was in frank decline at Jamaica and regarded as a nuisance. M. Pawson and D. Buisseret, *Port Royal, Jamaica* (Oxford: Clarendon Press, 1975), 33–36; Newton, *European Nations*, 276–77, 320–29; Haring, *Buccaneers in the West Indies*, 197–229.
102. CO 138/2, fo. 118, "State of Jamaica", 14 December 1675.
103. CO 138/3, fo. 283, Carlisle to Coventry, 24 October 1678.
104. CO 138/3, fos. 429–30, "Memorial of Spanish Ambassador", 6 September 1680; CO 1/52, fo. 67, Lynch to Jenkins, 26 July 1683.
105. BL Add. MS 11,410, fos. 685–743, "The Journal of our Intended Voyage into the South Seas". In 1680 to 1681 alone the Spaniards estimated the damage to their Pacific shipping and ports at over 4 million pesos; their merchant marine lost 25 ships and they suffered more than 200 fatal casualties. Lynch, 2: 197–200. In December 1684 Molesworth reported that at least 400 Jamaicans had been conveyed to Golden Island in island sloops and thence across the isthmus to join the privateers in the last three months. CO 138/5, fos. 15, 72, Molesworth to Committee, 30 December 1684, Molesworth to Blathwayt, 6 July 1685.
106. *CSP Col, 1675–77*, no. 537, Minutes of the Assembly of Jamaica, 26 April–15 May 1675.
107. BL Add. MS 11,410, fos. 623, 15, "Worsley's Discourse"; "The Cape of Tortudas".
108. CO 138/1, fo. 105, "A List of the Ships under the Command of Admiral Morgan".
109. A. Mass 60, fo. 73, "The Names of Captain Duglas' Men and Where their usual Being is".
110. When Modyford proclaimed peace in 1664 only one privateer came in; Capt. Swart "without men and money, his vessel out of all possibility to go to sea". CO 1/18, fos. 176b, 175, Modyford to Bennet, 30 June 1664, Edward Morgan to Arlington, 28 June 1664. Capt. Morris came in after his men mutinied and deserted him in 1671, CO

110. 1/28, fos. 15–15b, Lynch to Williamson, 27 January 1672; BL Add. MS 11,410, fos. 478–81, Lynch to Arlington, 28 January 1672.
111. CO 138/5, fos. 133–35, Molesworth to Blathwayt, 16 January 1685.
112. CO 1/28, fo. 7b, Lynch to Williamson, 13 January 1672.
113. BL Add. MS 12,424, fo. 7, "Beeston's Instructions to Lt William Ardany", 13 January 1672; CO 1/20, fos. 38–39, "Examinations of Morris, Fackman and Morgan", 20 February 1665.
114. CO 1/19, fo. 38, Modyford to Arlington, 20 February 1665; CO 1/31, fo. 214, Lynch to Williamson, 20 November 1674; CO 138/4, fo. 93, Lynch to Committee, 29 September 1682; Newton, *European Nations*, 34–38.
115. CO 140/3, fo. 495, Minutes of Council of Jamaica, 24 July 1676.
116. CO 138/3, fo. 40, Vaughan to Committee of Trade and Plantations, 28 January 1676.
117. Haring, *Buccaneers in the West Indies*, 227; CO 138/3, fo. 429, "Memorial of Spanish Ambassador", 6 September 1680.
118. CO 1/43, fo. 253, Letter of Intelligence, 18 October 1679.
119. William Claypole, "The Merchants of Port Royal, 1655–1700", unpublished PhD thesis, University of the West Indies, 1974, 174–95. Zahediah, "Trade, Plunder and Economic Development", 214, 221.
120. In 1680 Morgan sent an armed party to capture eight mutinous white servants who had intended to join a privateer. BL Sloane MS 2724, fo. 236, Morgan to Carlisle, 5 July 1680. In 1665 the Council of Jamaica ordered that no privateer should recruit any man without a ticket from the governor. Tickets would be available to free men, unmarried, without a plantation. CO 140/1, fo. 141, Minutes of Council of Jamaica, 10 October 1665. Similar orders were repeated.
121. CO 140/4, fos. 186b–187b, "A List of Injuryes and Damages Received and Done by the Spaniards and French to his most sacred Majesties Subjects of Jamaica".
122. CO 142/13, Naval Officer's Returns, Jamaica, 1680–1705.
123. PRO Chancery (hereafter C) 110/152, Brailsford vs. Peers, Chancery Masters Exhibits.
124. CO 138/5, fo. 68, Molesworth to Blathwayt, 15 May 1685. Dutch prizes were common as the Dutch played a major role in Spanish colonial commerce.
125. CO 140/4, fo. 225b, Minutes of Council of Jamaica, 3 May 1688.
126. CO 138/3, fo. 480, fos. 468–69, Morgan to Jenkins, 9 April 1681; Morgan to Committee, 27 January 1681.
127. CO 138/4, fo. 114, Lynch to Jenkins, 6 November 1682.
128. CO 1/40, fos. 195b, Vaughan to Coventry, 28 May 1677.
129. CO 140/3, fos. 474–511, Minutes of the Council of Jamaica, 24 July 1676.
130. CO 138/3, fo. 429, "Memorial of Spanish Ambassador", 6 September 1680; ibid., fos. 366–68, Carlisle to Committee, 23 November 1679; CO 140/2, fo. 54, *Journals of the Assembly of Jamaica*.
131. BL Sloane MS 2724, fo. 14b, Morgan to Carlisle, 14 June 1680.

132. Pawson and Buisseret, *Port Royal, Jamaica*, 43.
133. BL Add. MS 25,120, fos. 72–73, 132–33, Coventry to Morgan, 29 March 1676, Coventry to Carlisle, 16 November 1678.
134. In 1672 William Beeston captain of the *Assistance* embarked on a pirate hunting mission with four other island vessels in his fleet including John Morris, a reformed privateer, in the *Lilly*, BL Add. MS 12,424, fos. 8–14, "Beeston's Journal, 1671–1702"; CO 138/4, fo. 111, Lynch to Jenkins, 6 November 1682.
135. CO 142/13, fo. 11, Naval Officers Returns, May 1686. CO 138/5, fos. 323–24, Molesworth to Blathwayt, 9 February 1687.
136. CO 138/4, fos. 141–50, Lynch to Blathwayt, 22 February 1683.
137. BL Add. MS 12,424, fos. 8–23, "Beeston's Journal, 1671–1702".
138. Ibid., fo. 13b; BL Add. MS 11,410, fos. 540–41, Lynch to Arlington, 29 March 1672.
139. Johnson was one of the Jamaican privateers who ignored Lynch's proclamation. He captured a Spanish prize off Havana "an excellent ship, new and an admirable saylor build at Cartagena" which he manned with 100 men and 14 guns. He plundered Cuba claiming he had "a kind of commission of war" but Lynch treated him as a pirate reporting that he had done £30,000 of damage to the Spaniards. Beeston chased him for several months but could not catch him. CO 1/29, fos. 76, 92, Browne to Williamson, 28 September 1672; Lynch to Slingsby, 9 Oct. 1672; BL Add. MS 11,410, fo. 482, Lynch to Arlington, 28 January 1672; idem, 29 March 1672; BL Add. MS 12,424, fos. 8–23, "Beeston's Journal, 1671–1702".
140. CO 1/30, fos. 67b–68, 134, 213, King to Lynch, 15 January 1673, Lynch to Williamson, 12 August 1673, Lynch to Worsley, 12 August 1673.
141. IJ MS 159, fo. 20, "History and State of Jamaica under Lord Vaughan, 1679–80".
142. CO 138/5, fo. 135, Molesworth to Blathwayt, 16 January 1685.
143. CO 138/5, fo. 297, "Proclamation for suppressing Pirates and Privateers in America"; CO 138/6, fos. 44–47, 63–65, "Circular Letter for the Apprehending and Detaining Pirates", 13 October 1687, King to Albemarle, 22 January 1688.
144. All were Frenchmen except three, "an Irishman, a German and a Mulatto", CO 138/6, fos. 118, 134, fos. 129–32, 316–17, Albemarle to Committee, 11 May 1688, 20 June 1688; ibid., "Letter to the Duke of Albemarle touching Mr Lynch", 4 September 1688; ibid., Francis Watson to Committee, 22 April 1689; CO 140/4, fos. 225–30, Minutes of Council of Jamaica, 3 May 1688.
145. CO 138/6, fos. 215–16, 316–17, Francis Watson to Committee, 15 March 1689, 22 April 1689.
146. Zahedieh, "Trade, Plunder and Economic Development", 221.
147. BL Add. MS 11,410, fo. 636, "Mr Worsley's Discourse".
148. IJ, MS 105 II, fos. 503–4, "Taylor's History".

CHAPTER 3

Planters and Merchants

The Oliver Family of Antigua and London, 1716–1784*

RICHARD B. SHERIDAN

I

A significant number of London-West India merchants, members of established planter and mercantile families, came to the metropolis from the colonies in the eighteenth century. The late Professor Richard Pares told the story of Henry Lascelles, the Barbadian merchant, customs collector, and planter who became a London sugar factor and acquired one of the great fortunes of his age.[1] Recently, Mr D.W. Thoms has recounted the career of Thomas Mills, who lived some years in St Kitts as a factor, plantation manager, and renter before he came to London to join the family sugar firm.[2] With the possible exception of Jamaica, more merchants came from Antigua to London than from any other island. Antigua was not only larger than its neighbours, but it also had a more highly developed plantation economy and was the centre of the trade, shipping, finance, politics, and social life of the Leeward Islands. Numerous individuals capitalized on these advantages by establishing

---

*Originally published in *Business History* 13, 2 (July 1971): 104–13. Reprinted by permission of Taylor and Francis Ltd.

businesses in the metropolis: from 1740 to 1775 there were at least 41, including 27 London firms. There were 22 individuals with West Indian family origins, 24 who married into planter families, 25 who had been resident in Antigua, 12 who had been island merchants, and 20 who owned plantations. Antigua planter families represented in London by their kinsmen were the Banisters, Christians, Codringtons, Douglases, Dunbars, Fryes, Johnsons, Kerbys, Kirwans, Lovells, Lucases, Martins, Olivers, Skerretts, Tomlinsons, Turners, Udneys, Warners, and Watkins.[3]

One of the leading merchant-planter families of Antigua were the Olivers. Dr Vere Langford Oliver, a descendant and author of *The History of the Island of Antigua*, has compiled data on five Richard Olivers. The first two were brothers and partners who lived in Bristol; Richard I was a linen-draper and merchant who traded to Virginia and owned plantations beyond the seas while Richard II was also a linen-draper and merchant as well as burgess. Richard III, his second son, was born in Bristol in 1664. He was probably the Richard Oliver who became a merchant and planter in Antigua. That he was influential in the island community is evident from his election to the General Assembly, his appointment to the Council, and his posts as Speaker, Justice of the Peace, and Major of Militia. Richard III died in 1716, leaving three sons – Richard, Rowland, and Robert, and two daughters – Jane who died young, and Elizabeth who married Thomas Turner.[4] Richard IV, the eldest son, inherited half of his father's estate of 520 acres in Antigua. He too was active in the public life of the island, serving as Assemblyman, Counsellor, and Major of Militia. He was reported to be in England when a list of the Council of Antigua was published in February 1744/5. It may be presumed that he had established his London commission agency by that time.[5] In 1724, Richard Oliver IV married Mary, eldest daughter of Jonas Langford, a well-to-do Quaker planter of Antigua. Their children were Richard Langford and Elizabeth both of whom died young, Thomas and Mary, who married her first cousin Richard Oliver V. Samuel Langford lived at Greenwich near London where his sister and brother-in-law also lived. He provided in his will of 1747, that his mother should be his executrix, but that "if she die my brother-in-law Richard Oliver to be Executor". Jonas Langford the Younger was another kinsman and he appointed Richard and Rowland Oliver trustees of his estate in Antigua leaving instructions in his will of 1758 that "all produce of my plantations to be consigned to Richd Oliver if he shall continue the business of a sugar factor".[6]

The most prominent member of the family was the fifth Richard Oliver, Alderman and Member of Parliament for the City of London. Alderman Oliver was born in Antigua in 1735, the son of Rowland and Sarah Oliver but at an early age he came to London and entered his uncle's counting house. After taking up his freedom in the Drapers' Company, he was elected Alderman of Billingsgate Ward on 4 July 1771. A few days later he was returned to the House of Commons for the City of London. Together with John Wilkes and others, he became engaged in the famous struggle between the City and the House of Commons and he was a leader in the Society of the Supporters of the Bill of Rights. He was imprisoned in the Tower with the Lord Mayor for his defiance of the government. Subsequent to his release, he, with others, separated from Wilkes and formed a new association called the Constitutional Society.[7] Alderman Oliver and his wife are mentioned frequently in *The Diary of John Baker*. Baker was a London barrister who had been Solicitor General of the Leeward Islands. He was an absentee planter, a lawyer for numerous planters and London sugar merchants, and a man who led an active social life. On one occasion John Baker, William Manning, a sugar factor, and the Alderman "walked through the Minories to the Tower and round about many parts of it, particularly to where Mr Oliver lodged when sent by the H. of Commons". Baker heard on 24 October 1772, that "Messrs. Oliver, Smith and Tooke had given £29,000 for an estate at Grenada". On 3 May 1774, Baker met the Alderman at the Mansion House and talked with him about a debate on the Boston Port Bill in the House of Commons.[8] On 4 May 1777, Baker "met Mr Alderman Oliver, Mr Mich. Lovell, and Mr *Boston Oliver* – was Lt. Governor (or some such thing) there, has 6 daughters and no son".[9]

II

The history of the London partnership began in Antigua, where Richard IV accumulated capital and cultivated relations with planters and merchants who later became his correspondents when he moved to London. Wills and indentures indicate that his activities were widespread. In 1725, he and his brother Rowland divided their father's estate, consisting of 520 acres and an undisclosed number of Negro slaves in St John's Division and at the same time sold a plantation in Virginia and houses in St John's town on account of the father's heavy debts. In 1731, Richard leased a large sugar plantation which he improved by building a windmill and dwelling house.[10] Oliver lived at the port of St John's and combined planting with trade. A chancery case of 1741 reveals that Charles Goare, Richard Oliver, and Michael Lovell were merchants in company in St John's, trading as Goare and Company[11] while other records show that our subject was appointed executor of seven estates in the years prior to 1745.[12]

Richard Oliver IV transacted business in London as a single proprietor from about 1744 to 1761. On 25 April 1761, he took into partnership his son-in-law and nephew and gave him a mutual interest with himself in the business of the house, which was thenceforward carried on in the name and under the firm of Richard and Richard Oliver. Richard Oliver the Elder died on 10 June 1763 but "as the house was of long standing and the business advantageous", Richard Oliver the Younger determined to continue it and took into the house as partner Thomas Oliver, his first cousin and son of Richard Oliver the Elder. The firm then became known as Richard and Thomas Oliver. When Alderman Oliver retired from the firm to devote himself to politics, Thomas Oliver in 1770 took into partnership Michael Lovell, his first cousin who had been a merchant in Antigua. The firm of Oliver and Lovell continued in the sugar factorage business in London until about 1800.[13]

The house of Oliver nearly failed during the American War of Independence. *The Bath Chronicle* reported on 9 January 1777: "Another capital West-India House stopt payment last week, which makes the fourth, and 'tis imagined that others must follow. All this is the natural consequence of the American captures: upwards of 130 ships from the West India islands have been taken by their privateers in the course of the last year."[14] Several weeks later the same paper took pleasure in informing its readers that the above report about the Oliver's counting house in Fenchurch Street was unfounded, and that the firm was still in business but all was not well. Owing to the precarious state of his property in the West Indies, Richard Oliver resigned his gown as Alderman, but retained his seat in Parliament until the dissolution in 1780. *The Bath Chronicle* announced on 23 September 1779: "Mr Oliver, late an Alderman of the City of London, was on the island of Grenada when taken by the French. He has large possessions there, and went over on suspicion of what would happen. All sugars were sent to France and confiscated."[15] Several months later he was residing at Antigua, where he owned plantations and slaves, as well as at Nevis, Montserrat, and St Vincent. Alderman Oliver died a few years later on 16 April 1784.[16]

III

The London commission agent served his planter correspondents in a number of capacities. His mercantile and shipping duties consisted of receiving the planter's staples off the ship, paying custom duties, warehousing, and eventually selling the goods consigned to his care. He purchased plantation supplies and consumer goods that were ordered from England, chartered and insured vessels and cargoes, and in time of war petitioned the Admiralty for warships to escort the fleets of merchantmen. Miscellaneous services included the recruitment of indentured servants and artisans, the supervision of the education of children who arrived from the West Indies, and the collection and dissemination of commercial and political intelligence of concern to his correspondents.[17] The London factor was not only the planter's buying and selling agent but also his banker. He extended trade-credit by sending out plantation supplies before the planter's staples were received or sold. He accepted bills of exchange which his correspondent drew on him in payment for Negro slaves and other outlays. He granted loans to his correspondent with or without security such as promissory notes, bonds, judgments, or mortgages. If the balance of the sterling running account stood to the credit of the correspondent, the factor might accede to a request to purchase lottery tickets or to invest in public funds. Factors who operated on small capitals were bankers only in a deposit and transfer capacity. But those with funds of their own or with access to the money market (which included their own correspondents' credit balances) might be tempted by the high interest rates in the colonies to engage in extensive credit and loan transactions. Finally, the factor and his correspondents might decide to invest their income from the plantations in English or Scottish landed estates, or mercantile, mining, and industrial establishments.

Wills and indentures indicate that the Olivers had upwards of forty planter correspondents in the period from 1744 to 1780. Antigua seems to have accounted for almost all of the correspondents until about 1763, when the business expanded to Nevis, Montserrat, St Vincent, and Grenada. Oliver kinsmen who were loyal to the firm were the Langfords, Lovells, Turners,

Smiths, Watkins, Otto-Bayers, Murrays, Royalls, and Freemans. Scottish planter correspondents included the Tullidephs, Sydserfes, Hallidays, Dunbars, Jordans, and Dewars. Old Antigua families were represented in the firm's *clientele* by the Gilberts, Thomases, Martins, Tomlinsons, and Williams.[18] Unfortunately, only two of the outgoing letters of the firm are known to have survived. Richard Oliver IV wrote from London to John Tomlinson of Antigua on 31 October 1752, informing him that twenty hogsheads of his sugar had been sold at thirty eight shillings per hundredweight and another ten at thirty nine. The market had been slow owing to a combination of sugar bakers, "but they now buy tho' with great Complaints & are scheeming for Introduceing Forreign Sug^r Even upon the Double Duty".[19] On 5 October 1758, Richard and Richard Oliver wrote to Dr Walter Tullideph, an absentee living near Dundee, Scotland. The Doctor was informed of the receipt and sale of his sugars from Antigua, the report of short crops in the West Indies, the purchase of South Sea Company Annuities in his name, and the fact that Richard Oliver Senior had been a good deal confined to the country, presumably at his estate at Layton, county Essex.[20]

One of the Oliver's correspondents for some years was Colonel Samuel Martin, a leading planter of Antigua. Martin's connection with the Olivers becomes clear from the letters he wrote to his son Samuel Martin, Junior, Member of Parliament and Secretary to the Treasury Board. Colonel Martin began the correspondence on 12 May 1753 when he wrote that he had drawn upon the Olivers for £442 sterling for the purchase of Negroes. Martin consigned his sugars to two or more London factors. He wrote on 28 August 1755, that his crop would probably amount to 280 hogsheads, "113 of which are gone to Mr Oliver, 80 to Mr Whitaker, and 10 to Messrs Codrington & Miller . . .".[21] Martin ended his correspondence in 1762: in a letter of 20 March he complained that the Olivers had treated him "with the grossest ill manners, as they pretend on account of the badness of my sugar, but in fact because I consigned most of my crop to Mr Banister".[22]

IV

The letters which Dr Walter Tullideph wrote to the Olivers give an intimate view of relationships between a plantation in Antigua and a counting house in London. Tullideph came to Antigua from Scotland about 1726. For some years he practised medicine, engaged in trade, and by his marriage to a young widow he came into possession of a small sugar plantation. Between 1736 and 1754 he increased the size of his plantations from 127 to 571 acres, increased the number of his Negro slaves from 63 to 247 and rebuilt his sugar works.[23] Tullideph wrote more than 150 letters to the Olivers in the years from 1750 to 1765. His first letter to Richard Oliver, apparently a reply to a solicitation, said that his obligations prevented him from dividing his sugar consignments. "As soon as these Incumbrances are removed", he wrote on 20 March 1749/50, "I know of none more Capable than your self to serve me, and I ought when in my Power, to Acknowledge the favours I formerlie rec^d from you here."[24] Most of Tullideph's letters concerned consignments of sugar. The correspondence began on 27 June 1750, when the Doctor wrote that he was consigning ten hogsheads of choice sugar on the ship *Prince George* and he enclosed the invoice and bill of lading. From time to time the Doctor expressed his satisfaction with the sales of his sugars. Yet he frequently requested the Olivers to hold his produce in anticipation of a price rise after the bulk of the crop from the West Indies had been sold. The factor's willingness to accede to such requests depended very largely on the size of his correspondents' debt. Tullideph owed Richard Oliver several hundred pounds on 29 June 1751, when he wrote that he was consigning thirty hogsheads of sugar. "If my affairs would permitt it," he wrote, "I am inclined to think they would answear to be kept as last year, especially if Jamaica hath really failed but that I leave intirely to your direction & discretion."

Except in wartime, Tullideph shipped the greater part of his sugar to London and all but a fraction of it was consigned to the Olivers. From 1750 to 1757, when he retired to Scotland, Tullideph consigned a total of 731 hogsheads to the Olivers. Since each hogshead contained about fourteen hundredweight and the average London price of muscovado sugar was thirty-four shillings per hundredweight, the gross returns amounted to about £17,400, of which the Oliver's commission of two-and-a-half per cent was £435. The 731 hogsheads were carried on a total of thirty-three ships, usually in parcels of ten hogsheads to a ship. In peacetime Tullideph seldom insured his sugar which was divided between a number of vessels to reduce the risks. That some ships were favoured over others is suggested by the carriage of 426 hogsheads on eleven ships, while the other 305 hogsheads were transported on twenty-two vessels. The favoured ships were owned or chartered by the Olivers and their planter correspondents in the West Indies. Agents and planters exchanged current market information and crop reports and thus were able to adjust both the timing of ship arrivals and the supply of shipping to fluctuations in annual crop yields and seasonal leads and lags in sugar harvests. Tullideph was not only a "subscriber" but he also encouraged his relatives and friends to patronize the Oliver's vessels and assisted the captains in other ways to reduce the turn-round time in port. On 24 February 1755, he wrote to Richard Oliver that he had helped a captain secure a cargo, adding that "you need make no Apology's with me, every Vessell in your Interest shall meet with all the Assistance in my power". Despite these cooperative efforts, the Olivers were warned on 16 October 1756, that they would be sufferers in chartering a vessel since none of their friends had any sugar to ship.

Part of the Oliver's trade consisted of filling their correspondent's orders for plantation supplies and consumer goods which went out on vessels engaged in the London-West India shuttle trade. Tullideph purchased most of his iron and copper wares, groceries, and medical supplies directly from English tradesmen, but a variety of goods remained to be supplied by the Olivers who charged a commission of two-and-a-half per cent of the value of the goods purchased. Among other things, the London house supplied beans and oats, cheese, wearing apparel for his family, Negro clothing, branding irons, hoes, equipment and supplies for refining sugar, coals, bricks, hoops for hogsheads, and tombstones. On two occasions Richard Oliver was requested to send out tradesmen and indentured servants.

V

Commission agents were both merchants and bankers. Planters needed loans from time to time to purchase plantations and slaves, to settle existing plantations more fully, to purchase landed estates in Great Britain, and to pay absentees' expenses, annuities, legacies, and marriage settlements. Planters also incurred debts when they ordered supplies of greater value than that of the sugar they consigned to London. Planters were reluctant to risk their credit standing by mortgaging their estates and to keep their debts below the mortgage threshold, they worked diligently to increase their remittances which consisted of both major and minor staples, bills of exchange, bullion and coin.

Some remittances might reach London indirectly from the planter's consignees in North America and the English outports.[25]

Dr Tullideph's debt to the Olivers increased irregularly for nearly five years and then declined almost steadily during the nine years which followed. According to his first "account current" of 31 December 1750, the Doctor owed approximately £807. The debt had declined to £432 a year later and had risen to £653 at the end of 1752. The next two years saw a remarkable rise to £6,978 on 21 September 1754. The debt was reduced to £3,137 on 20 October 1756, and to £1,116 on 23 April 1759. From 5 May 1760 to 29 August 1763 the debt ranged from £1,543 to £1,095. London agents generally charged five per cent interest on their correspondents' debts, commissions of one-half per cent on insurances, and also on receipts and payments. Two-and-one-half per cent was charged on sugar and other colonial commodities, and the same rate on goods shipped from Great Britain to the Colonies.[26] The Doctor had reduced the London debts on his plantations when he commenced his correspondence with Richard Oliver. Part of the money had been borrowed from planter friends and relatives in Antigua. One of these friends, James Doeg, purchased a plantation in 1752 and asked that his loan be repaid. Tullideph responded by drawing bills of exchange on Richard Oliver which were made payable to Doeg, and by buying bills in Antigua and endorsing them to Doeg. Oliver was informed in a letter of 7 July 1752: "In the whole I have paid him [Doeg] £3000 which is nearly what I owe him. What now remains will be to you, Dr Sydserfe and about £300 to William Dunbar's estate." Sydserfe was Tullideph's cousin and Dunbar his uncle, a former London sugar factor.

Successful planters frequently achieved ambitions to marry their daughters to members of the gentry and aristocracy. Tullideph and his wife Mary had only one son who died young. The two surviving daughters made favourable matches which stretched their father's pocketbook. Charlotte Tullideph married Sir John Ogilvy, 5th Baronet, of Invercarity, Forfar, Scotland, in June 1754. Several years later the younger daughter Mary Margaret married Lieut.-General the Hon. Alexander Leslie. Both daughters had dowries of £5,000 sterling.[27] Having incurred debts of nearly £7,000, the greater part of which went to discharge his eldest daughter's dowry, Tullideph was put in a difficult situation a year later when an eligible young man sued for the hand of his younger daughter. Although this match fell through, Tullideph was prepared to mortgage one of his plantations to raise the marriage portion. From Antigua he wrote to Dr Sydserfe in London on 30 August 1755, giving him power of attorney to mortgage New Division Estate to raise money to pay the dowry. Tullideph said that he had "reason to hope that Oliver's demand on me for Principall and Interest will be under £3000 Sterl^g so that I hope he will not refuse lending the £5000 more, as he may depend on it I will use all my endeavours to discharge it as soon as possible . . .".

From arranging favourable marriage alliances for his daughters, Tullideph turned to the estate market in Scotland. From Edinburgh he wrote to Richard Oliver on 31 January 1758: "There is a small agreeable Estate to be sold that I have an inclination for, and if I should have occasion for £2000 or £3000 more than what I have of my own could you assist me with it abo^t. next May, if the present Crop proves favourable? I hope soon to replace it again." Baldovan Estate which cost Tullideph about £6,000 was located near Dundee; the mansion house on the estate was appropriately named Tullideph Hall.[28] Not content with the estate already acquired, the Doctor launched out on the purchase of additional lands in Scotland. For a time he entertained the thought of changing sugar factors if by so doing he could borrow £6,000 or £7,000[29] but he lowered his financial sights and remained with the Olivers. From Tullideph Hall he wrote to Thomas Oliver on 29 August 1763, that he might have occasion to borrow £1,000 or £1,500. "I would incline to know whether I may depend on your Assistance in the same manner as I could have done with my very worthy ffriend your ffather for whose Death I am heartily concerned."

Heavy outlays for dowries and landed estates made extraordinary demands on Tullideph's plantation attornies, and ultimately on his Negro slaves. Not only did he press for greater remittances from Antigua, but he also wrote dunning letters to his correspondents in North America, Ireland and the English outports. During his long residence in Antigua, Tullideph consigned refined sugar, rum, molasses, and occasionally a few slaves to merchants in Virginia and North Carolina. In most cases he instructed the consignees to remit the proceeds in bills of exchange to the Olivers. Similarly, Tullideph consigned rum and sugar to merchants in Dublin, Bristol, Lancaster, and the Isle of Man, with orders to remit the proceeds to the Olivers in London. Alternative markets with price and profit advantages were thus consistent with indirect remittances and the centralization of finance in London commission houses.

The last two years of Tullideph's correspondence with the Olivers was a time of frenzied finance. At the end of the Seven Years' War in 1763, the Doctor formed a West India company at Dundee; he and his partners purchased a sloop and a sugar-carrying ship and loaded them with merchandise to be sold in the islands. Leaving one partner in Dundee, Tullideph went to Antigua to handle mercantile affairs and oversee his plantations. Early in 1764 his business plans expanded to include a sugar factorage house in London, to be conducted under the style of Messrs. Walter and David Tullideph. The Doctor then began to make mortgage loans to planters in order to be assured of sugar consignments for his London house. Rather paradoxically, he drew bills of exchange on the Olivers and endorsed them to his mortgagers, which in effect was using the Oliver's credit to set up a rival sugar firm. Unfortunately, David Tullideph, the Doctor's brother, refused to enter the partnership and manage the London business. In the end Dr Tullideph found it necessary to persuade a firm of London merchants to assume the large debts he owed the Olivers. Thus, in May 1765 Tullideph's long business association with the Olivers came to an end.

VI

The Oliver case study sheds light on the rise of a London counting house during a prosperous era of the sugar industry. Physical, social, and economic circumstances were favourable to the growth of absentee proprietorship but not all absentees were the spendthrifts and idlers whose fictional counterparts populated the stage at Drury Lane when "The West Indian" and "The School for Scandal" were played. Numbered among the absentees were doctors, lawyers, clergymen, politicians, military officers, improving landlords, iron masters, ship-owners, and merchants. The Tullideph correspondence shows how close were the personal, family, and business ties between the planter and his agent. If Antigua was typical of the sugar islands, it would appear that most of the London sugar factors had previous planting and mercantile experience in the West Indies. One might employ conventional economic analysis to explain the Caribbean origins of the London sugar factors and miss the main point. The careers of the elder Richard Oliver and Dr Tullideph suggest that London afforded a wider stage for the display of entrepreneurial talent that had been discovered and schooled in the merchant-planter societies in the colonies. The wider stage was both political and economic, for Alderman Oliver became a leader in the City and Parliament and a defender of the Bill of Rights which was ironic for a man who was so deeply implicated in plantation slavery. No doubt the drive for wealth and power goes far to explain the translation from colony to metropolis. Some idea of the fortune acquired by the elder Oliver can be gained from the following extract of a letter written by Colonel Samuel Martin to another London factor in 1769: "Consider this O ye rich Merch[ts], who like old Oliver who died worth a Plumb in a little more than 20 years. He might have been a Planter 50 years and not worth a Pear." In the idiom of the time, the word "plumb" represented the sum of £100,000.[30]

Notes

1. Richard Pares, "A London West India Merchant House 1740–69", in *The Historian's Business and Other Essays*, ed. R.A. and Elizabeth Humphreys, 198–226 (Oxford: Clarendon Press, 1961).
2. D.W. Thoms, "The Mills Family: London Sugar Merchants of the Eighteenth Century", *Business History* 11 (1969): 3–10.
3. R.B. Sheridan, "The Rise of a Colonial Gentry: A Case Study of Antigua, 1730–1775", *Economic History Review* 13 (1961): 342–57.
4. Vere Langford Oliver, *The History of the Island of Antigua* (London: Mitchell and Hughes, 1894–99), 2: 318–23, 352–67.
5. Ibid., 318–36.
6. Ibid., 140–50.
7. Ibid., 318–36; *Dictionary of National Biography*, ed. Sidney Lee (New York, 1895), 42: 149–50.
8. *The Diary of John Baker, Barrister of the Middle Temple, Solicitor-General of the Leeward Islands*, edited by Philip C. Yorke (London: Hutchinson and Co., 1931), 64, 194, 208–9, 212–16, 226, 233, 236, 246, 282.
9. Ibid., 283, 287, 290, 293, 370–71, 390, 392, 394–95, 415, 473. Thomas Oliver was Lieut.-Governor of Massachusetts 1774–76. After being forced to resign his office by the rebels, he lived in England and later in Antigua. He was the son of Colonel Robert Oliver of Antigua and Massachusetts, and grandson of Richard Oliver III, who was also grandfather of Alderman Oliver. Oliver, *History*, 2: 346–51; *Caribbeana, Being Miscellaneous Papers Relating to the History, Genealogy, Topography, and Antiquities of the British West Indies*, edited by Vere Langford Oliver (London: Mitchell, Hughes and Clarke, 1909–19), 2: 305; 5: 107–11.

10. Oliver, *History*, 2: 333; 3: 170.
11. Oliver, *Caribbeana*, 4: 72.
12. Oliver, *History*, 2: 41, 141; 3: 44, 94–98, 129, 161–62, 210, 233, 254; Oliver, *Caribbeana*, 4: 126–27, 383; 5: 318; 6: 16–17, 147.
13. Oliver, *Caribbeana*, 4: 33.
14. Ibid., 1: 151.
15. Ibid., 1: 152.
16. Ibid., 1: 152.
17. Richard Pares, *A West-India Fortune* (London: Longmans, 1950), 163–238.
18. Ibid., 239–79; Sheridan, "Rise of a Colonial Gentry", 342–57.
19. Oliver, *Caribbeana*, 3: 47.
20. Letter Books of Dr Walter Tullideph of Antigua and Scotland. Three volumes, 1734–1767. Loose letter in vol. 2. I am indebted to the late Sir Herbert Ogilvy, Bart., for permission to quote extracts from these letters.
21. Letter Books of Colonel Samuel Martin of Antigua and England. Six volumes, 1750–1776. British Museum Add. MSS. 41,346, 1: 52–53, 71, 139, 194, 216.
22. Ibid., Add. MSS. 41,347, 2: 128.
23. For Tullideph's pedigree see Oliver, *History*, 3: 155–61. See also Richard B. Sheridan, "Letters from a Sugar Plantation in Antigua, 1738–1759", *Agricultural History* 31 (1957): 3–23; Sheridan, "Rise of a Colonial Gentry", 349–54.
24. Tullideph Letter Book, vol. 2. No further citations will be made of Tullideph's letters to Richard Oliver IV and his partners and successors since the folios are not numbered and the letters are entered chronologically. Vol. 2 runs from 1744 to 1758, and vol. 3 from 1759 to 1767.
25. Pares, *West-India Fortune*, 219–21.
26. William Beckford, *A Descriptive Account of the Island of Jamaica* (London: T. and J. Egerton, 1790), 2: 353–54.
27. Tullideph Letter Book, vol. 2. Letter to George Leonard in Tortola, dated Antigua, 5 April 1755: "As for my part I have dip't my self at home in order to Marry my daugr. Well, I gave £5000 St^g. ffortune, and propose giveing Miss Polley as much whenever a good Match offers."
28. Ibid., vol. 2, Letter to Dr Walter Sydserfe, dated Edinburgh, 25 February 1758; vol. 3, Letter to Dr James Russell, dated Tullideph Hall near Dundee, 22 February 1760.
29. Ibid., vol. 3, Letter to Henry Hancock, dated Tullideph Hall, 25 February 1760.
30. Martin Letter Book, 5: 101 (British Museum, Add. MSS, 41,350), Letter to Christopher Baldwin in London, dated Antigua, 25 September 1769.

CHAPTER 4

Incalculability as a Feature of Sugar Production during the Eighteenth Century*

DOUGLAS HALL

West India sugar planters, during most of their history, have described three general categories into which they may be divided: those who, enjoying extremely favourable conditions of production, can make a small profit; those who can barely cover their costs of production and marketing; and those who, for a host of reasons, must perforce produce at a loss. Few have ever claimed a place in the first category. The clearest statement of these divisions was made in 1830 by the West India merchants in London who pointed out:

> That many estates have not paid the expenses of their cultivation for the past year, without charging interest on the capital, or even interest on the debts with which the estate may be encumbered, or anything for the support of the families dependent on them; and that a debt has actually been incurred by the proprietors, in consequence of the expenses exceeding the sale of the crop.
>
> That many other estates, more favourably circumstanced than the preceding class, by making better sugar, or by being cultivated at less cost, have not produced enough to pay interest of the mortgages upon them.

---

*Originally published in *Social and Economic Studies* 10, no. 3 (September 1961): 340–52. Reprinted by permission of the Sir Arthur Lewis Institute of Social and Economic Studies.

> That the remainder of the estates, which are most favouarably circumstanced, have yielded so little net income, that upon the whole, great distress has fallen upon the families of proprietors, and upon all connected with or dependent on the West India Colonies.[1]

The main purpose of this paper is to show that however much they may have verbally deepened the shades of depression, the eighteenth century planters' groans were not entirely unreasonable. However excellent, well-equipped, and well-managed their estates might be, they could scarcely avoid a fundamental problem that although they were involved in a large-scale, capitalistic form of productive enterprise, they could indulge in little rational capital accounting. Consequently, they lacked the basic permissives of calculability of success or failure in their business. They seldom had any realistic idea of how the enterprise stood financially, or what its prospects were.

The method employed in this paper will be to take a few available late eighteenth century accounts of a sugar estate in the island of Grenada, to use these illustratively of the general state of affairs in British West India sugar production of the time, and to base the whole discussion on those "Conditions of Maximum Formal Rationality of Capital Accounting" laid down by Max Weber.[2] Clearly, it will not be sufficient merely to show a divergence from Weber's conditions which represent an ideal state of affairs. The attempt will be, rather, to discuss the West Indies in terms of Weber, Weber in terms of the West Indies, and to indicate significant rather than small divergences and incompatibilities.

Westerhall Estate in the island of Grenada belonged, in the early 1790s, to Sir James Johnstone who lived in England and employed Mr Robert Keith, an Englishman, as his resident manager in Grenada.[3] Sir James had inherited Westerhall from his brother Lt. Col. Alexander Johnstone, and although the property had come to him encumbered with a debt of nearly 400,000 guilders (about £33,300 sterling), it was undoubtedly a worthwhile inheritance. This is borne out by a detailed inventory and evaluation of the estate made in 1770, and by subsequent references to it in the 1790s. But, as the records also show, Westerhall eventually fell into the hands of creditors.

Westerhall Estate Inventory and Valuation, 1770 (Grenada Currency)*

Land & Crops

732 acres cultivable land, valued at	£48,880
250 acres indifferent land, valued at	£ 5,000
982 acres, of which 332 acres of canes valued at	£ 5,976
77 acres of provisions valued at	£ 1,386
101 acres of pasture valued at	£ 1,212
"Hedges, gates, yard"	£ 75
Lands, etc.	£62,529 Grenada currency
	(or £39, 08 sterling)

Buildings & Equipment

Water mill house, 37' x 32', masonwork and hardwood, valued at .	£1,800
Cattle mill house, 60' diameter, new masonwork	£1,300
Boiling house, 87' long, 3 furnaces	£1,000
Curing house, 160' x 28', for clayed & muscovado sugars, with cistern . . .	£1,500
Still house, 63' x 24', and equipment	£ 500
Dwelling house & Kitchen	**
Manager's house, kitchen & small store	£ 150
Bagasse houses (four)	£ 200
Hospital & yaws house	**
Storehouse, 47' x 18' (galleried)	£ 200
Mule pen, 108' x 20'	£ 120
Sheep, cattle, hog pens	£ 50
Stoves (two)	£ 400
Agricultural & manufacturing utensils	£ 2,404
Smith's house, furnace, tools	**
Canal of 1,000 feet, & masonry reservoir	£ 512
Buildings, etc.	£11,786 Grenada currency
	(or £7, 36 sterling)

Slaves & Stock

263 slaves, as follows:

3 drivers, 2 at £200 & 1 at £150	£ 550
82 Fieldmen at £85	£ 6,970

Slaves & Stock (cont'd)

62 Fieldwomen at £75	£ 4,650
5 Coopers, 3 at £150 & 2 at £100	£ 650
3 Carpenters at £150	£ 450
2 Boilers at £150	£ 300
8 Servants at £80	£ 640
20 Field boys at £55	£ 1,100
15 Field girls at £50	£ 750
31 Children at £30	£ 930
16 Old & infirm at £10	£ 160
6 Cattlekeepers & Sicknurses	£ 380
10 New Negroes at £37 (sterling)	£ 592
30 Cattle at £10	£ 300
51 Mules at £40	£ 2,040
4 Horses at £20	£ 80
Slaves, etc.	£20,542 Grenada currency
	(£12,84 sterling)

<u>Summary</u>

Land & Crops	£39,080 sterling
Buildings & Equipment	£ 7,365 sterling
Slaves & Stock	£12,840 sterling
Total	£59,285 sterling[4]

---

*The rate of exchange at the time was approximately £8 Grenada currency for £5 sterling.
** The valuations of these items unfortunately are not to hand but they are not important to the argument and the given total includes them.

In comparison with other British West Indian estates of the time Westerhall in 1770 was well-equipped, possessing all the essential facilities and machinery for the production of a large annual crop of cane and of sugar.[5] In 1793 it was apparently the same. In that year Keith wrote to his employer saying that he had purchased ten "fine stout young men and women", and five English mules "fit for draught". These had been paid for by "bills at twelve months sight" on London. He expected the harvest, about to commence, to yield 380 hogsheads or 650,000 lb. of sugar and a good quantity of rum, but, he added, rum was hard to dispose of locally, there being only a nominal offer of 4½d. (currency) per gallon. In fact, the sugar actually shipped to Britain in that year exceeded Keith's estimate by 16 hogsheads. By eighteenth century reckoning this would have been an excellent return, and it will be seen that Westerhall was, in the late 1790s, despite many losses and encumbrances, still worth the cost of proprietary litigation.

During the processes of cane cultivation and sugar manufacture, and before the sugar was shipped, certain expenses had to be met. Salaries became due to the free supervisory and skilled estate employees, taxes to the local governments, payments to the visiting sea-captains who brought slaves and various supplies of lumber, livestock and food to the sugar colonies, and payments to local merchants and other local creditors. Against these expenses the estate balanced its own local earnings from rent of land, or of slave-labour, from sale of secondary estate produce such as grass or firewood or livestock, and from the sale of molasses, rum, or sugar. Indeed, in most islands the scarce currency served largely as a standard of value while sugar and rum and other produce were used as means of payment. But British commercial regulations, the British merchant-houses, and the absentee-proprietors of the West Indian estates did not favour the local disposal by estate managers of exportable produce and particularly of sugar. The merchants and proprietors also disliked too many large "bills on London" which would eventually have to be met out of the proceeds of sales in London.

Once the sugar was on board ship in the West Indies the British merchant-house to which it was consigned took over the detailed accounting. From the proceeds of sales they deducted the costs of shipping and marketing, including their various commissions, payments of interest and principal on sums advanced by them or others to the estate, and all other charges with which the estate was annually burdened. The balance was then declared and paid or kept on account.

Consequently, unless absentee-owners or merchants supplied the necessary information, estate accounts kept by resident managers were restricted to local dealings, followed by a statement of the produce shipped. In 1793, for instance, we know that Keith purchased ten slaves and five English mules for Westerhall, and that his own accounts could be roughly summarized as follows:

Expenses
(Grenada currency)

(1) Miscellaneous expenditures on stores, equipment, labour, island taxes, salaries, 10 slaves, mules, coal, debts, etc.   £11,830
(2) Purchase of food provisions   £1,695
(3) Purchase of lumber   £<u>785</u>
£14,310

Receipts
(1) Sales of rum   £6,915
(2) Rent of land to Keith, and sales of sugar   £210
(3) Shipped to England 396 hogsheads of sugar (692,250 lbs)   <u>£?</u>
£7,125
+ ? Currency

    Messrs. J. Petrie, Campbell and Company, the merchant-house to which most Westerhall sugar was consigned and where the estate's accounts were kept, would thus have either added the local deficit of £7,185, Grenada currency (just under £4,500 sterling) to the charges against the 1793 crop, or informed Keith to carry part of the deficit locally and reduce it in the following year. Note that among Keith's expenditures in 1793 is an item "debts", which might refer to just such a carry-over from 1792.

    In 1794 Keith wrote to England telling of a scarcity and dearness in the island, of lumber.[6] Rum, he claimed, was still fetching only a nominal price, but it is hard to reconcile this with his accounted earnings from this source. He was unable to obtain the necessary quantity of staves for making hogsheads even though he was offering immediate delivery of rum in payment, and "this . . . will oblige me to draw further this year on the sugars than I expected". There had been other sources of much heavier expenditure. A new boiling house and curing house had been built that year. They were expensive, but "there are not two better buildings in Grenada".

    On 1 September 1794, Sir James Johnstone died and Keith returned to England, presumably to render his account in person to his new employer. By the terms of his will, Sir James left Westerhall in the hands of four appointed trustees, one of whom was Sir William Pulteney[7] who had previously taken over 300,000 guilders of the 400,000 borrowed by Lt. Col. Alexander Johnstone from Jean Osy of Rotterdam years before. The remaining 100,000 guilders were still not completely paid off, so when he died Sir James left at least two large creditors, Osy and Pulteney. The trustees of Westerhall, as from September 1794, were instructed to raise certain legacies and annuities mentioned in Sir James' will, to support the widowed Lady Johnstone for the remainder of her life, and to allow whatever remained from the annual proceeds of the estate to be passed over to Sir William Pulteney, who presumably undertook to see to the liquidation of the remaining debt to Osy.

But within months disaster had struck the estate. During a rebellion led by Julian Fédon,[8] Westerhall, like many other Grenada properties, suffered. The rebels were in control of the island from March 1795, until June 1796, when, on the re-assertion of British authority, many of the rebels, including slaves who had joined Fédon, were deported.

Immediately, John Ross, the newly arrived manager of Westerhall, set about the task of rebuilding the property. One of the mill-houses had been badly damaged, and there had been damage to other buildings, cattle, and crops. The slaves were put to work planting cane to be reaped in 1797. In 1796 the estate produced no sugar and its small earnings came from slave-labour hired out, when it could be spared, to government and other employers.

In England, in the meantime, the trustees sought to borrow more money to finance the restoration of Westerhall. By a special Act of Parliament (36 Geo. III) they were allowed to raise by mortgage on the estate a sum not exceeding £10,000 sterling, to be used to repair the damages resulting from the insurrection. The other terms were no less precise. The estate was to be vested in three trustees of whom Sir William Pulteney was to be one. During the lifetime of Lady Johnstone, the trustees would receive all income from the estate and meet its various annual liabilities in the following order of priority:

(1) Costs of production (but not re-habilitation which was to be financed out of the approved loan).
(2) Payment of interest and principal to Jean Osy, some of whose 100,000 guilders were still outstanding.
(3) Payment of interest on the new loan of £10,000 which had been advanced by Messrs. J. Petrie, Campbell and Company.
(4) Payment of a clear £500 a year to Lady Johnstone as from 1797.
(5) Payments of interest and principal to Sir William Pulteney.

(6) Payment to the trustees of £750 which they had advanced to Lady Johnstone, presumably during 1795–6 when Westerhall yielded nothing.

(7) Payments of the principal of the new loan.

When these commitments had been met, any remaining income was to go to Lady Johnstone; but there was a stringent proviso that defaults in any year, in respect of any of the liabilities listed, must be made good in the following year before any residual income could be declared.

In April 1797, Lady Johnstone died and there began a legal dispute whether her heirs were entitled to receive such residual income as might annually be declared. Westerhall's income, despite the charges laid upon it, still seemed worth arguing for. Many a lesser estate would have folded under the burden. Statements of account from John Ross and from J. Petrie, Campbell and Company illustrate the costs of marketing West India sugar in time of war, the inflated customs duties on colonial produce entering Britain, and the financial standing of Westerhall on 31 December 1797.

Local accounts in 1797, according to Ross, were as follows: the estate's expenditures in Grenada on staves, casks, lumber, wages, provisions, and other smaller miscellaneous items, totalled £5,525 Grenada currency. Receipts, totalling about £4,100, were:

(1) By pioneer and ranger hire (i.e. slaves)	£257. 0. 0.
(2) By sale 1 puncheon oats and 1 old nutwheel	£ 51. 11. 0.
(3) By sale 2 negroes to the 7th W. I. Regiment	£272. 10. 0.
(4) By 1 negroe kept with hire	£275. 0. 0.
(5) By sale 6,567 gallons rum (57 puncheons)	£ 2,995. 10. 3.
(6) By sale 2 puncheons rum	£ 107. 14. 0
(7) By sale 2,855 lbs. sugar	£ 140. 9. 9.
	£ 4,099. 15. 0

"Of the sugar I sent to England" wrote Ross, "I can give no account, there may be also some small sums paid by Messrs. Petrie and Company that should properly be charged to this account . . . "

Of the various statements issued by J. Petrie, Campbell and Company in 1797 we need only notice two. In one, they accounted for a shipment of Westerhall sugar received and sold by them in October:

Sugar received, 33 hogheads containing 477 cwt. 1 qr. 1 lb.

Charges:

(1) Duty, at 17s. 6d. per cwt	£417. 12. 0 sterling
(2) Freight, at 6s. 6d.	£155. 2. 2
(3) Insurance from fire	£ 1. 13. 0
(4) Warehouse rent, at 3d. per cask	£ 2. 17. 1 (*sic*)
(5) Other miscellaneous charges	£ 15. 19. 6
(6) Broker's commission, ½% on £1,820	£ 9. 2. 0
(7) Merchant's commission 2½% on £1,820	£ 45 10. 0
	£ 647. 15. 9
Proceeds by sale of sugar received	£1,820. 0. 0 sterling
Balance Credited to the Estate	£1,172. 4. 3 sterling

Three points about this statement are worth emphasis. First, it deals with only one of several shipments of sugar from Westerhall in 1797. Secondly, it illustrates the high cost of getting sugar from the West Indies to the British market during the war period of the late eighteenth and early nineteenth centuries. Thirdly, it indicates one of the main sources of loss by wastage. Ross had shipped 33 hogsheads. At 15¼ cwt. per hogshead this should have been about 510 cwt. of sugar. But the merchants acknowledged receipt of only a little over 477 cwt. Until better methods of manufacture were introduced in the nineteenth century, West India planters suffered from the leakage of their poorly cured "muscovado" from the hogsheads on route across the Atlantic. Here we see indicated a loss of about 6½ per cent of shipped produce, a high but not unusual figure.[9]

During 1797 J. Petrie, Campbell and Company received other shipments from Westerhall. Their other statement which concerns us was made on 31 December when they declared a balance to the estate of £11,055.18.7. Now would begin the procession of whittling charges established in priority and beginning with the payment to Jean Osy. Not much would be left for the heirs of Lady Johnstone if they won their dispute; but clearly Westerhall was recovering its full swing of production. The total sugar output for the year must have been well over 300 hogsheads, a rapid recovery from the disabling blows of the rebellion, and a tribute to the managerial skill of John Ross.

Here the description rests, with but one more revealing comment. In

December 1805, there was published by Robert Wilkinson of 58 Cornhill, London, "A Topographical Description of the Island of Grenada". It contained the relevant information: "Westerhall Estate; area, 951 acres; produce, sugar; proprietor, the heirs of Sir William Pulteney". Even in times of high prices many West India planters suffered disappointing net incomes from their estates after the burden of encumbrances was laid on them. In 1830, when prices were low, the merchants had cause to complain. They were the intermediary bearers of estate indebtedness. The costs of production and marketing (including their own not illiberal commissions) might be reducible, but interest on debts, and the fixed annuities to litigious dependents were not. These were among the mill-stones around the planters' necks which the various West India Encumbered Estate Acts of the later nineteenth century were intended to remove.

Indebtedness, of course, is a perfectly normal feature of business enterprise. The role of credit needs no stressing here. It is essential to the satisfactory functioning of any enterprise, however, that not only the amount of investment and the yield of profit, but also the amount, degree, and cost of any necessary indebtedness should be reasonably calculable in advance.[10] This property of "calculability" was strongly urged by Weber in his discussion of capitalist organization and capital accounting. The Westerhall documents indicate great difficulties in the way of any such previous calculation, and an examination of eighteenth century West India sugar production in the light of Weber's "Conditions of Maximum Formal Rationality of Capital Accounting" reveals a number of important points.

Weber's conditions can be summarized as follows: (1) the complete appropriation of all the non-human means of production by owners, and market freedom in disposal of the product; (2) complete autonomy in the selection of management by the owners; (3) no appropriation of jobs by workers or of workers by owners; (4) complete absence of substantive regulation of consumption, production, and prices, and of other regulations limiting freedom of contract; (5) the maximum calculability of the technical conditions of the productive process; (6) complete calculability of the functioning of law and government and a reliable guarantee of all contracts; (7) the most complete possible separation of the enterprise from the household or private budgetary interests; and (8) a rational monetary system. We shall discuss them in turn.

(1) The eighteenth century West India planter owned not only the non-

human, but also most of the human means of production in his enterprise. The complication of slavery will be discussed later. But the planter did not have freedom in the marketing of his product because he was bound by still existing British mercantilist regulations and, at various times in the century by war-time regulations and irregularities. It is not clear, however, why market freedom, or as Weber more fully described it "the complete absence of all formal appropriation of opportunities for profit in the market",[11] contributes to rational accounting. The securing of a market, whether by agreement with the buyer or by compulsion of the buyer, must tend to assure disposal of the product at a price agreed upon or compelled by the seller, and thus "calculable" in high degree. But this the West Indians did not have. They were secured to the British market by British regulations, but the market was not secured to them and there was no assurance by agreement, or otherwise, of the prices in that market. The possibility of any reasonably formed expectation of income or profit during a century of war-time fluctuations of markets and prices was consequently slight.

(2) Weber's second condition assumes a rigorous separation, in the mind of the owner, between business and personal interest. Complete autonomy in the selection of a manager allows the owner to appoint, say, his son to a managerial post. But whether he would do so because of a real confidence in his son's managerial skill, or for other reasons, is an important question from the point of view of the business. The eighteenth century West India planters generally enjoyed this autonomy in selection, but did not always exercise it free of personal interest. In this way they were not unlike most of their contemporaries who still also had not clearly distinguished between business and personal or family affairs. They suffered a handicap, however, in comparison with the owners of business in larger, unenslaved societies; for in the West Indies the ranks from which estate managers could be chosen were small and in Britain were confined to those who were prepared to go to the tropics. Perhaps when the West Indies were thought profitable this was no great limitation, but the essential point is that autonomy in selection is itself unrelated to the principles guiding the choice.

(3) Here the distinction of the slave force from the free labour market is obvious, and Weber advanced several cogent arguments to support his proposition that full-fledged slavery, especially, is "less favourable to rationality and efficiency than the employment of free labour . . .".[12] That the eighteenth cen-

tury planters suffered these hindrances is indisputable, but there remains an aspect of slave labour which has not been sufficiently emphasized. "Slave labour" is an unfortunately misleading term (from the economic point of view). That estate slaves were a form of capital investment, is beyond argument. Their "labour" was, consequently, not "labour" in the sense in which we use it in respect of "free labourers", but rather "power" in the sense that it is used of the efforts of livestock or the work of machinery. The eighteenth century planters' inventories almost invariably classified slaves with "stock".

Slave labour was mainly unskilled; consequently what the planter had at his disposal was a fund of power, which could be applied to any of a multitude of purposes. Slaves, far more than machines or the other livestock, could serve a variety of industrial (and other) ends. They were multi-purpose equipment, and when emancipation and the planters' compensation came these represented a forced liquidation of the planters' most flexible capital equipment. That is why emancipation was accompanied by a large exodus of planters from the sugar industry. A time of forced liquidation of capital is a good time to close down operations if future prospects seem disheartening.

Emancipation, therefore, was of industrial consequence not because it replaced "slave labour" by "wage labour", but because it introduced "labour" as a significant feature of production and of accounting, because it compelled those remaining in production to place future investments in far less "flexible" capital equipment and machinery, and because it brought, for the first time in the West Indies, significance and real meaning to concepts such as "labour-cost", "labour-productivity", and "labour-saving".[13]

(4) West India sugar producers were limited by no substantive regulation of consumption, production, or prices, except in so far as British commercial and maritime controls directed their transactions to the British market and subjected them to British laws and taxes. During the late eighteenth and early nineteenth centuries, planters and merchants cried out against the high import duties levied for revenue purposes, in time of war, on colonial sugars entering Britain, and argued that as duties inflated prices to consumers so the market was restricted. But it cannot be said that the duties were imposed in order to limit the market. Indeed, they were imposed because, as a tax on a necessary article of diet, evasion by consumers' abstinence seemed less likely to occur. Whether the rates of duties levied were such as to afford the maximum yield of revenue is a nice mathematical question which need not be discussed here.[14]

Restriction to the British market did, of course, limit freedom of contract with foreign dealers, but as long as British West Indian sugars were faced with an increasing demand and growing foreign competition this restriction and the protection which went with it gave security to an industry which, more and more, shouted its own inability to compete. The big question in the minds of the planters in the early nineteenth century was how much longer they would enjoy the protection offered by the mercantilist policies of which this restriction was a fundamental ingredient.

Within the industry and the British market, however, certain obstacles to freedom of contract between producers and merchants did arise. These were a consequence of planters' commitments, by family agreement, by custom, or, most important in this context, by indebtedness, to particular merchant houses. The connection between Westerhall and J. Petrie, Campbell and Company is a case in point. Westerhall sugar was sold in the market that Petrie, Campbell and Company chose for it and at prices they accepted. Westerhall needs were obtained through the agency of Petrie, Campbell, whose interests were not necessarily those of the estate. Westerhall's indebtedness, moreover, gave the firm a lien on the estate's produce. The freedom of the proprietor to search out the means of increasing receipts by selling produce to the highest bidders, and decreasing expenditures by careful purchases of needs, was thus limited by the commitment to a particular intermediary whose interests were not necessarily compatible with his own, and over whose actions he had little control as long as he remained a debtor.

(5) The incalculability of the technical conditions of sugar production in the eighteenth century scarcely needs further emphasis. Slave labour, as Weber pointed out, was unwilling, uncertain, impossible to cost in any meaningful manner, and subject to social, political, and biological influences which the slave owner had to take account of but could not account for. But even within the manufacturing process itself uncertainty prevailed as a consequence of inefficient techniques. The quantity of sugar shipped was not the same as that received by the merchants. There was always a loss, of unpredictable extent, on route, depending on the quality of the sugar, the state of its containers, the time-length of the voyage, the manner of ship storage, and the time lapse between arrival in a British port and release to a purchaser. Of this, and also of the prevailing uncertainty of the public administration and law, the Westerhall documents offer clear illustrations.

(6) One need only remember the numerous naval and military assaults in the Caribbean in the eighteenth century to realize how incalculable were the continued functioning of the public administration and the legal order, and how unsafe was any formal support by governments of terms of contracts. Between 1759 and 1814, only Barbados, Antigua, and Jamaica, of the British sugar colonies in the Caribbean remained uninterruptedly in British ownership. St Kitts and Nevis changed hands twice, St Lucia nine times, and Grenada five times. Apart from these external disruptions of the local administrations, moreover, there were local uncertainties arising out of fears of foreign invasion, long internal strife such as between the Maroons and the colonists in Jamaica, or shorter but sometimes violent disagreements, riots or slave rebellions.

(7) Weber's seventh condition required the most complete separation of business and private family interests and accounts. Of this, something already has been said, and again the Westerhall accounts are illustrative of a general pattern. By generous gifts bestowed in times of prosperity and optimism about the continuing profitability of sugar, many estate owners encumbered their properties with charges on expected profits. When the profits declined the beneficiaries, accustomed to and often dependent on their gratuities, pressed impossible claims upon reduced and insufficient means, and often enjoyed, as Lady Johnstone did, a prior right of satisfaction over the business needs of the estate.

(8) Finally, the eighteenth century sugar planters operated in a confusion of currencies and money exchanges. Spanish, American, British, and other coins were openly used. A variety of negotiable papers exchanged hands. And where and when coins and papers were scarce, money served as a standard of value by which commodities were exchanged one against the other. It will be remembered that Keith tried to purchase lumber with rum. Not until the middle nineteenth century did the foreign coins begin to disappear from circulation as British currency was more generally brought into use, and even today business can be done (though not always legally) in the market-places with £sterling, £Jamaican, $USA, $Canadian, $BWI, and, in some islands, with guilders and francs. In part, the present situation reflects an increasing sophistication in currency affairs, such as is demonstrated in "black market" dealings; in part also it reflects an historical familiarity with an irrational monetary system. The irrationality in the eighteenth century arose not simply out of the

use of a variety of currencies, because in most cases the rates of exchange were fixed; the difficulty came rather from abrupt price fluctuations, and from variations in the volume of currencies in circulation which made currency of any kind difficult and often expensive to secure.

Uncertainty must in some measure attend all productive enterprise. Much has been written of the profits of sugar in the eighteenth century, but not enough has been said to emphasize the high degree of uncertainty and incalculability which faced every proprietor who might have sought to engage in any formal accounting of his investments and their probable yields. There can be little doubt that many of the financial encumbrances assumed by the planters were entered upon in moments of blind optimism. Current prices may have seemed to justify the optimism, incalculability provided the blindfold. Risk was ever present and always acknowledged by the eighteenth century European farmer-manufacturer in a tropical slave society. Where calculability is possible, risk can be reduced by insurance against disaster. But where even probabilities cannot be reasonably calculated, insurance, which is itself calculated on the basis of probability, cannot be bought, or must be priced high, and risk must remain unmitigated or too dearly avoided.

For the West India planter, unlike many other producers of his time, the amount of capital to be risked was considerable;[15] costs were swollen by high shipping and marketing charges; the prices of his products fluctuated violently with wars, hurricanes, and the state of the British home and re-export markets; and his major operations were carried out in the fretful environment of an unstable local government and a slave society. These conditions had much bearing on the planter's apparently sole concern to exploit while the opportunity allowed, and to shut his eyes to plans and preservation for the future. These last were beyond his limited range of calculation.

During the nineteenth century, the emancipation of the slaves, currency reform, corporation finance and limited liability, improving techniques of agriculture and manufacture, laissez-faire and Pax Britannica, all helped to bring the conditions of production nearer to those observed by Weber. Later developments, on the other hand, have questioned the validity of certain of his conditions, and have modified others in the light of departure from the principle of untrammelled economic enterprise.

In the twentieth century, sugar producers, in common with producers of other agricultural staples, have sought to avoid the incalculability of unpredictable price fluctuations by negotiating for guaranteed markets, quotas, and firm prices, and by setting up "stabilization funds". In this, they have implied doubt of the validity of Weber's contention for "the complete absence of all formal appropriation of opportunities for profit in the market". Also, the growth of trade unionism and the formidable demonstrations of power, and not infrequently of irresponsibility, by trade unions, have certainly modified Weber's conditions of complete autonomy in the selection of management by owners, no appropriation of jobs by the workers, and freedom of contract.

However this may be, it appears reasonable that in discussing the West India planters and their sugar industries of the eighteenth century we should emphasize, not only the inefficiencies supported by slave production and a highly protected market, but also the great deficiency of the possibilities of calculation and capital accounting.

Notes

1. *Statements, calculations, and explanations, submitted to the Board of Trade relating to the commercial, financial, and political state of the BWI Colonies, 1830–31*, comp. Thomas Lack (Printed by Order of the House of Commons, 1831).
2. Max Weber, *The Theory of Social and Economic Organization*, trans. A.R. Henderson and Talcott Parsons; rev., ed. and intro. Talcott Parsons. (London: Hodge and Co., 1947), 252. The purpose here is simply to show that BWI sugar production of the time lacked rational accountability. Whether Weber would consequently not have admitted it to be an example of industrial capitalism is another matter.
3. All references to Westerhall are based on MSS. West India documents at the University of Bristol. The call numbers of the documents used are: 41/21/1–2, 41/32, 41/59/6, 41/59/12, 41/59/13, 41/59/16, 41/60/2, 41/60/4, 41/61/1, 41/61/17, 41/62/2, 41/65/3, 41/70/9–11, 41/70/14, and 41/70/39–40.
4. Bryan Edwards' account, in the 1790s of the capital necessary to establish a sugar estate in Jamaica provides a useful comparison. Edwards recommended for an estate to produce annually 200 hogsheads of sugar of 16 cwt each: Land: 600 acres, of which 300 would be planted in cane, 100 in provisions, 100 in guinea grass, and 100 left in its natural woodland state . . . £10,071 sterling; Buildings: a list very closely akin to that of the Westerhall inventory of 1770 . . . £5,000 sterling; Stock: 250 negroes, 80 steers, and 60 mules . . . £14,557 sterling. Such an investment, Edwards contended, would yield an annual "£2,150 sterling, and no more, clear profit to the

planter, being seven per cent on his capital, and £50 over, without charging, however, a shilling for making good the decrease of the negroes, or for the wear and tear of the buildings or making any allowances for dead capital, and supposing too that the proprietor resides on the spot . . . " Edwards, however, was illustrating that sugar was less profitable than supposed. See his *History, Civil, and Commercial, of the British West Indies*, 5 vols., 5th ed. (London: 1819), 2: book 5, chapter 3.

5. This was also borne out by the testimony of William Dickson of Barbados who knew Sir James Johnstone. See Wm. Dickson, *Mitigation of Slavery* (London, 1814), 294.
6. As a consequence of limitations on trade with the United States of America.
7. A brother of Sir James Johnstone, according to William Dickson, but a creditor none the less.
8. In sympathy with French revolutionary movements in other islands of French control or previous French control.
9. As late as 1845 this loss was estimated at 15 per cent of sugar shipped from Jamaica. See A.G. Fyfe, *Suggestions for Separating the Culture of Sugar from the Process of Manufacture; with a Plea for Establishing a Central Sugar Factory at Annotto Bay, Jamaica* (London, 1846).
10. By "satisfactory" I do not mean profitable (which many estates were, as the continuance of the sugar industry clearly indicates), but responsive to managerial scheme and control.
11. Weber, *Theory of Social and Economic Organization*, 252.
12. Ibid., 253.
13. Reasonable objections to negligence in this discussion of the social and human aspects of slave production emphasize how complicated this matter is, and how inadequate have been the many pre- and post-emancipation attempts to account for the comparative costs of free and slave labour.
14. The following figures are illustrative of the growth of the market during a period of rapid population growth in Britain:

Year	Imports (to the nearest 100 cwt.) of BWI Raw Sugar into Britain	Import Duty per cwt.	Prices offered (per cwt.) in London, excluding duty		
1780	1,300,000	6s. 7½d.	59s.	and	45s.
1795	1,672,800	15s.	64s. 7 ½d.	"	54s. 10d.
1800	2,312,500	20s.	59s. 11 ¼d.	"	37s. 5 ¼d.
1805	2,583,000	27s.	51s. 2 3/4d.	"	47s. 9 ½d.
1810	2,964,700	29s.	53s. 9 3/4d.	"	44s. 2 ¾d.
1815	3,381,800	30s.	64s. 2 3/4d.	"	57s. 2 ¼d.
1830	3,682,900	24s.	34s. 2 ¼d.	"	25s.

Sources: Edwards, vol. 5, and L.J. Ragatz, *Statistics for the Study of British Caribbean Economic History, 1763–1833* (London, 1927).

Note: Prices in 1780 are the highest and lowest offered that year. Other prices are the highest and lowest average monthly prices offered.

15. As illustrated by the Westerhall inventory and valuation, and by Bryan Edwards' accounts.

CHAPTER 5

Women in the Trinidad Cocoa Industry, 1870–1945*

KATHLEEN PHILLIPS LEWIS

Introduction

Traditionally the role of women in Caribbean agriculture has been undervalued and underestimated when at all recognized. Historically it was in agriculture that women made their most telling economic contribution. In the pre-contact era, indigenous island societies relied heavily on the ceaseless toil and productive input of their women in the fields. While men hunted and waged war, women planted, tended the growing cultivation, harvested and found creative ways to transform these agricultural products into palatable foods and beverages, alcoholic drinks, baskets, apparel, household utensils, ornaments and bodily decorations. In island Carib, Tainian and Arawak societies women were responsible for 70 per cent of the agricultural food production and over 30 per cent of the entire food supply for their communities. It is safe to say that women were the most productive economic resource.

During the era of slavery women came to constitute the greater percentage of the field hands, proving themselves more than capable of performing the most strenuous jobs in the first gang, as well as the relatively lighter tasks of

---

*Originally published in the *Journal of Caribbean History* 34 (2000): 20–45. Reprinted by permission of the Departments of History, University of the West Indies.

the second and third gangs. The post-emancipation era witnessed the rise of a vibrant peasant sector, kept afloat by the contribution of women from the ex-slave and time-expired East Indian immigrant groups. Many of them also offered their labour for wages on neighbouring estates. Much of this contribution to agriculture and the economy over the centuries has gone unnoticed in the historiography of the Caribbean.

This paper argues that, as exemplified in the cocoa industry, any analysis of women's importance in agriculture cannot be restricted to their direct labour input nor measured merely in volume of production or income returns. In the first place, it is not always possible or desirable, in terms of historical analysis, to separate their contribution into meticulously delimited spheres or sectors: private or political; domestic or public; formal or informal; peasant or wage labourer. An examination of the development of the Trinidad cocoa industry illustrates this fact. Women were involved in all sectors and at all levels of this industry: as labourers, contractors, own-account peasant farmers, large-scale planters and employers, exploiters of labour, produce dealers and intermediaries in the marketing process, sometimes filling more than one role simultaneously.

At a time when their Anglo-Saxon sisters were still struggling for recognition of property-ownership rights of married women, Caribbean women were already owners of productive cocoa properties of considerable acreage and annual yields. This did not, however, provide them with access to political rights of participation or representation, which did not come until the 1940s. Yet, despite their heavy involvement in the cocoa industry, women were restricted by more clearly differentiated gender labour roles than in the sugar industry. Gender-role division tended to become less well defined higher up the socioeconomic ladder within the industry; little or no legal distinction was made between male and female cocoa plantation owners or male and female produce dealers. Gender differentiation was evident, however, in patterns of ownership and management styles. A gendered analysis, therefore, is essential to our understanding of the internal dynamics of the cocoa industry, which sustained the Trinidad economy for much of the post-emancipation period and the twentieth century.

Generally, information on women's involvement in the cocoa industry, particularly for this period, is minimal. Statistical records are not gender specific, and official reports did not make the specific role, experiences and concerns of women their primary preoccupation. With in-depth reading and asking new questions of existing sources as well as the use of non-traditional sources it becomes clear, however, that women formed the backbone of the cocoa industry and contributed significantly to its economic success.

Cocoa growing, by nature, established different parameters for internal gender structure and relations from those obtained in the sugar industry. For the most part, cocoa occupied land unsuitable for the growth of sugar cane. Cocoa tended to be grown not in flat, open expanses as sugar but in the damper, more shaded valleys and foothills of the mountain ranges in Trinidad. This implied spatial separation from the sugar plantations. Initially, therefore, cocoa and sugar tended to attract different types of labour. The Spanish-speaking peon or *conuquero* labourers from Venezuela provided the early labour force for cocoa estates. With emancipation, many liberated slaves offered their labour on cocoa estates, which provided both spatial separation from sugar plantation life and the chance for economic improvement toward self-reliance. Time-expired Indian indentured labourers, too, found that the cocoa estates provided good wage-earning opportunities. All of these groups of labourers came to the cocoa estates more as families than as individuals, both men and women as well as children, finding employment on these estates. The application of the concept of the family as a male-headed unit of production worked to marginalize the role of women in the industry.

Accommodation

In the aftermath of emancipation, labouring families were usually provided with rent-free accommodation on cocoa estates as additional inducement to full-time labour. Cocoa estates tended to be located some distance away from villages and therefore housing for labourers was a foremost concern. Bachelors were given a barrack room of 10 feet by 12 feet. Men with families were allowed a barrack room of twice that length (20 feet by 12 feet) in which their entire family was housed. No provisions were made for single women or mothers with families; women were expected merely to accompany their husbands or common-law mates.[1] The average size of a family housed in one of these barrack-rooms was five members.[2] Lack of privacy and overcrowding were problems which impacted significantly on women's lives as labourers and wives of labourers.

By the turn of the century a solution to the problem of overcrowding on many estates came with the construction of two-room detached houses for families when barracks were found to be unsatisfactory. Even these houses catered inadequately to the needs of large families. Estate housing was preferable to the cocoa planters for it allowed easy access to and control over labour. At first it did provide some advantages for workers fresh out of slavery or indentureship, or from the mainland, who were given, along with rent-free housing, rent-free provision grounds to ensure their families' supply of basic food items. In their spare time, women worked on provision grounds cultivating vegetables and ground provisions, which formed their dietary staples. Many opted to work full-time on the provision grounds rather than to offer their labour to the estates. Men, too, despite free housing, offered their labour to the estates on a casual basis, few working the full 5–5½ days per week, although their names were registered on the list of full-time workers.

General home furnishings were as sparse and spartan as in the workers' kitchens. For peon contractors and peasant farmers, even more so than for those accommodated in estate barracks, accommodation was rough and basic. Oftentimes a small four-sided hut built with wood and palm fronds sufficed. The roof was thatched with "carrat" palm fronds, loosely fitted around cross pieces of wood nailed to posts. The sleeping area was cordoned off by pieces of jute sacks used as curtains. Bedroom furniture, when it existed, was a crude makeshift wooden couch which served as a bed and an old Carib-type clothes basket. In the adjoining room, the living room, there was a bench or two and a soapbox in which non-perishable foodstuffs were kept away from mice and rats.

Health and Education

Another concern for women workers on the cocoa estates was health. Accommodation lacked even the basic sanitary requirements and occupants had to rely heavily on improvisation. Overcrowding and cramped barrack conditions did nothing to promote healthy practices. Some cocoa estates had very limited hospital facilities, particularly those estates that employed Indian indentured immigrant workers. Smaller estates could not afford to provide such facilities. In times of lowered cocoa prices when recession hit the estates, even those that had once provided hospitals or some free medical attention for workers often ceased to do so. In many cases workers had to travel, on foot or pack animal, great distances to see a doctor, sometimes as many as 14 miles each way. These journeys were accomplished on foot or mule back because of the deplorable and often impassable condition of the "bridle paths", Crown traces (unpaved roads on Crown lands) and trunk roads, especially during the rainy season.[3] Emergency cases were "toted" in hammocks by able-bodied co-workers the entire distance. Estates that employed indentured labourers and did not have any medical facilities kept a small four-wheeled ambulance to send patients to district hospitals when necessary. Again these were rendered less effective by the conditions of the roads.

Since women did not have timely access to hospitals and trained medical practitioners, they generally had their babies at home with the aid of a midwife or many "self-delivered" and were back on the job within days. The manner in which births were announced denoted the differential allocation of value placed on female and male children. The birth of a girl was announced by two shots from a musket elevated on a block in the yard, while the birth of a boy was announced by three shots.[4]

Women were the main health workers, however untrained, among estate labouring populations. Estate workers and their children were highly susceptible to contagious diseases, given the conditions under which they lived. Malaria, hookworm, dysentery, small pox, influenza, tuberculosis, cholera, yaws, ankylostomiasis, ground itch and venereal diseases, especially syphilis, accounted for high debility and mortality rates. Employers provided some basic medicines, such as quinine, Epsom salts and iodine, free of charge for resident employees. Every other medical treatment was left to worker initiative and resourcefulness. Women possessed knowledge of the medicinal properties of herbs and employed them in homeopathic concoctions, a different one for each ailment. These were said to be highly effective in the treatment of everything from menstrual cramps to venomous snakebites. As one cocoa labourer observed in reference to garden herbs and wild roots, "Everything was good for something."[5] Estate owners' wives and women labourers provided first aid in case of injuries or accidents on the job. For medical, as for other purposes, networking and mutual assistance and support among women on the estates proved valuable.

Women resident on estates were also concerned about their children's education. The lack of educational facilities on the estates and the deplorable state of Crown traces restricted estate children's access to village schools. This encouraged migration to nearby village centres. Women favoured this move, despite the resulting loss of rent-free accommodation. It was a small sacrifice for providing their children with an opportunity to escape the hardships and poverty of life as cocoa labourers. The move to village centres increased their disinclination to send their children out to work on the cocoa estates even as part-time wage labourers. This meant a reduction in the pool of cheap labour available to planters.[6]

Diet and Food Preparation

Poor diets and the drinking of unpurified river and rainwater increased the labourers' susceptibility to disease and infection. The staple diet was starch-based – plantains (*buc-buc*), rice, cassava and very large quantities of flour – and this led to malnutrition. The short time allotted for lunch, sometimes only half an hour, meant that labourers preferred to take their meal with them to work. Flour-based foods proved easiest for this purpose and most substantial. *Panyol* labourers and contractors relied heavily on homemade products from cassava. The other option, breadfruit, was held in great contempt by many because its consumption was regarded as a sign of extreme poverty. As a dietary supplement *bhaji*, a type of spinach, was stewed with coconut oil, pork fat or salted codfish.[7] It was easier for the labourers to base their daily diet on whatever was produced in the provision gardens or among the cocoa trees themselves, for example, tannias, plantains, yams and some vegetables. Employers allowed workers to take whatever they needed in lieu of paying them higher wages. Women had to be very creative in culinary skills for meal preparation. They did so with limited or crude homemade cooking utensils and a monotonous list of basic ingredients.

Food was prepared on makeshift stoves, *firesides,* constructed out of dirt and stones in pans made out of kerosene tins. Ovens, too, were large dome-shaped, earthen constructions. Peon women used *temite* (a long-leafed plant), bamboo and dried grasses to manufacture cooking and other household utensils and accessories. Every home had a mortar and pestle, a *couleve* and other woven baskets of various sizes. Early morning coffee was sipped from tin-cups made out of discarded milk cans, to which handles were added. Water was ladled with dugout gourds or calabashes, which also served as soup bowls and often as plates or general food containers. Cocoa workers and peasants sat on rough benches or on the bare floor to eat their meals and used tin soup spoons, forks or their bare hands.[8]

Meal preparation consumed much of women's time away from the fields or provision grounds. Peasant women of the *Panyol* peon group spent much of their time preparing cassava bread for the family and many of them sold the excess to nearby village shops. The making of cassava bread was a complicated process. Women had to get up at 4 a.m. to begin the process. The "skin" or protective covering on the cassava roots had to be scraped off; then the roots had to be washed, grated, squeezed, strained and broken up into fine particles. The farine thus produced then had to be passed through a sieve, baked in round discs on a hot iron griddle, and dried in the sun. If the rain interrupted the drying process and the bread became wet, women often spent all night drying it again on the griddles. Not only was the process tedious, backbreaking and time-consuming, but it required considerable know-how.[9]

Estate Labour

The life of a female labourer on a cocoa estate was not easy. Work began at 7 a.m. and continued to 5 p.m., with lunch break being taken usually between 12 noon and 12.30 p.m. For women with young children there was seldom any provision for organized child-care on the estates. Older children stayed at home to attend to younger siblings. Ordinance 26 of 1916 passed during governor J.R. Chancellor's administration required employers of female Indian immigrant workers to provide suitable nurseries for infants. The greater percentage of cocoa estates did not, however, employ indentured immigrant labourers but rather those whose indentureship had terminated and therefore did not feel as strictly bound by such laws.[10]

Women cocoa workers did backbreaking work for long hours on the cocoa estates but were always compensated at the lowest levels of the remuneration scale. There was a clear gender division of labour among wage workers on cocoa estates. Men did the clearing of forest trees and the planting; weeding, trimming and pruning; draining; picking and breaking the cocoa. Mostly women performed the work of gathering the cocoa into small heaps, extracting the beans, spreading them out to dry and polishing or "dancing" them. Yseult Bridges, the daughter of a cocoa planter, describes how the "*Negroes,* equipped with cutlasses and *goulettes*, blades on long poles, severed the stout stems of the pods while others gathered them up, deftly sliced them open and tossed them on to a heap around which squatted women who scooped out the slimy beans and threw them into panniers woven from lianes . . ."[11]

Female and male juveniles sometimes accompanied the crook animals (donkeys and mules) to the sweating boxes where the beans were fermented to free them from the "slime" or pulp. Women held shared responsibility for preparing the beans for sale and "dancing" the cocoa but were singularly responsible for drying the beans.[12]

Girls over the school-leaving age of twelve were employed on the cocoa estates. They were assigned the tasks of sifting the cocoa in cocoa houses, catching cocoa beetles and keeping an eye open for evidence of witchbroom and other fungi and pests. Children were preferred for these tasks because of their alertness and sharpness of vision.[13] Girls worked alongside boys in gangs, which were supervised by a male driver. Women were very seldom given the position of driver. Such positions of great responsibility were generally reserved for men.[14] Sometimes girls and boys were made to work in the same gangs as men and women.

Women provided, on the average, 150 days per year in wage labour on the cocoa estates (2½–3 days per week), while men worked 200 days per year (3½–4 days per week). During the crop time there was usually an increase in the number of women workers. These extra workers were mainly wives of permanent or full-time male labourers.[15] In Trinidad, cultivating a cocoa estate "from scratch" took approximately 221 man-days per acre. When women were used as labourers, women-days were converted to man-days on the basis of five man-days being considered equal to six woman-days.[16]

Clearly, women's work was considered less productive than man's work and women less valuable as workers. Accordingly, women received lower wages than men received. Wages were paid either per day's work or per task. On most estates, wage levels were structured according to task rather than gender, but tasks were designated according to gender, women being assigned the less remunerative tasks. In 1886 wages for a day's work ranged from 30 cents for women to 50 cents for men. For picking cocoa, a task assigned to men, wages

Table 5.1: Rate of Pay in Cocoa Industry (cents per day)

	Pre War	1920	1935	1939
Day's work				
Men	35–40	50–60	30–40	45–50
Women	30	30–35	25–30	25–35
Juveniles	15–25	15–30	15–25	25–35
Task work				
"Cutlassing"	35–40	50–75	35–40	40–45
Draining	50–65	70–90	50–60	55–65
Round–ridging	30–45	40–60	30–40	35–45
Pruning	–	50–90	40–60	50–65
Picking	–	60–90	40–60	45–65

Source: PRO, CO 950/953, Memorandum submitted to the Moyne Royal Commission by the Imperial College of Tropical Agriculture, January 1939.

could be as high as 50 cents per day. Gathering cocoa beans into small heaps, a woman's job, brought wages of no more than 35 cents per day.[17]

Most of the tasks done by women were assigned as day's work rather than as task work. Those who performed task work had better opportunities for maximizing their earnings. Women, however, were rarely able to increase their incomes by task work. Forty years later, things had not changed significantly. Women's wages had registered negligible increases, which were quickly eroded with the onset of World War I. During the post war period wage levels for women were even lower than they had been in 1886, as table 5.1 illustrates.

Men were able to perform, on average, 1¼ to 1½ tasks per day. "Cutlassing" was normally done per 100 trees per task which fetched 40–50 cents, and could be completed in 4–6 hours. Pruning (100 trees per task) could be performed in 6–8 ½ hours and paid 50–65 cents for light pruning and 80 cents–$1.20 for heavy pruning. Draining (100 feet per task) brought in 40–60 cents and could be done in 5–8½ hours. Picking and breaking (combined task per barrel) took 1–4 days to complete and could fetch as little as $2.40. Picking and breaking were tasks done by men.[18]

As table 5.1 shows, by 1939 women at the upper end of the scale were paid only slightly better than juveniles who did lighter work. If they were provided with any kind of rations, provision grounds or other facilities, these were deducted from their pay at the rate of 10 cents per day, leaving them with minimal personal disposable income.

The welfare of women workers on cocoa estates was not ensured, neither was that of their families. The hardship of women's lives increased proportionately with declining cocoa prices and export earnings. Unlike wage rates, the allocation of, and deductions for, weekly rations, were not gender-differentiated. Both men and women received 1½ lb rice, 2 lb maize, ½ lb salted fish, salted meat or dried uncooked meat, and 1 oz. coconut oil, the cost of which would be deducted from their pay. Deductions therefore represented a greater burden for women than for men. The general ratio of female-to-male Indian indentured immigrant workers employed on cocoa estates was 1:2. Returns for 1901, for example, show that 218 female indentured workers were employed on all cocoa estates, as opposed to 481 males. Their mortality rate was reported as 0.76 per cent.[19] This in itself does not, however, give us a clear and accurate indication of the actual quality of their lives. Laws governing rations existed for Indian immigrants, but these were not always strictly enforced and many instances of abuse of the regulations went unreported. Only a vigilant Protector of Immigrants could restrict the incidence of non-compliance with the codes. No such laws existed for African or *Panyol* workers.

With the end of Indian immigration and falling market prices for cocoa, employers became increasingly lax in the provision of rations and in generally ensuring decent and acceptable workers' standards of living. Figures for 1939 show that not all estates provided additional provisions, rations or facilities to enhance the workers' standard of living: 15 per cent of all estates did not provide housing; 47 per cent did not provide gardens; 25 per cent provided fuel but no provisions.[20]

It was not customary for cocoa estates to provide any form of insurance or compensation for workers injured on the job. Planters claimed that cocoa workers, especially the women, were usually casual estate employees: some worked only two or three days per week, others for half a day, and spent the rest of the time in their provision grounds, vegetable gardens, cocoa pieces or rice fields. Planters opposed the idea of insurance and injury compensation for workers because of the additional cost of such a provision, especially without the assurance of their full-time labour or of reduced wages.[21]

Access to Land Ownership

Women did not view wage labour on the cocoa estates as a permanent feature of their lives. Their ambition was to improve their living standard and quality of life through land-ownership and own-account small-scale agriculture. The steadily increasing proportion of casual and part-time wage labour vis-à-vis regular and full-time employment on the cocoa estates bears witness to their increasing disinclination to pursue this economic option. This did not mean, however, that they were opposed to working on cocoa cultivation but merely that they preferred other options within the same industry besides wage labour.

One attractive option was contract work, which gave them some modicum of control over their labour and allowed them an opportunity to increase their savings and eventually to purchase their own cocoa holdings, either individually or as a family. Another option was to work on their own lands, planting cocoa and other crops. When land was not readily available for purchase in small parcels either privately or from the Crown, they squatted. Squatters led very spartan lives. The insecurity of their tenure was partly responsible for the nature of their existence. They could be ejected from their homes and lands at any moment and/or imprisoned for squatting, and therefore had to be constantly on the run from the authorities.[22]

To defend their homesteads and prolong their tenure, women resorted even to ploys geared to deter vigilant though superstitious Crown land agents, bailiffs and surveyors. They placed obeah symbols such as blue bottles and miniature coffins along the boundaries of their holdings to ward off the authorities. The tenuous nature of their residence made life difficult and hazardous. It also limited their ability to develop their holdings to their full productive potential.

With the liberalization of the Crown land disposal and management policies since the time of Sir Arthur Hamilton Gordon in 1869, the attainment of smallholder status in freehold tenure became a less unlikely possibility. Many squatters were able to regularize their tenure by purchasing small plots of alienated Crown land for development of peasant agriculture. For the most part, they planted cocoa, interspersed with food crops.

Cocoa in Trinidad was perceived more as a garden (family) crop than a field (plantation) crop, as was sugar. This meant that cocoa lent itself well to cultivation by smallholders who could neither afford to invest in more than a few acres at a time, nor to employ additional labour outside of the family. Women in smallholder families, therefore, toiled alongside their men in their cocoa holdings without cash remuneration. The number of family smallholdings increased gradually over time. By 1931, 41,656 acres of cocoa were being cultivated by smallholders. Of these 23,906 were ten acres or less in size, and 17,760 were between 11 and 50 acres.[23]

Women provided a significant share of the labour for peasant farms, growing, besides cocoa, tannias, plantains, pigeon peas, sweet potatoes, yams, corn, cassava and sometimes rice, interspersed with cocoa or grown on separate garden plots. While even on family farms work in cocoa cultivation remained gender differentiated, women almost totally monopolized the cultivation of vegetables and ground provisions in the cocoa pieces. Subsistence food production helped families meet the cost of living and of imported foodstuffs, which supplemented their diet.

Wives of contractors and peasant farmers were in an insecure position as regards tenure of their lands. The death of a husband entailed untold financial difficulties. Widows of contractors did not themselves have legal standing with respect to contracts and were frequently ejected. Over an extended period many of these contractors had purchased undeveloped forest land from the Crown and were awaiting the end of their contractual period to begin cultivating their own holdings. In the event of the death of her spouse, the woman often found herself unable to manage on her own the clearing of such land, teeming with snakes and other wild animals. Many of them lacked the money to hire labour or even continue paying the ward rates and taxes.

In order to avoid forfeiting their land to the Crown for non-payment of rates, and also to feed their families, women had to supplement their incomes with additional estate labour or with employment as carriers at nearby sand pits or quarries. As these jobs did not bring high levels of remuneration, the consequence was often increased indebtedness to estate and village shops. Weekly repayment left them with little to feed their families. The choice was either further debt or an unhealthy diet of boiled, salted rice or *buc-buc*. Widowed mothers had to keep older children from school a few days each week to assist in necessary household tasks or in various income-earning pursuits, for example, taking provisions or cassava bread to the village for sale.[24]

Additional labour was necessary, too, when food prices increased out of proportion to wages. From the commencement of World War I in 1914, the

Table 5.2: Changes in Food Prices for Selected Years, 1914–1938 (cents)

Commodities	Prices		
	1914	1920	1938
Beef (per lb)	10	21	10–14
Salted Cod Fish	8	20	10
Wheat Flour	3½	8	4–5
White Rice	4½	9½	3
Brown Rice	3½	9	2½
Dhal	4	9	6
Red Beans	10	20	8
Spilt Peas	5	12	4
Pigeon Peas	5	6	6
Sweet Potatoes	2	3	3
Yams	3	4	4
Milk (per tin)	11	29	7–10
Milk (per quart bottle)	8	12	12–18
Butter	33	72	32

Source: PRO, CO 950/953, Memorandum of the Trinidad Chamber of Commerce to the Moyne Royal Commission, January 1939.

cost of imported food increased while incomes declined. Food prices of basic imported staples jumped an average of 30 per cent from 1914 to 1937 as table 5.2 demonstrates. The increased cost of living led to a decline in living standards and an increase in the economic demands on women.

Apart from these food items, smallholder families had to purchase other necessities such as candles, tallow, matches, building materials and items of clothing. In the Golden Age, 1870–1920, when cocoa enjoyed high returns, small-farming was a popular option. When prices fell, however, many female smallholders allowed their cocoa to grow by itself temporarily while they sought work on nearby estates. A small cocoa farm of about ten acres employing strictly family labour would bring in about $60.83 per annum, that is about 17 cents per day, excluding allowances for tools, bags, and so on.[25] This meant that a mother/wife with a family of five (the average size of cocoa peasant families) would have to maintain her children on about three cents per day per person. Given inflationary prices of imported food and other items, this was an almost impossible task. Small properties fell into neglect as women gave increasingly more time to estate labour.

Another factor that affected the incomes of women cocoa farmers was mounting indebtedness to local shopkeepers/produce dealers. With reduced ready-cash they had to accept credit on manufactured and/or imported food items, wearing apparel and even building materials, which were retailed in local shops. In return they either pledged their properties or their future crops, or agreed to sell a portion of their crop to the local dealers, regardless of price. Small-farmers would then have to pay whatever was demanded for imported goods, which was generally higher than the going prices. However, many smallholders remained oblivious to this fact. Over time they increased their indebtedness. The ease with which credit was obtained on imported provisions from local shopkeepers also acted as a deterrent to small cocoa farmers to grow their own food supplies and this increased their cost of living.

The prices they were paid for their raw cocoa were also much lower than the prices paid by dealers in the towns. The arrangements established eliminated meaningful bargaining between buyer and seller and prevented small-farmers from fixing profitable prices for their produce.[26] Average prices paid for cocoa in country districts were frequently 2 to 3 cents less per pound than Port of Spain prices. This did not encourage small-farmers to produce the best quality cocoa possible. It also served as a disincentive to increased productivity. Women who farmed cocoa smallholdings, or who were wives of farmers, found their cocoa undervalued and many who pledged their estates were faced with forfeiture if unable to meet their debt payments.

For many reasons they were unable to access the larger market in the capital where more competitive prices were paid for raw cocoa. Means and cost of transportation to Port of Spain markets created very real problems for them. Large estates utilized railway or lorry transport, which cost about 4–5 cents per ton for each mile, that is about 40 cents for a bag of cocoa weighing 165 lb to Port of Spain, a distance of approximately 40 miles.[27] Small-farmers, however, were not located within easy access to main roads. The Crown traces which traversed or ran near their properties were so poorly maintained that small-farmers were forced either to "tote" their produce on their heads to the main roads or leave it to rot on the land. Crown trace surfaces were often destroyed by oxen used to drag logs or lumber purchased from the Department for Crown Lands.

Another option opened to them was to become members of the Cocoa Planters Association, the Association of Cocoa Growers or their district-affiliated branch of the Trinidad Agricultural Society (founded in 1894), which arranged collective marketing of cocoa and paid more remunerative prices than the local dealers. Membership fees were about 50 cents per annum for smallholders. Their deep indebtedness to local produce dealers and shopkeepers, however, restricted their full exploitation of the better prices and marketing facilities provided by these cooperative organizations. It is for this very reason that they were also unable to utilize the service of the cooperative fermentaries established at Biche and Penal primarily for their use. Few smallholders owned any technical drying and fermenting equipment or machinery.

Women cocoa farmers were granted loans by agricultural credit societies for the rehabilitation of their properties, particularly with the onslaught of the witchbroom epidemic, but this was another route for finding oneself hopelessly in debt. Agricultural credit societies borrowed money from the state at 6 per cent interest, then lent to small farmers at double that rate. The borrower had to pay the interest up-front: if she borrowed $100, she would only receive $88. She was often unable to repay the principal and debt, and eventually it became impossible to liquidate it.[28]

Loans from the Agricultural Development Bank, which were designed primarily for smallholders, were equally risky. Each year the borrower had to pay 8 per cent of the original loan in two half-yearly instalments, in June and December. Of this amount, 7 per cent went toward interest payments and 1 per cent toward reducing the principal. When cocoa prices dropped, there was little hope of meeting the loan obligations. Compound interest was charged on arrears. Some who managed to make their payments did so by reducing the cost of production or by abandoning or curtailing production and leasing their lands to oil companies. Others combined their production of cocoa with other crops which were more marketable and which seemed to harbour good prospects: bananas; Robusta coffee; tonca beans; mangoes; avocado; citrus; fruit trees; and food crops such as tomatoes, corn, sweet potatoes, tannias, yams and cassava.[29]

Despite the difficulties, women continued to enter the ranks of peasant proprietors or smallholders either as individuals or in conjunction with their spouses. Networking and informal means of providing mutual support assisted women in accumulating savings, which could be used to purchase small acreage. Women, more so than men, fully utilized the informal cooperative savings mechanisms of the *susu* and the *chitty*, as well as the formal ones such as friendly societies and government and post office savings banks.[30] The advantage was that, unlike wage labour, it did allow them some measure of control over their labour and their destinies. As female peasant cocoa cultivators they were able to manage their time more effectively and determine time allocations to their various duties and responsibilities. Their communities were heavily patriarchal and women's roles in the family were clearly defined. Women had to divide their time between their domestic duties, including parenting, and their cocoa holdings and food-crop gardens.

The question remains as to how women came into possession of cocoa lands at a time when metropolitan women were not allowed to own property. The Married Women's Properties Act was not passed in Britain until 1881 but registered deeds and various returns show women owning cocoa properties long before this time. Records for 1870–71 show women already in possession of valuable cocoa properties. Over the period 1870 to 1945 the incidence of female cocoa proprietorship, large and small, became increasingly more frequent, despite some legal and social restrictions.

In the years after the abolition of slavery, women were part of the gradual movement from plantation labour to family peasant proprietorship. Their contributions within the peasant family concerns were counted not as individual productive economic contributions in their own right, but as the performance of non-productive domestic labour. In 1869, when Governor Gordon took the decision to make land grants instead of return passages to time-expired Indian indentured immigrant labourers, women were not included in this concession. Between 1869 and 1888 inclusive, of 5,652 Indians who had their return passages commuted, 3,872 were men and 1,780 were women. However, of that number, 2,643 men received land grants of between five and ten acres. No women received land grants; they were given money grants instead.[31] However, most of these women were wives, who indirectly gained control of family land for agricultural purposes. Many opted to grow cocoa as well as other marketable food crops.

The Trinidad *Blue Books of Statistics* do not readily yield gender-specific data for the ownership of cocoa holdings, and for the acquisition of Crown

Table 5.3: Cocoa Estates Owned by Women in Ten-Year Intervals, 1905–1945

Ward Union	1905	1915	1925	1935	1945
Arima	1	0	2	2	4
Lower Caroni[a]	3	–	–	–	–
Upper Caroni[a]	4	–	–	–	–
Caura[a]	1	–	–	–	–
Cedros	1	2	2	2	–
Chaguanas	2	7	6	5	7
Diego Martin	6	9	3	6	8
Guanapo	1	–	–	–	–
La Brea/Oropuche	4[b]	2	3	4	7
Manzanilla	4	2	–	3	5
Maracas/Tacarigua	2	12	12	11	11
Mayaro	4[b]	–	11	4	8
Montserrat	8	–	1	3	4
Naparima	2	–	–	–	–
St Ann's	1	–	2	2	–
Savana Grande/Moruga	4	–	3	5	10
Toco	2	10	4	6	6
Turure	2	–	9	10	9
Total	52	44	58	63	79

[a]Lower and Upper Caroni were counted with the ward of Chaguanas in successive years. Caura was counted with the ward of Tacarigua after this time.
[b]On some of these estates both cocoa and coconuts were cultivated.
Source: Compiled from C.B. Franklin, *The Trinidad and Tobago Yearbooks* (Port of Spain: Franklin's Electric Printery, 1905–1945).

lands during the late nineteenth and early twentieth centuries. However, the regular publication of the register of deeds in the *Trinidad Royal Gazette* and other less conventional sources provide valuable insights. Close examination of these sources reveals that methods of cocoa land acquisition by women varied. Purchase, either individually or jointly with spouses (legal or common-law), widow's inheritance from deceased spouses and inheritance from deceased parents (sometimes jointly with other siblings) were the most frequent methods of acquisition. Through one of these ways women frequently became proprietors of sizeable cocoa estates. In some cases inheritances were as large as 200 quarries (640 acres). Lucy Agnes Gonzales was listed in 1945 as owning the 820 acre San Carlos estate in the Caura district, in the Ward of Tacarigua.[32] In some cases women were able to purchase, individually or jointly, several small cocoa acreage and amalgamate them to form estates of considerable size. In 1905 women owned 51 of the 635 cocoa estates in various parts of the island. Table 5.3 shows ownership of cocoa estates by women according to Ward Union distribution in ten-year intervals from 1905 to 1945.

The pattern of cocoa proprietorship by women reveals interesting similarities and departures from the patterns of male ownership. As in the case of male cocoa proprietorship, the pattern of female proprietorship showed an increasing tendency toward ownership of multiple estates and amalgamation of estates or smallholdings to form one large estate.

In at least six of the cases documented in 1905, women owned two or more estates, eight women owned multiple estates in 1915, three in 1925, four in 1935 and six in 1945. However, unlike those owned by men, these estates tended to be located in a single Ward Union. Over time, too, there was no significant increase in multiple ownership by women, while amalgamation became the norm in the case of male-ownership. This indicates a preference by women to remain close to their estates and to opt for the personal touch and micro-management. Men, on the other hand, held no compunctions against owning estates scattered throughout the island, wherever gain was to be had, and existing as absentee owners, relying on managers, overseers and agents.

It appears that widows who inherited multiple estates sold most of them, particularly those which were too remote from the one on which they were resident. This would explain to some extent why proprietresses disposed of large, seemingly thriving cocoa estates for no apparent reason. In some instances, however, women had to dispose of inherited estates because they were heavily encumbered. Sometimes joint inheritors who were disinclined to work the estates themselves allowed one of the owners to look after the estate while retaining a share in the ownership and profits instead of selling the property outright. In this way some properties were retained within the same family for several generations.[33]

Married as well as unmarried women were cocoa proprietresses. Until the

1970s, single women far surpassed married/widowed women as owners of cocoa estates. Between 1905 and 1925 the ratio was 2:1, and by 1945 it had increased to 4.5:1.[34] For the most part they were indentified in the records of ownership according to marital status. Married women were identified as "Mrs", followed by their marital surname and rarely a first name (initials sufficed). Widows were either identified as "Mrs" Or "the widow of . . . " Unmarried women of some social status were identified as "Miss" followed by their father's surname.

Women retained respectability, it seems, by identification with the male next-of-kin. Those proprietresses referred to by first and last names minus the titles were generally the matriarchs, females of independent means or younger women/girls. Designations tended to point to class origins. Miss Devenish and Legge, Mrs E. Lange and Mrs Kavanagh, all belonged to the elite "French Creole" class of Trinidadian society. Those with lowly origins were always referred to by their names minus the titles of respectability, for example, Mary Bagwandeen (who had Indian indentured immigrant roots), and Josefita deLeon (of Cocoa *Panyol* peon origins).

Over the entire period 1905 to 1945, only three names appeared that were recognizably those of Indian women. This had much to do with the laws governing Indian marriages, and consequently legitimacy and inheritance. Most Indian marriages were not recognized by law until 1945. This meant that neither the wives nor the children of these marriages were recognized as legal heirs. In the event of the man dying intestate, as was frequently the case, his lands reverted to the possession of the Crown. Sometimes parents tried to arrange deeds of transfer for children while they were still alive.[35]

In 1881 an Ordinance was passed recognizing Indian Christian marriages that were duly registered, provided the man was at least 16 years of age and the woman 13 years. These two stipulations disqualified all but a few Indian marriages. An additional complication was that Hindu marriages were performed "under the bamboo" by Brahmins (pundits) or Sadhus, and Muslim marriages by Kazis, who were not recognized as legal marriage officers. In 1935 Muslim marriages finally received legal recognition, but Muslims constituted only a small minority of the Indian population. Hindus outnumbered them by more than 7:2. It was not until the passage of the Hindu Marriage Ordinance in 1945 that all Indian marriages received legal recognition, legitimizing the rights of spouses, widows and children.[36]

Although the laws allowed women to buy or lease lands, most women inherited their lands. In the years after 1945, female ownership of cocoa estates, and particularly smallholdings, increased significantly. In 1970, 91 per cent of all cocoa producers were smallholders. Of these farms, women owned 26 per cent and men 23 per cent, while the remainder was jointly owned.[37] More significantly, women managed most small farms whether or not they were the sole owners. Women managed two-thirds of all small farms, while men managed the remaining one-third. The farms also differed in their use of hired labour and manual or mechanical operations. Women hired male labourers to clear land and drains and to spray pesticides, while men usually did not. Women also used manual methods of irrigation while men used mechanical.[38]

The foregoing discussion is indicative of the extent to which women of all classes and ethnic groups were getting into the business of cocoa cultivation. Class, race and marital status determined to a large extent, the nature, extent and scale of operations. The ownership of large cocoa estates by both men and women continued to be mainly the preserve of the French Creole elites, while the lower classes –*Panyol* peons, Indians and Africans – owned small plots. However, the number of females owning cocoa lands registered steady increases. One might conclude that the cocoa industry offered women the chance for some measure of economic self-reliance, and sometimes financial independence and upward social mobility.

Marketing and Manufacturing

Another interesting feature of the Trinidad cocoa industry in the late nineteenth and early twentieth centuries was the increasing involvement of women in the marketing and manufacturing branches of cocoa production on the island. As the discussion on indebtedness to local shopkeepers seems to indicate, cocoa "dealing", that is, the purchasing of cocoa beans from small producers and marketing it in Port of Spain for shipment overseas, was lucrative business and attracted those who had an eye for quick turnovers and sizeable profit margins. In order to make a good profit in the intermediary cocoa-dealing business, the rural cocoa dealer had to pay greatest attention to the "margin" and the "mark-up", over which he or she had some control, rather than the prevailing national or international market prices which were beyond his or her control. The rural cocoa dealer could easily pass on inflationary overhead costs to those at his or her mercy, that is, the small cocoa contractors and peasant proprietors who were also their creditors. The ready credit system ensured a steady flow of business shopkeeper/intermediaries, through built-in guarantees, assurances and pledges from creditors. Women were not above entering this business and exploiting these smallholders' needs for credit, cash advances and an easy means of marketing their cocoa.

According to the Report of the Trade and Taxes commission of 1886, to obtain a dealer's licence one had to pay £15 ($72) to do business in the town, and £5 ($24) to do business in the country districts.[39] This was a small price to pay for the returns such licences brought. By the end of 1937 an average of 17 women were applying for licences and licence renewals each year.[40] Interestingly enough, most of the women applying for licences to deal in cocoa and other licensable produce were of Chinese origin.

The Chinese have traditionally been stereotyped in Trinidad as being astute and oftentimes corrupt shopkeepers. This stereotype carried over into their involvement as cocoa dealers. They were alleged to be masters in the illegal art of adulterating and claying the cocoa beans to enhance their market value.[41] There is no concrete evidence either to corroborate or disprove this allegation. The business of shopkeeping and produce dealing did, however, attract an inordinate number of persons of Chinese origin for some unexplained reason. Many of these, including women, owned premises in more than one location and came into possession of vast acreage of cocoa as a result of forfeiture of pledges through the credit system.

One of the ways used by cocoa dealers, male and female, to maximize their profit-earning possibilities was to purchase raw, wet, unfermented cocoa beans from persons who were not cultivators and who were not required to identify the origin of their cocoa. The likelihood was that those persons were stealing cocoa from other persons' lands and offering it for sale. An indication of this was their inability to dry and ferment the beans. Cocoa dealers looking to turn a quick penny asked no questions. Many of them did the drying themselves and benefitted from the value added through resale to urban dealers. Female cocoa dealers were as involved in this process as their male counterparts.

This form of exploitation was curtailed by the passage of laws declaring the sale and purchasing of wet cocoa beans a criminal offence, tantamount to praedial larceny and acceptance of stolen goods. But the practice remained so prevalent that laws had to be revised and reinforced repeatedly. Penalties for the commission of such offences were severe and did not attempt to differentiate between female and male offenders.

Licensed cocoa and other produce dealers were, by law, required to keep ledgers in which they had to enter immediately the receipt of any cocoa and the date on which it was received, the name and address of the person offering it for sale. Local constables were empowered to enter dealers' premises at any time to inspect the premises and the ledgers. Refusal to allow a constable to execute this search was a punishable offence. Any dealer, male or female, found guilty of receiving stolen cocoa was eligible for any term of imprisonment and/or a fine of between £10 and £20. It was left to the judge or magistrate to order the offender to undergo corporal punishment as he saw fit. Again, women were not exempt from any of these penalties and punishments.[42]

A few women applied annually, too, for licences to manufacture cocoa on a commercial basis. Most small-scale cocoa proprietors manufactured crude "stick-cocoa" for home consumption. "Stick-cocoa" was grated and boiled, then strained of its fat and granular residue, and sweetened to make a hot beverage called "Creole cocoa". Few attempts were made to manufacture chocolate on a commercial scale and most of these proved unsuccessful.[43] There were never more than four chocolate factories at one time in Trinidad during this period.

In 1937, seven women applied for licences to manufacture chocolate. These applications generally came from persons living in urban districts or small town centres rather than from rural districts. Of the seven women who applied, four were resident in Port of Spain and its suburbs, one in the town of Tunapuna, one in Carapichaima, and one in Couva.[44] A few of them were listed as hucksters. This indicated that they had previously been in the business of selling home-manufactured sweetmeats and other items on a retail basis, the list most likely containing some form of cocoa and/or chocolate. Chocolate manufacturing, however, failed to achieve any significant or successful levels during this period. Nevertheless these efforts demonstrated women's willingness to experiment with various levels of involvement within the cocoa industry.

Class and race affected the way in which women within the cocoa industry perceived and interacted with each other. On large estates French and British Creole women were proprietresses; Africans and Indians formed the bulk of both the labouring population and the small-scale proprietary/contractor class; Chinese (and sometimes Portuguese) women opted for cocoa dealing and shopkeeping. Even on the cocoa estates working together as wage labourers did little to bridge the cultural gaps and differences in perception which separated Africans from Indians and both groups from the whites.

Yseult Bridges, the daughter of a cocoa planter, relates how her mother's failure to understand the differences in the Indian and African woman's perception of the institution of marriage led to disastrous results, and the termination of what had previously been a perfectly happy, long-standing, common-law union between Mr and Mrs Morgan, both of African descent. Even in the aftermath of the fiasco she failed to see the light, consoling Mrs Morgan (and herself) that present woes "were as nothing to what she would have had to endure in the world to come, had she not been saved from living in a state of mortal sin".

Conclusion

Much remains unclear about the nature of women's involvement in the cocoa industry during the period of its rise to prosperity and its decline into virtual insignificance. Oral research into their involvement and contribution in the present-day industry shed some light on their historical role and the changes that occurred over time. Questions still arise as to why their heavy involvement in agriculture (in Trinidad and elsewhere in the Caribbean) did not simultaneously produce changes and legislation to recognize and encourage their participation as equal citizens in every aspect of sociopolitical life. When, for instance, agriculture was introduced in the 1960s as an integral part of the elementary school curriculum, it was made available only to boys. Instead, girls were taught home economics, which meant in reality needlework and cookery. In a country whose livelihood was almost totally dependent on agriculture, this was inexcusable.

Although change has come, it was slow in coming and in many respects it merely has succeeded in disguising or rewriting in less blatant manner the age-old patriarchal sexual division of labour. Men clear the land, dig drains, weed, plant, spray, prune, crack pods and transfer the cocoa beans from the field to the house. Women are solely responsible for drying. They remove weeds and gather the pods with the help of children (boys and girls). Both men and women prepare cocoa for sale, and "dance" the cocoa; a few women also assist the men in selling the beans. Women are still largely responsible for the cultivation of ground provisions, rice, *bhaji,* and vegetables for home consumption. In the last three decades the sexual division of labour on family-owned farms has been even more glaring than it was in the first half of the twentieth century.

Notes

1. Interview with John Thomas, cocoa labourer, Lopinot, Trinidad, 1982; interview with Lucille Dollabaille, Lopinot, Trinidad, 1982; cocoa labourer and smallholder, Lopinot, Trinidad, 1982.
2. CO 950/953, Memo to Moyne West India Royal Commission (WIRC) submitted by the Association of Cocoa Growers of Trinidad and Tobago, January 1939, 19.
3. CO 950/808, Evidence of the Agricultural Society of Trinidad and Tobago to WIRC (1938).
4. Pedro Valerio, "Sieges and Fortunes of a Trinidadian in Search of a Doctor's Diploma", in *The Book of Trinidad*, ed. Bridget Brereton and Gerald Besson (Port of Spain: Paria, 1991), 325.
5. Interview with Sylvestre Guerrero, cocoa worker and later smallholder, Lopinot, Trinidad, 1982.
6. CO 950/952, Memo of Rufus Garcia to the Moyne WIRC, Port of Spain, December 1938.
7. Ibid.
8. James Henry Collens, *A Guide to Trinidad: A Handbook for the Use of Tourists and Visitors*, 2nd ed. (London, 1888), 212–22.
9. Interviews with Lucille Dollabaille Guerrero, Paulina Hernandez, Alice Hernandez, John Thomas, Sylvestre Guerrero, Trinidad, 1982; Valerio, "Sieges and Fortunes of a Trinidadian", 325–26.
10. CO 297/21, Trinidad Acts, 1916, 82.
11. Yseult *Bridges, Child of the Tropics: Victorian Memoirs* (Port of Spain: Aquarela Galleries, 1988), 183–84.
12. Indra S. Harry, "Women in Agriculture in Trinidad: An Overview", in *Women and Change in the Caribbean,* ed. Janet H. Momsen (Kingston: Ian Randle, 1993), 214.
13. CO 950/790, Evidence of Mr H.E. Robinson of the Association of Cocoa Growers to the WIRC, February 1939.

14. Ibid.
15. CO 950/953, Submission of Imperial College of Tropical Agriculture (ICTA) to WIRC, 65, 81.
16. D. Urquhart, *Cocoa* (London: Longman, 1955), 197.
17. D. Morris, "Cacao: How to Grow and Cure It", ch. 5, *Public Opinion* 11, no. 169, 17 August 1886.
18. CO 950/790, Memorandum of the Cocoa Planters Association of Trinidad to WIRC (January 1939).
19. CO 295/404, Trinidad Despatch no. 390, 7 September 1901, Report of W. Coombs, Protector of Immigrants, re Immigrants on Cocoa and Coconut Estates.
20. Ibid.
21. CO 950/808, Evidence of the Agricultural Society of Trinidad and Tobago to WIRC (1938).
22. CO 295/272, Longden to Kimberley, 14 February 1874.
23. CO 950/952, Memo of Rufus Garcia to the Moyne WIRC (December 1938).
24. Interviews (see notes 1, 6 and 9); Valerio, "Sieges and Fortunes", 325–26.
25. CO 950/953, Memorandum of the Association of Cocoa Growers of Trinidad to WIRC (January 1939).
26. CO 950/952, Memo of Rufus Garcia to the Moyne WIRC (December 1938).
27. CO 950/953, Memo of ICTA to WIRC (January 1939).
28. CO 950/933, Evidence of J.R. Wortley, Director of Agriculture to WIRC (1939).
29. CO 950/953, Memo of ICTA to WIRC (January 1939), 12 & ff.
30. Maureen Warner-Lewis, *Guinea's Other Suns: The African Dynamic in Trinidad Culture* (Dover, Mass.: Majority Press, 1991), 24; Col. Research Publication no. 15 *Friendly Societies in the West Indies. Report on a Survey by A.F. Wells and D. Wells* (London: HMSO, 1953), 75, ff.
31. CO 295/324, Trinidad Despatch no. 332, Fowler to Knutsford, 19 December, 1889.
32. "San Carlos Lands Arbitration", *Trinidad Guardian*, 14 February 1946, 2.
33. C.Y. Shepherd, *The Cocoa Industry: Some Economic Aspects*, Part IV (Trinidad: ICTA, 1937), 4.
34. Compiled from James Henry Collens, *The Trinidad and Tobago Yearbooks* (Port of Spain: Franklin's Electrical Printery, 1905–1945), see table 5.3.
35. Interviews; J.C. Jha, "Background to the Legalization of Non-Christian marriages in Trinidad and Tobago", in *East Indians in the Caribbean: Colonialism and the Struggle for Identity*, ed. Bridget Brereton and Winston Dookeran (London: Kraus International, 1982), 117–40.
36. Jha, "Background", 117–40; K.O. Laurence, *A Question of Labour: Indentured Immigration into Trinidad and Tobago 1875–1917* (London: James Currey, 1994), 236–51.
37. Harry, "Women in Agriculture", 209.
38. Ibid.

39. Report of the Trade and Taxes commission, Schedule D, *Public Opinion*, 30 December 1886, 4.
40. *Trinidad Royal Gazette*, 1930–1938.
41. A.W. Knapp, *Cocoa and Chocolate: Their History from Plantation to Consumer* (London: Chapman and Hall, 1920) 2; Extract from an Early Trinidad publication "How Jose Formed His Cocoa Estate", n.d.
42. CO 297, Trinidad Acts, Ordinance 54 of 1921, enacted under Ag. Governor Bart.
43. *Trinidad Blue Books of Statistics and Colonial Reports Annuals*, 1870–1938.
44. *Trinidad Royal Gazette*, December–January 1938.

SECTION 2

Bankers and Financiers

CHAPTER 6

Patterns of Investment and Sources of Credit in the British West Indian Sugar Industry, 1838–1897*

RICHARD A. LOBDELL

In this essay we attempt to describe the pattern of investment and identify the sources of credit in the British West Indian sugar industry between 1838 and 1897. During those years sugar planters faced three separate crises: Emancipation in 1838, Free Trade in 1846, and bountied beet sugar competition in 1884. In order to examine the response of the sugar industry to each of those crises, it is convenient to divide this study into three time periods. The first deals with the period 1838–45; the second examines the years 1846–83; and the last considers the period 1884–97. Within each of those sections, we attempt to discuss (1) the pressures on the industry to undertake technological improvements, (2) the pattern of capital investment as a result of those pressures, and (3) the major sources of credit which enabled that investment to proceed. In a concluding section we offer a brief summary of our findings and reflect upon the consequences of the industry's attempts to reduce production costs over the period.

*Originally published in the *Journal of Caribbean History* 4 (1972): 31–53, this essay was awarded the Newcomen prize for essays in Material History at McGill University in 1971. Reprinted by permission of the Departments of History, University of the West Indies.

The Post-Emancipation Crisis, 1838–45

The British West Indian sugar industry had been in recession for several years prior to the Emancipation Act of 1834. Responding to wartime demand in the British markets, West Indian planters had expanded production throughout the first decade of the nineteenth century, and in the process new and only marginally productive land had been brought under sugar cultivation in an effort to capture the profits of a distant war. With the peace of 1815, however, sugar prices plummeted, profits disappeared, and planters were faced with the difficult task of reorganizing production. As prices continued to fall, many marginal estates ceased production altogether as sugar cultivation retreated to more suitable lands.

Understandably, the Act of 1834 tended to complicate this rationalization of the sugar industry. Although emancipation was not immediate, few planters held much hope for the future prosperity of the sugar industry. Feeding on each other's wildest fears and recalling the generally unfortunate experiment called Apprenticeship, most British West Indian planters gloomily awaited the collapse of the economy with the coming of full emancipation in 1838.

In the light of such forebodings, it is not surprising to discover that plantation accounts tend to show increasing costs of production following the Act of 1834. But as can be seen in table 6.1, most planters argued that during Apprenticeship production costs were only slightly higher, and in some cases even lower, than under the last few years of slavery. Predictably, the most spectacular increases in costs uniformly belong to the period immediately following 1838.

The accuracy of the data in table 6.1 may be questioned. Since this evidence was presented to a committee of the British House of Commons with the hope of winning aid for the sugar industry, it was obviously in the planters' interest to show clearly "the high cost of freedom". Even if planter honesty and good faith are assumed, it is doubtful whether the costing of production was very sophisticated on most estates.[1] Nonetheless, although these estimates may be somewhat inaccurate, there is little reason to suppose that overall costs of production did not rise as labour was transformed from a slave to a wage basis. Antigua was probably not exceptional when its leading planters claimed that in 1848 somewhere between one-half and two-thirds of total production costs arose from wages.[2]

Table 6.1: Estimated Annual Average Cost of Producing a Hundredweight of Sugar (Exclusive of Capital Charges)

Colony	Slavery	Apprenticeship	Freedom
Jamaica[1]	10s 5½d	9s 2¼d	29s 2d
Trinidad[1]	9s 5d	8s 3d	32s 6½d
Tobago[1]	8s 5½d	11s 2d	27s 10d
St Vincent[2]	7s 3½d	7s 1d	19s 7d
Grenada[2]	9s 5d	9s 8d	24s 3d
St Kitts[3]	4s 5d	6s 7d	21s 10d
Antigua[4]	7s 8d	7s 6d	19s 7d

Sources and explanations:

[1]Slavery – 1832–34; Apprenticeship – 1836–38; Freedom – 1838–40. (*The Sugar Question: Being a Digest of the Evidence Taken Before the Committee on Sugar and Coffee Plantations* [London: HMSO, 1848], 2: 62.)
[2]Slavery – 1831–33; Apprenticeship – 1834–38; Freedom – 1838–40. (*The Sugar Question*, 2: 62.)
[3]Slavery – 1828–34; Apprenticeship – 1834–38; Freedom – 1842–46. (*The Sugar Question*, 2: 19–20.)
[4]Slavery – 1829–33; Apprenticeship – 1834–36; Freedom – 1837–46. (*The Sugar Question*, 2: 10, 14–15.)

It is interesting to note that not all planters were convinced that labour was the chief cause of increasing production costs in the mid-1840s. According to one authority, the increased costs of sugar production in St Kitts were mainly the result of mismanagement arising from absentee ownership of estates.[3] A planter in Trinidad believed that the principal cost of production was not high wage rates, but instead arose from "waste, loss, destruction and damage" in field and factory operations.[4] In both men's view the situation could not be expected to improve until fresh capital, new management practices, and improved prices were forthcoming.

By 1840, therefore, most British West Indian planters were convinced that costs of production were rising as a result of emancipation and that some remedial action was urgently required if the sugar industry were to survive. Thus, when it began hearings in 1842, the Select Committee on the West India colonies encountered a variety of proposals designed to check the declining fortunes of sugar. Without question the most frequently heard complaint dealt with the "labour problem" and possible solutions to it. Mr Burnley, whose particular interests were in Trinidad, echoed the opinion of many when he declared that if only labourers could be induced to work regularly, then profits could still be made in spite of the high wage rates.[5]

The Committee of 1842 also considered the usefulness of capital investment in reducing overall costs of production. Of course, certain improvements in field operations had been made long before emancipation. In Grenada, for example, ploughs had been employed since 1815, although they were not extensively used until after 1838.[6] This wider use of field implements after emancipation seems to have been common in most of the West Indian colonies. Hence, in Barbados it appears that more extensive use of artificial fertilizers and better drainage systems were undertaken mainly after 1838.[7] Similarly, cultivation machinery is said to have become widespread in Trinidad by the mid-1840s,[8] and certain estates had clearly improved production through the use of ploughs and harrows in Jamaica after 1838, but capital needed to finance further improvements was very scarce.[9]

It was in British Guiana that cultivation techniques were most advanced before 1845. Although extensive use of ploughs was limited by the layout of estates and soil conditions, British Guiana could easily boast the best cultivation and transportation systems in all the British West Indies. Steam engines, cane carriers, and megass carriers were widely employed in the transportation of estate products, while new techniques of fertilization and irrigation were known and used before 1845.[10] Indeed, the only obstacle to even greater employment of machinery in field operations (e.g. relaying of fields to facilitate steam ploughs) was the acute shortage of finance capital.[11]

Capital investment was not limited to field operations during the period 1838–45. Indeed, it is not unlikely that most new capital was invested in factory equipment during those years. One obvious innovation was the introduction of steam-powered mills for the crushing of cane. Although they were expensive, a number of estates installed these new mills in order to reduce overall production costs. In St Kitts, for example, only one steam engine was to be found in 1833, but by 1847 some twenty-three were employed on the island.[12] Likewise in British Guiana a good number of steam mills were employed during the period 1838–45, though some planters seemed unwilling to risk capital in sugar's dubious future.[13] Barbadian planters ordered over £14,000 worth of factory equipment from one manufacturer alone in the two years ending in 1846.[14] Steam mills were widely employed in Trinidad in 1842. In fact, Mr Burnley reported that while others might speak of a capital shortage, he was of the opinion that in Trinidad there was much more capital in relation to labour than prudence dictated.[15]

Nonetheless, steam mills remained the exception on most of the less prosperous sugar estates before 1845. In Antigua, for example, only six or seven steam mills were employed on more than 125 estates in 1842.[16] Virtually all sugar mills in Grenada were turned by water power in that same year,[17] and even in the previously most prosperous colony of Jamaica, investment in factory equipment was concentrated on a few estates, most notably at Worthy Park in St Catherine.[18]

These attempts to reduce the costs of sugar production were not dramatically successful before 1845. Planters generally found it difficult to economize on labour as it became virtually impossible to make substantial reduction in wage rates. On those estates where new factory and field machinery were introduced, the costs of transition, as well as inadequate accounting systems usually put an intolerable strain on finances. On the surface at least, costs of production continued to rise in spite of planters' efforts to rationalize production before 1845. And yet, there is some evidence that capital investment made during this period was useful in reducing costs of production in later years. Mr Greene of St Kitts, for example, reported that the previous introduction of machinery on certain local estates had led to a marked fall in production costs by 1848.[19] In 1850 Lord Stanley argued that Barbadian planters who had made capital improvements before 1846 were in a stronger financial position than their less adventurous neighbours.[20] Even the ultra-cautious Guianese planter Henry Barkly admitted that some neighbouring estates' cost of production had been reduced through the employment of new machinery during this period.[21] In short, those estates which made substantial capital investment in field and factory improvements before 1845 were generally in the best position to withstand subsequent crises.

A British West Indian planter interested in continuing the operation of his estate, or in making capital investments in the hope of future profits, might acquire financial support from a number of sources after 1838. He might try to continue previous credit arrangements with his agent in Britain. Under this system a planter acquired on credit from a British merchant the supplies necessary for the operation of his estate. The subsequent crop would automatically be consigned to the same merchant who would arrange its sale on the British market. Once the crop had been sold, deductions were made for supplies shipped to the estate on credit, commissions were subtracted, and the balance credited (or debited) to the estate's account. At the end of the Napoleonic Wars, however, many consignee creditors began to despair of such arrangements as the indebtedness of planters grew with declining prices. Consequently, advances were limited to the barest necessities and following emancipation only the financially strongest plantations could safely rely on this traditional source of credit for investment funds.

A second possible source of investment funds was the £17 million voted by Parliament in 1834 as partial compensation to British West Indian planters for emancipation of slaves. Had this money been used for rational investment, the productivity of sugar estates would have undoubtedly improved. Although a few planters did invest their compensation payments in sugar estates,[22] the greatest share of the compensation money seems to have been used to reduce indebtedness previously contracted. In so far as these debt payments increased creditworthiness, they may be considered to have established a potential source of credit for future capital investment. But as suggested above, many consignee merchants had grown suspicious of West Indian plantations and viewed the compensation money as a last chance to make good an increasingly worthless planter indebtedness.[23]

Thirdly, planters might have financed capital improvements from savings accumulated during periods of past prosperity. Unfortunately, only estates free of debt in 1838 and in possession of sizeable savings could consider such an undertaking. Although not unheard of, this alternative was not a very real one for the vast majority of planters.[24]

Finally, sugar planters might turn to the newly established local banking system for help in financing estate operations. Of the local banks, by far the largest was the Colonial Bank of the West Indies which was granted a royal charter in May 1836. By the mid-1840s branches had been established in most of the British West Indies, as well as in Cuba and North America. Under its Charter, the Colonial Bank was empowered to carry on the normal operations of a commercial bank, including dealing in bills of exchange, accepting deposits, and advancing money on commercial paper and government securities. However, the bank was expressly forbidden "to lend or advance money on the security of lands, houses, or tenements, or upon ships or to deal in general wares or merchandise of any nature or kind whatsoever".[25] Consequently, the bank was legally forbidden to undertake substantial loans to sugar estates. It might advance money to meet some working expenses of the estates if owners were willing to sign a personal guarantee of liability. But long term capital improvements were quite impossible for the bank to finance. Hence, although it prospered throughout the nineteenth century, the Colonial Bank had little beneficial effect on investment in the British West Indian sugar industry. Indeed, through its excessively high discounting rates, the Colonial Bank may have seriously hindered the industry's development.[26]

Other local banks followed the practice of the influential Colonial Bank and refused to lend money on the security of sugar estates. By the mid-1840s there was only one rival to the Colonial Bank in British Guiana. Established sometime in 1836, the Bank of British Guiana was granted a Charter very similar to that of the Colonial Bank.[27] There is no evidence that this smaller bank lent money to finance capital investment in sugar during the years preceding 1846.

Jamaican local banks appear to have adopted the same policy towards estate financing as did their counterparts in British Guiana. For example, an institution known as the Jamaica Planters' Bank was formed in 1839, but was never given a charter. There is no evidence that it undertook estate financing, but instead seemed particularly interested in financing commercial activities. It is not surprising, therefore, that the Planters' Bank fell victim to the British financial crisis of 1848 and was forced to close its doors in Jamaica.[28]

A final example of the kind of banking institution which existed during these years is the Bank of Jamaica which was founded in 1837 and closed in 1865. Like the Planters' Bank, the Bank of Jamaica was refused a formal charter. But unlike other local banks, the Bank of Jamaica's Deed of Settlement hints at a more liberal policy towards advances and credit. According to the Deed, the Bank was allowed to "give credit or make advances to any person or persons whomsoever, to such amount, at such rate of interest, and upon such terms, as the Directors may think fit, and such credit may be given, and advances made, with or without security, at the discretion of the Directors ...".[29] Whether in fact the Bank of Jamaica did pursue such a liberal credit policy is not known. From the lack of planter comment and enthusiasm, however, it is probably safe to assume that the Bank of Jamaica did little to finance capital investment in that island's sugar industry.

In summary, those British West Indian planters interested in capital improvement before 1846 had either to rely upon their own meagre savings or upon consignee credit which was becoming increasingly restricted. Undoubtedly, many planters and merchants had lost confidence in the future of sugar in the West Indies. The steady decline of sugar prices, the mounting indebtedness of estates as profits diminished, and the alluring prospects for investment elsewhere[30] all acted to divert capital away from the British West Indies between 1838 and 1845.

The Free Trade Crisis, 1846–83

Before 1825 British West Indian planters enjoyed a near monopoly in the British muscovado market. British import tariffs were such that the lowest rates applied to West Indian muscovado, slightly higher rates were levied on muscovado coming from elsewhere in the empire, and prohibitively high duties were placed on the muscovado of foreign planters. Beginning in 1825, however, slight alterations in the structure of the sugar tariff were introduced. In that year muscovado produced in Mauritius was allowed to enter the British market at the same tariff rates as West Indian muscovado. Ten years later muscovado made in the East Indian colonies was similarly admitted.[31]

Between 1836 and 1844 the British sugar duties were altered almost annually, though for most of the period the "B.W.I. group"[32] muscovado paid 24s per cwt in duties, as against 32s for other empire producers, and a staggering 63s duty on foreign muscovado. In 1844 all foreign muscovado not grown by slave labour was admitted to the British market at the rate of 34s duty, and a year later rates were reduced on all categories of imported sugar.[33] Thus, even before the Act of 1846, alert British West Indian planters must have seen their preferential market slowly disappearing.

The Sugar Duty Act of 1846 announced the intention of the British government to reduce preferential duties so that by 1854 a single rate would apply to sugar of a given quality, regardless of its origin. The Act further prescribed that eventually all sugar would be admitted free of any duty. Consequently, beginning in 1846 British West Indian muscovado entered the British market with only a seven shilling tariff advantage over all foreign-made muscovado. And, as the Act had promised, all muscovado was admitted to the British market at a single rate beginning in 1854.

It is important to note, however, that even after 1854 different quality sugar was taxed differently when imported into the United Kingdom. The British government, anxious to protect its home sugar refining industry, introduced a tariff that progressively increased duties as the quality of imported sugar rose. Hence, the highest duties were paid by refined sugar and successively lower duties were charged on partially refined and muscovado sugar.[34]

This arrangement clearly favoured West Indian planters who had always concentrated on the production of muscovado. Even the vacuum pan yellow crystals made in British Guiana was allowed to enter at relatively favourable rates after 1854. Having installed a good deal of modern machinery after 1840, foreign competitors (e.g., Cuba, Brazil, Mauritius) produced relatively refined sugar, which almost always entered the British market at higher rates of duty. The duties were so favourable to muscovado that some West Indian producers, especially those in British Guiana where modern equipment had recently been employed, found it profitable to spoil refined sugar and export it as muscovado.[35]

This peculiar advantage disappeared only after 1874 when all sugar was admitted to British markets free of any duties. Some West Indian estates were abandoned as a result while others sought more satisfactory markets for their produce. Hoping to encourage a domestic sugar refining industry, the Americans restructured their sugar duties in 1872 and it became advantageous for West Indian planters to sell muscovado in the American rather than the British market. Between 1879 and 1883 exports of West Indian sugar to the United Kingdom fell by 25 per cent, whereas by the early 1880s nearly half (47 per cent) of all British West Indian sugar exports went to the American market.[36] Nonetheless, planters fully recognized that the American market was inherently unstable since muscovado prices were entirely dependent upon the whim of Congress which set the tariff in a generally unpredictable manner.

Between 1846 and 1883, therefore, British West Indian planters were faced with declining prices in the British markets and great uncertainty in the American markets. Although total British West Indian sugar exports had more than doubled over the period, on the whole it was difficult to maintain total revenues as prices continued to sag.[37] The only obvious way to earn even modest profits was to reduce overall production costs.

As most planters saw the situation after 1846, there were three possible ways by which sugar production costs might be significantly reduced. First of all, a new source of cheap and efficient labour would greatly lower production costs. After a good deal of experimentation, East Indian indentured immigrants were brought to the British West Indies and were found to be suitable estate workers. Considerable sums of money, both private and public in origin, were required for such immigration which may be considered an investment of sorts in the industry.

A second strategy used by planters to reduce costs of production between 1846 and 1883 involved the mechanization and rationalization of field and factory operations. Immediately following the Act of 1846, significant capital investment seems to have fallen off in the West Indian sugar industry, though it did not completely disappear. Between 1803 and 1851, for example, the firm of Boulton and Watt sent to the British West Indies at least 129 sugar mill steam engines, some of which must surely have been ordered and installed after 1846.[38] Furthermore, one witness before the Committee of 1848 claimed that "2,500 agricultural implements have been sent out to the West Indies during the last few years".[39] Nonetheless, it is difficult to find much direct evidence of massive capital investment in sugar during the first few years following the Act of 1846.

By 1850 the immediate shock and panic had begun to subside and West Indian estates which were still in operation increasingly turned to newer techniques of production. In spite of hardships in Barbados, for example, most estates were running profitably in the years after 1850, primarily as a result of "investment of fresh capital in improved machinery, drainage, and expensive concentrated fertilizers".[40] Indeed, between 1865 and 1883 a mild prosperity seems to have visited the West Indian sugar industry. With the momentary prosperity came renewed interest in investment. To be sure, some of the smaller islands seemed to prosper without undertaking capital improvements, but those same colonies were virtually ruined when the last remnants of preference in the British market disappeared in 1874.

It was in the large, relatively "new" colonies of Trinidad and British Guiana that capital investment was most impressive during the period 1846–83. The Colonial Company in Trinidad made substantial investments in all kinds of new equipment. Vacuum pans, centrifugals, steam powered crushing mills, better techniques of cultivation, and a modern central factory were the main elements of the new investment in Trinidad. Similarly, in British Guiana large sums were invested in the sugar industry between 1846 and 1883. Especially in the latter years of that period, sugar machinery imports often averaged over £100,000 annually.[41] Vacuum pans, centrifugals, improved steam mills, better irrigation schemes, hybrid cane, and improved transportation represented the major areas of capital investment in British Guiana over those years.[42] Indeed, the capital stock of the industry was so improved by 1883 that estates in British Guiana were justly noted for their "utility, economy, and latest manufacturing appliances".[43]

The third method planters saw for reducing costs between 1846 and 1883 lay in the amalgamation of small estates into larger, well-managed, commercial enterprises. Such consolidations allowed for more efficient use of existing factory equipment, available labour supplies, and marketing facilities. In addition, as more acreage was absorbed by the consolidated estate, costs could be lowered by carefully concentrating cultivation on the most productive lands. Finally, and perhaps most importantly, these consolidated estates usually enjoyed the availability of sufficient credit necessary to undertake other cost-saving innovations.

Small inefficient muscovado-producing estates were often consolidated through direct purchase. In Trinidad these small estates usually found it financially impossible to modernize operations by investing in expensive machinery.[44] Consequently, many turned to cocoa or coconut production where soil and climate permitted. Still others were simply sold to buyers who wished to continue sugar production. Mainly through direct purchases, the joint stock company known as the Colonial Company had by 1871 managed to expand its Trinidadian holdings to such a degree that a central factory was considered economical.[45] Other companies and even some individuals in Trinidad followed this tactic in consolidating sugar estates during these years. By 1884 estate consolidation had proceeded so far that a huge proportion of Trinidadian sugar was being grown, manufactured, shipped and marketed by a mere handful of companies.[46]

As in Trinidad, estates in British Guiana were systematically consolidated during the period 1846–83. Thus, the 404 estates producing sugar in 1838 had by 1870 been consolidated into 135 units of production, of which the greatest part was owned by non-resident companies. The Colonial Company, Messrs Daniels of Bristol, and a few other British merchant houses controlled "nearly all the largest, finest, and best cultivated estates"[47] in that colony by 1883.

The amalgamation of estates in St Lucia proceeded in a slightly different manner. The multiple crises following 1815 had driven many muscovado estates into bankruptcy. In order to facilitate the liquidation of these debts, a local law was passed which allowed for the seizure and sale of immovable property. As might have been expected, these sales tended to concentrate land ownership into fewer hands.[48] Consolidation had proceeded so far by 1871 that the next logical step in the rationalization of production, the construction of a central factory, was undertaken. However, the central factory was unable to reduce substantially the costs of production before 1883, as it suffered from mismanagement and poor organization of cane deliveries.[49]

In the other areas of the British West Indies, systematic amalgamation of small estates was hindered by the legal peculiarities of indebtedness. The law did not make it easy to bring about the forced sale of insolvent estates. No strict priority of encumbrances was generally recognized, and that difficulty aside it became almost impossible after 1846 to find buyers willing to assume the estate's outstanding liabilities. Hence, it was often in the interest of insolvent proprietors to abandon production altogether and default on their debts.

In order to expedite the sale and legal transfer of land held by insolvent owners, the West India Encumbered Estates Act was approved by the British Parliament in 1854. By passing an appropriate local ordinance, any West Indian colony[50] could make use of the encumbered estates courts whose duties were to order the sale of land hopelessly in debt. In addition to courts in the various colonies, the Act provided for a central court in London in order to ensure equal protection to all litigants. The courts were most active between 1857 and 1883, although they were not formally abolished until 1895.

Estates processed under the courts were generally sold in London. Only rarely were such estates purchased by individual planters. Instead, the vast majority came into the hands of various British merchant houses. In St Vincent, for example, the thirty estates sold by the courts were mostly bought by Porter and Sons or by Cavan Bros., who also held plantations in British Guiana, Trinidad, and Barbados. Similarly, court-processed estates in Montserrat, Antigua, and St Kitts were usually purchased by the estate's former consignee merchant. By 1883 most of the land in these smaller colonies was controlled by non-resident proprietors.[51]

The courts were most active in disposing of insolvent estates in Jamaica. In that colony some 148 estates were sold by the courts, including some of the largest and best known plantations. Many of these estates were taken out of sugar production, but some were cultivated while muscovado continued to enjoy an advantage in the British market. However, only a limited amount of new machinery was introduced on these estates which often tended to concentrate on rum production.[52] As elsewhere, the sale of encumbered estates tended to concentrate ownership in the hands of non-resident merchants.

In summary, the consolidation of estates after 1846 tended to concentrate plantation ownership in the hands of British merchant houses specializing in sugar. The non-resident nature of these companies, which possessed considerable non-estate assets, gave them a creditworthiness which the smaller estates could not hope to rival. The extensive use of such credit and the more thorough organization of existing assets enabled these new enterprises to dominate the industry by 1883.

Moreover, the consolidation of sugar estates demonstrates a change in attitude towards plantation production. In former times a surprising number of estates had been operated by a curious combination of sentiment and family pride. With the crises of the first half of the nineteenth century, however, it was increasingly apparent that a more commercial approach to estate production was required.

Finally, consolidation of estates generally led to lower costs of production during the years 1846–65. The new creditworthiness of the amalgamated estates made possible the introduction of machinery and other improved techniques of production. It must be noted, however, that production costs were not significantly reduced during the years 1865–83.[53] Nonetheless, the consolidation of estates across the whole period 1846–83 laid the foundation for remarkable savings in cost after 1884.

Apart from consolidation under non-resident merchant ownership, other credit sources were available for the financing of capital investment between 1846 and 1883. In spite of a general hesitancy to do so, a few consignee merchants seemed willing to continue the advances on which planters had always relied. This traditional system of credit seems to have been particularly important in Barbados. Unlike neighbouring colonies, Barbados exhibited no tendency towards estate consolidation. Even as late as 1897 only 14 of 440 sugar estates were owned by public companies.⁵⁴ By virtue of their excellent quality muscovado and relatively low costs of production, Barbadian planters were usually able to earn modest profits, which in turn allowed them to finance their operations in the traditional manner. To planters in other West Indian colonies, however, merchants showed great reluctance to advance credit.

Secondly, planters might try to finance day to day operations through credit secured from the local banking system. Unfortunately, the Colonial Bank still refused to loan money on the security of land and so it was of little assistance in financing major capital investment. Nevertheless, the Colonial Bank could usually be relied upon to provide working capital in the form of personal loans to well-known and highly respected planters. Other local banks were of no more help in the financing of major investment. Moreover, many of these smaller banks closed their doors before 1884. In short, local banks might grant small loans to cover working expenses, but they would not provide the financing required for significant capital investment during the years 1846–83.

Finally, planters in a few colonies were able to take advantage of indirect financial aid offered by local governments. During these years many colonial governments employed skilled engineers to advise planters on improved manufacturing techniques, thus indirectly encouraging capital investment. In addition, many local governments had established, at least on paper, a Department of Agriculture which gave advice and some assistance to planters interested in improving production techniques. The St Lucian government undertook an even bolder course of financial assistance to the sugar industry by granting some £40,000 for the construction of a central sugar factory in the 1870s.⁵⁵ The governments of Trinidad and British Guiana expended considerable sums of public money on the importation of indentured immigrants which may be considered a form of assistance extended to the industry. On balance, however, it would be difficult to argue that substantial government credit was available to planters interested in capital investment during the period 1846–83.

The Beet Sugar Crisis, 1884–97

Taking advantage of rapid technological developments, European beet sugar producers were able to reduce costs and increase output substantially during the second half of the nineteenth century. Better crop yields, more efficient manufacturing, and more systematic marketing placed beet sugar in a position to threaten cane sugar by 1870 when nearly one-third of total world sugar output was beet in origin. Only ten years later, beet producers were turning out 50 per cent of the world's sugar.[56]

Although total world sugar production increased by 44 per cent between 1870 and 1880, sugar prices in Britain remained reasonably steady at or near 20s per cwt. Beginning in 1884, however, European beet sugar was "dumped" in massive quantities on the British market. Protected by a disguised export bounty and enjoying the absence of a British tariff, beet sugar soon swamped the British market. Prices began to fall so precipitously that by the end of 1884 sugar was selling at 13s 3d per cwt; by 1897 prices had fallen below 10s.[57]

The reaction of British West Indian planters to the threat of bountied beet sugar was immediate and frantic. Countless petitions, innumerable pamphlets, and seemingly endless interviews with government officials proved futile during the twelve years following 1884. Wedded to the principles of free trade and cognizant of the political advantages of inexpensive sugar for home consumption, the British government remained serenely indifferent to colonial complaints. Only after another round of bounty increases in 1897 was the British government prevailed upon to send a Royal Commission to their West Indian colonies.

Most planters of the time did not require a Royal Commission to point out the difficulties confronting their industry. By 1870 hardly anyone seriously believed that West Indian sugar would ever again be protected in the British market. Consequently, more and more West Indian muscovado found its way into the more attractive American market, especially after the revision of the American tariff in 1872. By the end of the century more than 65 per cent of all British West Indian sugar was being exported to the U.S. markets.[58]

Furthermore, few planters needed a Royal Commission to explain that profits were determined as much by costs of production as by final product prices. As it became increasingly obvious that British prices were not likely to improve and that the American tariff was subject to the uncertainties of partisan politics, West Indian planters took more interest in reducing their overall costs of production.

In 1884 the least expensive British West Indian sugar cost 16s per cwt to produce.[59] After that year, however, those sugar estates which were still in oper-

Table 6.2: Estimated Least Costly Production of Sugar, by Colony (Exclusive of Capital Charges)

Colony	Cost per cwt, 1897
Barbados	8s 7½d
Trinidad	8s 10½d
Jamaica	7s 4d
St Kitts	9s 5½d
British Guiana	9s 0d

Source: Royal Commission of 1897, *Report,* appendix A.

ation managed to reduce costs of production dramatically. The Royal Commission of 1897 found Guianese producers making sugar for about 9s per cwt;[60] two years later costs were said to have been lowered to 8s.[61] Similar reductions were found in the principal sugar producing colonies by 1897, as can be seen in table 6.2.

These relatively low production costs were the result of several important improvements. Firstly, significant economies had been realized in field operations between 1883 and 1897. In British Guiana, for example, cultivation costs involved in making one hundredweight of sugar had fallen from 6s 4d in 1883–4 to 4s 3d in 1896–7.[62] The Royal Commission believed that improved species of cane was the single greatest cause of such falling cultivation costs. Reductions in the wage rates had also been important, though by 1897 it was difficult to imagine that additional savings of this type could be expected. More widespread use of modern cultivation implements, more thorough application of artificial fertilizers, and better irrigation schemes also made significant contributions to lower cultivation costs.[63]

Secondly, improved factory operations helped reduce overall production costs after 1884. In British Guiana, for example, factory costs associated with the making of a hundredweight of sugar were calculated to be 9s 9d in 1883–4, but had fallen to 4s 9d by 1896–7.[64] This remarkable decline in factory costs must be laid to the heavy investment which proceeded even after the crisis of 1884. Hence, the value of sugar machinery imported into that colony during the period 1879–97 has been estimated at between £1.4 million and £2.2 million.⁶⁵ In 1890 alone some £130,000 worth of sugar factory equipment was imported into British Guiana.⁶⁶

In similar fashion capital investment played a large role in reducing production costs in Trinidad after 1884. By 1897 some £2.5 million had been invested in the sugar industry, of which at least 75 per cent represented machinery of the most modern nature.⁶⁷ After 1885 these improved factories began to produce an increasing proportion of Trinidadian sugar exports. In 1891, for example, about 43 per cent of sugar export earnings was vacuum pan produced; by 1896 that figure had increased to 53 per cent.⁶⁸ Indeed, capital investment in Trinidadian factory equipment was so extensive that the Royal Commission could find little to recommend by way of improvement.

On the other hand, capital investment in sugar industries of other British West Indian colonies virtually ceased after 1884. In the technologically backward islands of Grenada, Dominica, Montserrat, and St Vincent sugar production had all but disappeared by 1897. Certainly after the crisis of 1884 no major improvements were undertaken in sugar, though a few merchant companies with land in these colonies turned production to limes, cocoa, and sea cotton.⁶⁹ Even the more prosperous islands of St Kitts and Barbados saw little capital investment in sugar after 1884, though relatively cheap labour held production costs within manageable limits.⁷⁰ After 1884 even Jamaica ceased to be a major exporter of sugar, choosing instead to concentrate on the production of rum, bananas, and citrus. To be sure, a few extraordinary Jamaican plantations still profited from sugar production,⁷¹ but methods of production were primitive and sugar investment negligible.⁷²

Finally, production costs were reduced after 1884 through various economies resulting from consolidation of estate lands. Although interest in consolidation waned in some of the smaller islands after 1884, amalgamation of estates continued in Trinidad and British Guiana. We have already seen that such consolidation helped to reduce costs of production by co-ordinating various estate activities in the years between 1846 and 1883. Similar economies were realized after 1884 as amalgamated properties became better organized and new techniques of production were steadily introduced. In Trinidad, for example, the central factory built by the Colonial Company in the 1870s had reduced production costs by more than 50 per cent between 1884 and 1894.⁷³

The availability of credit to finance capital improvements was a major difficulty for most planters after 1884. The traditional sources of credit, the consignee merchants, had been almost unapproachable before 1884 and the events of that year offered little inducement to merchants to provide estates with additional capital. Increasingly, planters had to look elsewhere for the credit needed to finance their operations. The reluctance of consignee merchants to extend credit did not close the sugar industry to inflows of foreign capital. As noted earlier, by the mid-1880s most of the best estates had come under the control of a few British-based merchant houses. Relying on their own creditors in London, these enterprises were able[74] to secure the credit necessary to undertake modernization, and after 1884, if not before that date, this type of credit was the most important available to the British West Indian sugar industry.

A second source of credit for the industry lay in the availability of local investment funds. Some local capitalists were apparently willing to loan funds at 8 per cent interest when the liability was secured by a mortgage on a large estate; smaller, less secure estates were often required to pay 40 per cent interest for similar local financing.[75] Perhaps even more important, however, local capital available for such loans at any rate of interest was strictly limited. Giving evidence to the Royal Commission of 1897, the mayor of Port of Spain and other prominent Trinidadians bemoaned the lack of local credit for small independent planters.[76] Similar complaints were heard by the Commissioners in all of the colonies visited. Although it cannot be completely disregarded, local credit did not seem to play a very important role in the financing of sugar investment during this period.

The increasingly sophisticated banking system of the West Indies might have provided a third source of credit for the sugar industry after 1884. Unfortunately, although the banks continued to prosper, they provided little financing of investment in sugar. In most colonies the Colonial Bank held a monopoly on banking transactions, but the bank was still bound by its original charter which explicitly prohibited the extending of credit on the security of land. Even the personal credit that had proved so useful during the years 1846–83 had been severely restricted after 1885 as prices continued to fall and confidence waned.[77] Only in British Guiana was there to be found a bank willing to underwrite estate operations after 1884. But the Bank of British Guiana was too small, overambitious, and overextended to remain solvent for long. By 1897 it had been forced to seek government help in meeting its commitments and its role as a financier of sugar had all but ended.[78] In short, the banking system after 1884 could no longer aid planters with even the most temporary advances. That the banks, as they were then constituted, might have financed major capital investment was completely beyond question.

Finally, financial assistance to the sugar industry was occasionally made available by various colonial governments after 1884. The colony most active in the public support of sugar was Barbados, a colony which had little access to corporate financing so important to Trinidad and British Guiana. When credit became tighter and more expensive following the events of 1884, the Barbados government approved the Agricultural Aids Act of 1887, which allowed planters to borrow money on the security of their growing crop. The Act was so enthusiastically received that by 1896 some 138 estates comprising over 30,000 acres (about one-third of total plantation acreage) had borrowed more than £100,000 under the scheme. It is important to note that these funds were not governmental in origin; rather, they were loans made by private individuals whose confidence had been bolstered by the obvious interest of the government in the sugar industry. Unfortunately, the poor harvests of the 1890s placed many of these advances in danger of default.[79]

Government aid in other West Indian colonies was less significant. St Lucia continued some public support for the central factory, but nothing on the scale of the 1870s. Most colonies had agricultural officers who advised planters on new techniques of sugar production and increasingly urged diversification into the production of bananas, cocoa, and limes. Large governmental expenditures were involved in the indentured immigrant programmes in Trinidad, British Guiana, and a few other colonies after 1884. Nonetheless, except for the policies of the Barbadian and St Lucian governments, it is difficult to find much direct assistance given by governments to the sugar industry between 1884 and 1897.

Summary and Conclusions

Confronted with declining sugar prices during the last two-thirds of the nineteenth century, British West Indian planters desperately sought to reduce production costs. As we have seen, a number of possible economies presented themselves to the enterprising planter. Attempts to reduce wage rates and fevered efforts to secure an adequate and predictable supply of labour were the initial responses of most planters to rising unit costs of production. Although wage rate reductions proved difficult, the use of indentured immigrants did reduce labour costs of production in some colonies.

Most thoughtful planters were convinced that overall production costs could be lowered if field and factory operations were made more efficient. Consequently, newer milling machinery, more efficient use of factory equipment, and less costly transportation systems were employed after 1840. Improved species of cane, more enlightened use of fertilizers, widespread use of irrigation, and the introduction of new cultivation implements also contributed to lower production costs.

More importantly, overall production costs were reduced through the consolidation of small inefficient estates into larger units of production. Such amalgamation allowed for the more complete employment of factory equipment, more thorough organization of planting and cultivation, and more profitable marketing of final products.

We have seen that these strategies for reducing costs were most successfully undertaken in British Guiana and Trinidad during the period 1838–97. Of those colonies which undertook the importation of indentured immigrants, Trinidad and British Guiana probably benefited most. Heavy investment in modern factory equipment and improved cultivation tools was widespread in both colonies. Perhaps because they were less encumbered, possessed more fertile soil, and were generally more suited to large scale production, estates in Trinidad and British Guiana were steadily amalgamated so that by 1897 the sugar industry in those colonies was controlled by a mere handful of foreign based merchant companies. Although these strategies were attempted in the other islands, the newer colonies of Trinidad and British Guiana had by the end of the century succeeded in dominating the West Indian sugar industry. More convincing proof of the efficacy of these strategies would be hard to imagine.

During these years planters searched frantically for the massive credit with which to finance capital investment. As we have seen, the traditional system of consignee credit, savings from past profits, small loans from local banks, and occasional governmental assistance were all useful (though highly restricted) sources of capital. The most important sources of finance capital were the British merchant companies which came to dominate the West Indian sugar industry after 1880. Relying on credit secured by non-estate assets, these merchant firms alone possessed the capital necessary for significant investment in the newer techniques of production.

The rise of these large, foreign based, vertically integrated companies is the single most important development in the West Indian sugar industry during the last two-thirds of the nineteenth century. Indeed, the emergence and success of these companies mark the beginning of a fundamental change in the institutional organization of the West Indian economies. Dispassionately shifting production and investment from estate to estate and colony to colony, these new enterprises were no longer bound by the tradition, nostalgia, and status considerations which had proved so important to earlier planters. With consummate skill and almost ruthless efficiency, these firms combined their ability to command massive outside credit with their talent for vertical integration. The ultimate result was the transformation of family based plantations into modern, impersonal, industrial enterprises. Indeed, their vertical integration, ability to command credit, reliance upon advanced technology, and foreign ownership may qualify these sugar companies of the late nineteenth century as the first modern multi-national corporations in the Caribbean.

Notes

1. Douglas Hall, "Incalculability as a Feature of Sugar Production during the Eighteenth Century", *Social and Economic Studies* 10 (1961): 340–52.
2. *The Sugar Question: Being a Digest of the Evidence Taken Before the Committee on Sugar and Coffee Plantations* (London: HMSO, 1848), 2: 12, 14.
3. Evidence of Mr Pickwood in *The Sugar Question*, 2: 21.
4. Evidence of Mr Burnley in *Report of the Select Committee on the West India Colonies* (London: HMSO, 1843), 91–92. Hereinafter referred to as *Report* (Committee of 1842).
5. Ibid., 92ff.
6. Evidence of Mr Barkly, *Report* (Committee of 1842), 205.
7. Earl of Derby, *Further Facts Connected with the West Indies* (London, 1851), 28, 41.
8. Evidence of Mr Bushe, *Report* (Committee of 1842), 287–88.
9. Evidence of Mr MacCornock, *Report* (Committee of 1842), 359. N.B. Alexander Geddes disagreed, believing that little machinery had been introduced in Jamaica and was of no value to those estates where it had been employed. See his evidence, ibid., 477.

10. Evidence of Mr Campbell, *Report* (Committee of 1842), 152ff.
11. Evidence of Mr Barkly, ibid., 187–88.
12. Evidence of Mr Greene in the *Report of the Select Committee on Sugar and Coffee Planting*, 8 reports (London, 1848), *Third Report*, 138.
13. Evidence of Mr Barkly, *The Sugar Question*, 2: 86.
14. Evidence of Mr Moody, ibid., 121.
15. Evidence of Mr Burnley, *Report* (Committee of 1842), 76.
16. Evidence of Mr Nugent, ibid., 227.
17. Evidence of Mr Barkly, ibid., 205.
18. Evidence of Mr Price, *Second Report* (Committee of 1848), 62–70.
19. Evidence of Mr Greene, *Third Report* (Committee of 1848), 138.
20. Derby, *Further Facts*, 27–28, 41.
21. Evidence of Mr Barkly, *The Sugar Question*, 2: 82. See also the evidence of Dr Rankin, ibid., 74–76.
22. Evidence of Mr Barkly, *Report* (Committee of 1842), 188.
23. That most consignees viewed suspiciously the future of sugar in the BWI during these years is beyond dispute. The evidence collected by the Committees of 1842 and 1848 is full of such suspicions. See for example the evidence of Mr Innes in *The Sugar Question*, 2: 53, and that of Mr Hankey in the *Third Report* (Committee of 1848), 26.
24. Although the evidence is not conclusive, Mr Barkly seems to have been one of those who did so (*Report* [Committee of 1842], 187–88). On the other hand, Mr Tollemache's estates in Antigua were debt free and reasonably profitable, but he flatly refused to invest in new equipment (*Third Report* [Committee of 1848], 247).
25. As quoted in Robert Montgomery Martin, *History of the Colonies of the British Empire*, 6 vols. (London: William H. Allen, 1843), 4: 20–21. See also, Barclays Bank, *A Banking Centenary: Barclays Bank, 1836–1936* (Plymouth, UK: Mayflower Press, 1938).
26. R.W. Beachey, *The British West Indian Sugar Industry in the Late 19th Century* (Oxford: Basil Blackwell, 1957), 159; J.W. Root, *The British West Indies and the Sugar Industry* (Liverpool: the author, 1899), 12–14.
27. Martin, *History*, 4: 134.
28. Douglas Hall, *Free Jamaica, 1838–1865* (New Haven: Yale University Press, 1959), 122–24; Gisela Eisner, *Jamaica, 1830–1930: A Study in Economic Growth* (Manchester: Manchester University Press, 1961), 196, 199.
29. Bank of Jamaica, *Deed of Settlement of the Bank of Jamaica* (Kingston, 1837), 15.
30. Evidence of Mr Barkly, *The Sugar Question*, 2: 85. When one planter was asked by the 1848 Committee why investment was lacking in the BWI sugar industry after emancipation, he replied: "[Investors] preferred India and Mauritius . . ." (Evidence of Mr Higgins, *Fourth Report*, 101.)

31. Noel Deerr, *History of Sugar* (London: Chapman and Hall, 1949–50), 2: 430, 442–43.
32. Meaning muscovado originating in the British West Indies, Mauritius, and the East India colonies.
33. P. Curtin, "Sugar Duties and West Indian Prosperity", *Journal of Economic History* 14 (1954): 159–61.
34. Deerr, *History of Sugar*, 2: 442.
35. Beachey, *British West Indian Sugar Industry*, 45–48.
36. Calculated from Beachey, *British West Indian Sugar Industry*, 57.
37. Deerr, *History of Sugar*, 1: 194–203; Curtin, "Sugar Duties", 160–61.
38. Noel Deerr and Alexander Brooks, "The Early Use of Steam Power in the Cane Sugar Industry", *Transactions of the Newcomen Society* 21 (1940–41): 11–21.
39. Evidence of Mr Miles, *Fifth Report* (Committee of 1848), 260.
40. Derby, *Further Facts*, 41.
41. *Report and Evidence of the West India Royal Commission of 1897*, Appendix A, 84–85.
42. A railway was begun in British Guiana in the early 1840s and substantial sums of money (£100,000) were invested by local planters. However, after 1846 English capitalists refused to pay in their subscribed funds as their confidence in the colony's future declined. See *The Sugar Question*, 2: 66.
43. Beachey, *British West Indian Sugar Industry*, 120.
44. One authority in 1848 placed the cost of installing a modern factory capable of producing a modest output of 500 hogsheads of sugar at £8,000. (*The Sugar Question*, 2: 120–21.)
45. Beachey, *British West Indian Sugar Industry*, 84–85.
46. Ibid., 42, 84, 122, 127.
47. Ibid., 118–21.
48. Royal Commission of 1897, *Report*, Appendix A, 116–17.
49. Beachey, *British West Indian Sugar Industry*, 84–85.
50. With the exception of St Lucia, Barbados, Trinidad, and British Guiana, all the West Indian colonies eventually passed such an ordinance.
51. Beachey, *British West Indian Sugar Industry*, 8, 36–38.
52. See both Beachey, *British West Indian Sugar Industry*, 6–9, 36, and Eisner, *Jamaica*, 196–97. Both these authors suggest that during these years there was some absolute reduction of the industry's capital stock as some sugar factories were dismantled and sold to Cuban planters.
53. Beachey, *British West Indian Sugar Industry*, 53.
54. Ibid., 125–26.
55. *Report* (Royal Commission, 1897), 45.
56. Deerr, *History of Sugar*, 2: 490.
57. Ibid., 2: 505.

58. About £2 per ton more revenue could be earned in the American market during most of the last thirty years of the nineteenth century. See Beachey, *British West Indian Sugar Industry*, 128–29.
59. *Report* (Royal Commission, 1897), Appendix A, 84.
60. Ibid.
61. Root, *British West Indies*, 50.
62. *Report* (Royal Commission, 1897), Appendix A, 84.
63. Ibid., 14.
64. Ibid., 84.
65. Ibid., 84–85; Root, *British West Indies*, 16, 24.
66. Beachey, *British West Indian Sugar Industry*, 176.
67. *Report* (Royal Commission, 1897), Appendix A, 100.
68. Calculated from data found ibid. In St Lucia the central factory and other modern factories had all but eliminated muscovado by 1897.
69. *Report* (Royal Commission, 1897), Appendix A, 110, 120, 122–23, 127.
70. In Barbados between 1886 and 1895 nearly £70,000 was spent annually on artificial fertilizers. Strictly speaking this may not qualify as capital investment, but it clearly shows a willingness to adopt technology suited to the Barbadian circumstance. See, *Report* (Royal Commission, 1897), Appendix A, 97.
71. For example, Mesopotamia estate averaged some £2,000 profit annually between 1874 and 1891 and other estates in the parishes of Westmoreland, Hanover, and Trelawny seem to have been equally prosperous. See, Beachey, *British West Indian Sugar Industry*, 159.
72. *Report* (Royal Commission, 1897), Appendix A, 137.
73. In St Lucia similar reductions in costs were claimed for these years as the central factory began efficient operation. See, Beachey, *British West Indian Sugar Industry*, 86.
74. Though they were not always willing to do so. In St Kitts, for example, foreign owners whose credit was excellent refused to undertake necessary investment after 1895. See, *Report* (Royal Commission, 1897), 57.
75. *Report* (Royal Commission, 1897), Appendix C, 282.
76. *Report* (Royal Commission, 1897), Appendix C, 237, 241, 276, 282. See also, Root, *British West Indies*, 16–17; Eisner, *Jamaica*, 196.
77. *Report* (Royal Commission, 1897), Appendix C, 44–45.
78. The government's commitment to the Bank of British Guiana stood at £145,000 in 1897. See the letter from Gov. Hemming dated 26 April 1897, found in *Report* (Royal Commission, 1897), Appendix C, 148–49.
79. *Report* (Royal Commission, 1897), 30, and Appendix C, 151–53, 157; Beachey, *British West Indian Sugar Industry*, 34.

CHAPTER 7

Financing Agriculture and Trade

*Barclays Bank (DCO) in the
West Indies, 1926–1945**

KATHLEEN E.A. MONTEITH

It is generally agreed among historians that the lending policies of the British banks that were established overseas in the nineteenth and early twentieth centuries, were highly selective and restrictive, engaging in a certain amount of discrimination. What remains debatable is the basis for this discrimination; that is, whether it was racially motivated or based on the more benign factor of creditworthiness.[1] Geoffrey Jones in his broad coverage of British multinational banking in the nineteenth and twentieth centuries, has indicated that while the banks based their lending decisions on commercial criteria, their assessments of risk and creditworthiness were also based on assumptions about ethnicity. Among these assumptions was that people of non-European ancestry in general lacked sufficient monetary and commercial responsibility.[2] This chapter extends this discussion to the British West Indies through an examination of the products and services offered by Barclays Bank (Dominion, Colonial and Overseas) during the period 1926 to 1945. It begins with a brief discussion of some of the business entities who would have formed the most important client base of the bank. This is followed by a discussion

---

*Extracted from *Depression to Decolonization: Barclays Bank (DCO) in the West Indies, 1926–1962* (Kingston: University of the West Indies Press, 2008).

of the credit facilities and arrangements provided by the bank, noting the degree to which the bank was prepared to be flexible.

The focus on financing trade and that of servicing the requirements of merchant companies involved in the West Indian trade reflected the underlying principles that governed conventional British multinational banking practice in the nineteenth and early twentieth centuries. British banking practice mandated that credit was made available only on a short-term basis. In the nineteenth and early twentieth centuries this was usually three months.[3] Bills of exchange were the usual instrument of credit. The British merchant, instead of waiting for money to arrive from the planter or merchant in the West Indies, might sell the bill to a bank at a discount. The British merchant would then receive prompt payment for his services and goods, while the planter in the West Indies would have a period of credit during which time it was hoped proceeds would be realized from the sale of his produce.[4] In the event of an exporter in Britain sending goods to a wholesale or retail merchant in the West Indies, a bill requiring payment after a given period, normally sixty to ninety days, would be drawn by the exporter. The bill would be presented to the overseas customer, who would "accept" it, arranging payment before taking delivery of the shipping documents giving title to the goods in the case of bills drawn on a "Document against Payment" basis, or taking immediate delivery of the shipping documents upon acceptance, in the case of bills drawn on a "Document against Acceptance" basis. The merchant in the West Indies could request a bank in Britain through its branch in the West Indies to pay the exporter in Britain, and in turn pay this bank in local currency in his own country.[5]

Related to the requirement that the credit advanced should be self-liquidating was the premium placed on what was considered suitable security. Generally, bills of exchange and bills of lading, which represented goods in transit, were the preferred forms of security.[6]

Over the course of the nineteenth century, the Colonial Bank, the predecessor to Barclays Bank (DCO) in the West Indies, extended credit for the growing of export crops. So that by the time of its reconstitution as Barclays Bank (DCO) in December 1925, its largest financial propositions were with respect to accommodation for the cultivation of sugar cane and the manufacture and export of sugar, the region's major export commodity during this period.[7] This development, however, did not mean any significant departure

Table 7.1 Annual Average Sugar Exports (Tons) from the West Indies, 1920–1929, 1930–1939 and 1946

Territory	1920–29	1930–39	1946
British Guiana	96,000	152,000	164,000
Trinidad & Tobago	63,000	108,000	110,000
Barbados	62,000	101,000	134,000
Jamaica	48,000	68,000	178,000
St Kitts	13,000	25,000	34,000
Antigua	15,000	19,000	17,000
St Lucia	4,000	6,000	6,000
St Vincent	200	1,000	–
Total	301,200	480,000	643,000

Source: B.W. Higman, *Abstract of Caribbean Historical Statistics* (Kingston: Department of History, University of the West Indies, 1985), v/i; Kathleen Stahl, *The Metropolitan Organisation of British Colonial Trade* (London: Faber and Faber, 1951), 39.

from conventional banking practices, especially in terms of the banks' customer base. Despite the existence of a sizeable peasant and small-farmer class – mainly the descendants of African slaves brought to the region between the seventeenth and early nineteenth centuries – as well as a sizeable East Indian community, particularly in Trinidad and British Guiana, all of whom were engaged in the cultivation of sugar-cane for processing and export, a substantial amount of land remained under the province of plantation agriculture.[8] Plantation land was not only under the auspices of the ruling merchant-planter elite, who during the course of the late nineteenth and early twentieth centuries had usurped the position of the traditional planter class, but also under the control of British companies.[9] Indeed, these companies were primarily responsible for a significant proportion of the production of the nearly 500,000 tons of sugar exported from the West Indies between 1930 and 1939 (see table 7.1). In the main, they were also responsible for the increase by 28 per cent to approximately 640,000 tons exported from the region in 1946.[10] It was to this group that the bank gave the bulk of the provision of finance for sugar production, as was noted in 1930 by O. Barritt, then-manager of the

Table 7.2 Barclays Bank (DCO), Breakdown of Advances (£) in the West Indies, 1948

Category	Secured	Unsecured	Total	% of Total
Agricultural	1,896,371	243,837	2,140,208	23.6
Retailers	963,871	431,571	1,395,442	15.4
Wholesalers	714,688	561,764	1,276,452	14.1
Personal/ professional	303,574	105,196	408,770	4.5
Industry & manf.	436,768	365,654	802,422	8.86
Motor trade	226,118	7,893	234,011	2.58
Local govt., etc.	25,275	2,103,777	2,129,052	23.5
Mining	4,132	–	4,132	0.045
Brokers, private individual	217,029	713	217,742	2.40
Executive trust companies, building society	9,575	25,000	34,575	0.38
Cooperative societies	187	–	187	0.002
Other banks	–	559	559	0.006
Sundries	258,749	147,841	406,590	4.49
Total	5,056,337	3,993,805	9,050,142	100.0

Source: International Departments, General Manager's Office, BBA 11/551. Sundries category included loans to religious bodies; personal and professional included loans to staff, architects and lawyers, and other private individuals.

Colonial Section of the bank: "[L]arger financial propositions are in respect of concerns for which the accommodation granted includes the growing of canes, purchase of canes from smaller farmers, the manufacture of the sugar, and in some cases general business purposes also. These clients are practically all large firms growing the bulk of the sugar themselves."[11]

The wholesale and retail sectors in which many of these same large sugar producing firms were engaged also accounted for a substantial proportion of loans and advances made by Barclays Bank (DCO). Table 7.2 provides a breakdown by category of loans and advances made by the bank as of September 1948 which, though three years beyond the period of discussion for this chapter, is still a fairly accurate representation. Loans and advances for agricultural purposes and to wholesalers and retailers together accounted for over half, 53.1 per cent, of the total disbursed by the bank. Retailers and wholesalers accounted for almost 30 per cent of total loans indicating Barclays Bank (DCO)'s emphasis on financing trade.

British Firms

The emergence of British corporate ownership of property in the West Indian sugar industry was a process that had begun in the late nineteenth century and continued into the early twentieth century. The opening up of newer plantation areas, particularly in the East following the dismantling of long-standing policies which had given protection to West Indian produce within the metropolitan market, caused recurrent fluctuations in the price of plantation produce. As a result, many West Indian planters found themselves becoming heavily indebted with many of the properties being acquired by their consignees owing to the heavy mortgages held against them.[12] It was through this avenue that many of the British merchant companies involved in the sugar trade became directly involved in the production of the commodity in the West Indies.[13] Many of them were also motivated to enter into the production of sugar as a result of the development of an intense competition within the trade during this period. The failure of a number of British merchant houses and the fact that a number of them decided to transfer their investments to the more lucrative trade in the East as a result of the sharp fall in the price of sugar in 1884 and 1885 led to a severe restriction of credit to the West Indian sugar industry.[14]

Subsequently, keen competition developed among the surviving companies and speculators who were prepared to buy commodities directly from producers and merchants in the producing areas. Indeed, many planters generally abandoned the system of shipping produce on consignment, preferring to sell directly to merchants and other speculators on the spot.[15] In light of this development, the merchant houses which remained in the trade were also motivated to engage in production with a view to gaining better control of supplies of the commodity. To raise the capital necessary for such investments, several British merchants and commission agents organized themselves into what Stanley Chapman termed as "investment groups", or business groups. The capital raised was then used to establish companies which managed the sugar-producing properties so acquired in the West Indies.[16] Undoubtedly, many of these companies were representative of the "free-standing" type of foreign direct investment which characterized many of the British multinational firms in the nineteenth century.[17]

While most of British foreign direct investment in the region's sugar industry during this period took the form of the "free standing" firm, Tate and Lyle, the giant British sugar refining firm in 1936 marked the entry of the first modern type of British multinational enterprise to the industry in this period. This company's history of operations in the West Indies as producers began then, as its business before that was confined to large-scale refining in Britain. Prior to that date, the only significant modern multinational that was involved directly in the sugar industry in the region was the giant American fruit company, the United Fruit Co. Ltd (UFCo.) which acquired Bernard Lodge and Monymusk estates in Jamaica in 1929. In 1930 both estates together accounted for just over 25 per cent of the total crop produced in the island in that year.[18]

From Barclays Bank (DCO)'s point of view, the increased concentration of West Indian properties under British corporate control provided for an attractive customer base. Such companies brought a certain amount of credit-worthiness to the properties, given their access to the London capital markets. These companies were therefore able to raise the necessary share capital for the reorganization and centralization of production on the properties, thereby making them more efficient and profitable.[19]

British firms were not only merely involved in plantation production. They also operated substantial wholesale and retail businesses in the region. For example, in addition to its extensive holdings of sugar estates in British Guiana, Booker Brothers, McConnell and Co. Ltd in the 1930s operated as an important ancillary, a large general merchant business.[20] This aspect of its business represented about 25 per cent of the entire commerce and industry of British Guiana.[21]

British capital was also prominent in the Trinidadian oil industry which underwent spectacular growth during this period.[22] A number of British mercantile firms which had remained involved in the West Indian trade concentrated primarily on the import/export trade. One such firm was the London based firm of Thomson, Hankey and Co., which had a long-standing connection with the Windward and Leeward Islands dating back to the eighteenth century.[23] This company maintained a branch of its business at St George's in Grenada where a substantial wholesale business in provisions, hardware, liquor and lumber was carried on. Branches were also maintained outside the capital at Grenville and at St Andrew from where it controlled a large proportion of the export trade in cocoa and other produce from Grenada.[24] The Scottish mercantile and shipping firm of Thom and Cameron Limited, which had been in existence from the early nineteenth century, also maintained a business at Bridgetown in Barbados, shipping sugar and molasses and importing a wide selection of British and North American manufactured goods.[25]

West Indian Firms

In terms of their value as a customer base for the bank, the British firms involved in production and trade did not overshadow the West Indian firms and individuals involved in agriculture and commerce in the region.[26] Despite the British firms' extensive hold over sugar-producing property during the first half of the twentieth century, a significant number of sugar-based plantation properties remained in the control of local concerns, particularly in Trinidad, Jamaica and Barbados. Most of these were owned by merchants who operated commission agencies and acted as representatives for British, European and North American manufacturing firms whose goods they imported and sold in their wholesale and retail establishments. Many had acquired property using the profits from such business and took advantage of the depressed state of the industry in the late nineteenth and early twentieth centuries when the value of property was low.[27] Properties were also acquired as a result of the financial accommodation which many of them made to planters who did not qualify for loans from the commercial banks.[28] For example, Gordon, Grant and Co. Ltd, of Port of Spain, Trinidad, acquired a substantial amount of cocoa and sugar estates through defaulted payments on loans.[29] In Jamaica, Lascelles Demercado and Co. Ltd, a large mercantile and commission agency house located at Port Royal Street in Kingston, owned and controlled Vere sugar estate through its subsidiary, Vere Estates Co. Ltd. Other Jamaican merchants involved in the sugar industry included W.N. Farquaharson who owned Holland and Rasheen estates in St Elizabeth, and H.V. Lindo who owned United Estates.[30] Many of the properties that were acquired were reorganized and incorporated as limited liability companies. The capital that was raised was used to make technological improvements which included the centralization of the production process thereby increasing the efficiency of the factories that were established.

The commercial sector in the West Indies also included a number of West Indian commercial firms and wealthy merchants who operated on their own account and who preferred to remain outside the ambit of agricultural production, specializing in the procurement and export of various agricultural produce. Many of them were also wholesalers, and functioned as representative agents for a number of British and North American manufacturing firms. One such individual was the very successful and wealthy merchant, J. Stephen Miller from Christiana, Manchester, in Jamaica, who had begun trading on his own account in 1907. By the early 1920s he had established the Jamaica Import and Export Co. at 22–28 Orange Street in Kingston. This was in addition to his principal business, Williamsfield Trading Co., in Manchester.[31]

Some of the West Indian firms had their origins in the liquidated assets of collapsed foreign-owned merchant firm's holdings in the region. In Jamaica, the large general trading company Grace, Kennedy and Co. Ltd was born from the liquidated assets of the American firm of W.R. Grace and Co.[32] Many of the Barbadian firms were also established out of parent British firms in the late nineteenth and early twentieth centuries. An example of this was A. Cameron and Co., which was founded by Alister Cameron in 1891. Another is that which was established by John Hadely Wilkinson, the son of a partner in the London firm Wilkinson and Gaviller, who in 1920 formed a partnership with an old-established Barbadian planter family by the name of Haynes, creating the large commercial concern Wilkinson and Haynes Co. Ltd.[33]

Clearly, favourable demand conditions for Barclays Bank (DCO), with respect to both the British and local West Indian firms, existed in the West Indies. The business activities of these firms were directly related to the region's foreign trade, which grew significantly during this period: the total value of imports to the region between 1936–38 and 1948 increased by 73 per cent, and the total value of exports by 67 per cent (see table 7.3). These increases testified

Table 7.3: Import and Export Trade, British West Indies (£ million sterling), 1936–1938 and 1948

Territory	Imports (total)		Exports (total)	
	1936–1938	1948	1936–3198	1948
Trinidad & Tobago	6.8	27.5	6.9	27.6
Jamaica	5.8	19.9	4.6	11.5
British Guiana	2.2	10.0	2.7	7.7
Barbados	2.1	6.4	1.5	3.0
Windward Islands	0.7	3.2	0.7	1.9
Leeward Islands	0.7	1.9	0.7	1.5
Total	18.3	68.9	17.1	53.2

Source: E.F. Nash, "Trading Problems of the British West Indies", in *The Economy of the West Indies* ed. G.E. Cumper (Westport: Greenwood Press, 1974), 224.

to a flourishing import/export sector which presented tremendous business opportunities for Barclays Bank (DCO) in this period.

Credit Facilities: Flexibility and Conservatism

In the early twentieth century, loans in the form of overdrafts and transactions involving various types of bills of exchange were used to facilitate the import of various types of manufactured goods and the export of agricultural produce. Usually, a portion of the negotiated loan would be allocated for the overdraft portion and the larger portion in bills of exchange. The most common type of bills included documentary bills, clean credit bills and bills for collection (d/a or d/p). Barclays Bank (DCO) also provided credit by discounting bills. The provision of credit involving documentary bills entailed an arrangement whereby the bank undertook to pay the price of the goods being exported or accept a bill of exchange for the invoiced amount.

For example, a major Jamaican general produce and commission mercantile establishment was granted a £130,000 loan in September 1938. Of this total, £40,000 was allocated for overdraft facilities and the rest for various types of bills.[34] The bank in return for the service received a percentage commission. The security normally required for this type of credit were the documents to the goods, such as the bill of lading and invoices, thus documentary bills.[35] Clean credit involved credit provided by the bank for a customer for the payment of bills of exchange drawn upon the customer for which there were no supporting documents attached.[36] Transactions involving bills for collection entailed an arrangement whereby bills of exchange drawn by an exporter, usually at a term, on an importer overseas, were brought by the exporter to the bank with a request to collect the proceeds. The bank would send the bills to its agent overseas where the importer was located and have them presented for acceptance, or payment, or both. The bank would then bring back the proceeds and credit the customer's account. If such a bill had documents of title attached, it was called a documentary bill; if not, it was a clean bill. The customer had to instruct the bank whether documents were to be released against acceptance by the importer, that is, document against acceptance (d/a), or only against payment (d/p).[37]

Credit in the form of discounts entailed the discounting or buying of bills of exchange drawn by the customer, usually an exporter on an overseas importer of the goods. By discounting the bill, the bank paid the face value of the bill less a discount, which was essentially its charge for the service.[38]

The most predominant type of security accepted by Barclays Bank (DCO) in the West Indies in this period continued to be bills of exchange. These included bills drawn on reputable American and European manufacturing firms and on reputable local names and firms. The bank also accepted accommodation bills, wherein a person added his name to accommodate another person, thereby acting as a guarantor.[39] By the late 1920s the bank in the West Indies was also accepting life insurance policies, mortgages against real estate, and stocks and shares held in local and American businesses.[40]

Credit facilities advanced for the growing and processing of cane into sugar were referred to as crop advances and covered expenses. These covered expenses, including labour and plantation supplies, such as fertilizers and other necessary equipment required on the estate for the duration of the season. They also covered the expenses associated with the marketing of the crop.[41] They were short-term in nature and were therefore expected to be recovered at the end of the crop season, which usually lasted six months, by which time it was expected that the crop would have been sold and the proceeds realized.

Security for such advances included a lien held by the bank against the crop.[42] In addition, mortgages on factories or estates, or both, were sometimes required for such advances. The type of mortgage that was required was more often than not an equitable mortgage, which was created by a deposit of the deeds with or without a memorandum, or by a memorandum of charge which gave the bank an equitable interest in the property.[43] If the mortgage value of the property plus the value of the crop was less than the crop loan required, the bank accepted additional security in the form of life policies and colonial government bonds.[44]

Credit facilities advanced for sugar production in the West Indies were predicated on the basis of what the price of the commodity would be at the time of sale. The hope was that the sale would take place soon after shipment. Consequently, an element of risk was involved. The market conditions of the period which saw sugar prices plummeting, particularly in the late 1920s, made bank managers extremely cautious, and Barclays Bank (DCO) often requested considerable security for crop advances for sugar production. For example, a Trinidad client in 1928, on securing a crop advance of £100,000 for the 1928/29 season, was required to render as security first mortgages on sugar, cocoa and coconut estates, and a lien on the sugar crop, which had a total value of £305,000.[45] The requirement for such extensive security was no different in Jamaica, where in 1936 a report was made on an account for which £46,000 had been advanced for the 1936/37 crop, along with a £9,000 loan repayable from crop surpluses at the end of the 1937/38 season. The proposed security consisted of the usual lien on the crop, which was estimated to value £48,659, along with mortgages against two sugar estates which together were valued at £15,000. In addition, a prior existing charge of £10,000 was postponed in favour of the bank, being available for any shortfall that might have arisen.[46]

Weather added to the risk factor involved in the provision of credit for crop production.[47] As hurricane and drought conditions were liable to cause shortfalls in projected yields, the likelihood always existed that the loans advanced against such crops would not be recovered entirely, or not at all, at the end of a crop season. Given this uncertainty, some measure of flexibility was imposed upon Barclays Bank (DCO) in its lending terms in the event of such vicissitudes. In the event of a shortfall on a crop produced, the bank was prepared in some cases to give what was termed a "policy" advance to cover the shortfall, in addition to the accommodation that was required for the forthcoming crop season.[48]

Generally, easier terms on loans were restricted to the British firms. For example, one such company, a major owner of sugar producing properties in British Guiana, in 1940 required financial accommodation amounting to £385,000 in the form of credits and overdraft. At least £350,000 of this loan was unsecured, with the remainder, £35,000 being secured by produce.[49] A similar level of leniency was given to a significant British company in Jamaica in 1937, which was allowed to draw £20,000 in the form of clean drafts on sight on its parent company in London.[50] Its sister company in Trinidad was allowed £50,000 in the form of clean unconfirmed credit for twelve months for which no security was required.[51] Such leniency, however, towards British companies engaged in the West Indian sugar trade was not a standard feature of Barclays Bank (DCO)'s operations; generally, some form of security was requested by the bank, even if it did not cover the full extent of the loan being granted.[52]

A degree of flexibility with regard to the terms on loans was also forthcoming for the large, well-established West Indian companies. Such was the case with a Jamaican company which maintained its account with Barclays Bank (DCO) from the time of its founding in 1922.[53] This company was involved in the heavy importation of foodstuffs, particularly salted and pickled fish, flour and rice which were staples of the Jamaican diet. The company also imported other manufactured goods, representing at least thirty-two foreign manufacturing companies in the 1930s. In 1939, the company was allowed a loan totalling £46,500 in the form of an overdraft and documentary and clean bills, as well as indemnities for which no security was required. At the time of application, a current unsecured loan for £26,809 was due to run off at the end of September of that year.[54]

In general, credit facilities to the sugar industry in the West Indies were restricted to the production and marketing of the crop, and were short-term, running for a maximum of six months, the duration of a crop season. However, on at least one occasion Barclays Bank (DCO) extended credit towards the purchase of property on a medium-term basis for three years. This occurred in Barbados in 1937, when a loan of £20,000 was advanced by the bank towards the purchase of a sugar estate comprising 450 acres and valued at £23,255. The deeds for the estate were required as security, and repayment of the loan was expected to be made on the basis of £4/5,000 per annum with full repayment by 1940. The bank retained the option of calling in the loan on demand and kept a close watch on the account with a review undertaken every six months.⁵⁵

Similarly, a substantial sugar and banana plantation owner in Jamaica was given crop advances of £60,400 for the 1938/39 season and £53,000 for the 1939/40 season. On the strong recommendation of the branch manager, the Central Board sanctioned the proposal for the repayment of £18,000 of the total loan over a three year period, with £7,000 repayable at the end of 1940, another £7,000 at the end of 1941 and the balance of £4,000 at the end of 1942. Security included mortgage against a sugar estate and factory in the amount of £45,000 equity in a banana estate in the amount of £14,000, a life insurance policy for which the surrender value was £2,500 as well as lien against banana crops estimated at £44,000.⁵⁶

Plantation owners were not the only recipients of medium term loans in this period. Approval was granted in May 1941 for a "three to four year" £35,000 unsecured loan to a large drygoods mercantile establishment in Kingston, Jamaica, whose average estimated surplus capital was £111,200 in January 1940.⁵⁷ The retail and wholesale establishment was the largest of its kind in Jamaica in the early twentieth century.⁵⁸

This deviation in lending policy by Barclays Bank (DCO) in Barbados and Jamaica can be partly explained with reference to the customers involved. In the case of the Barbadian client, the bank's local adviser on West Indian operations recommended approval given the valuable connection between the company and the bank.⁵⁹ The client was among the most wealthy and influential property owners in Barbados. The company also operated a major commercial business, importing general estate supplies and operated as a commission agent and manufacturers' representative for British and North American firms and was a member of the island's largest trading conglomerate, often referred to as the "Big Six".⁶⁰

The bank's willingness to accommodate the Jamaican clients is best understood within the context of the then prevailing competitive environment in the commercial banking market in Jamaica. Barclays Bank (DCO) was severely criticized in the early to mid-1930s for its stringent policy on loan facilities and security requirements that contrasted with its competitors' more flexible approach. Its rigidity had resulted in the loss of valuable clients to the Canadian banks, forcing the British bank to review and amend the way control on advances and loans was exercised. Barclays Bank (DCO)'s concern about the loss of clients to its rivals in Jamaica is exemplified by its acceptance of an unaudited balance sheet as testimony of the business transactions of a client who had requested loans and advances totalling £52,500 and US$20,000 on one account, and £11,397 on another – after the client declined to submit an audited balance sheet, in spite of the bank's repeated requests. The customer, who operated a substantial wholesale general mercantile business on Harbour Street in Kingston, importing a wide variety of drygoods from Europe and North America, responded to the bank's first request by stating that he was "quite satisfied that [the] accounts as then [set] out indicated a conservative estimate of the position, and that the additional expense was unnecessary". The branch manager, in imploring the London Committee of the Central Board of the bank to drop the matter, stated that "to press the matter further might jeopardize the accounts . . . as Mr ————'s integrity is undoubted".[61]

The bank sometimes made accommodations for the purchase of an existing business. This was not a general feature in the loan portfolio of the bank in the West Indies, and such requests appear to have been only considered for highly regarded and reputable accounts. This was the case in 1939 when a major Jamaican commercial firm bought out a local retail rum business for £10,000. However, the terms of the loan granted for this transaction called for the loan to be repaid in six months. The average estimated value of this firm in June 1939 was £49,000.[62]

Barclays Bank (DCO) sometimes provided accommodation for the purchase of machinery, but again, this was more the exception than the rule – only one instance of this was identified in the bank's loan registers for this period. In 1936, in addition to crop loans for the period 1936/37 and 1937/38 amounting to £65,000, a Jamaican firm in control of a major sugar estate borrowed £40,900, £5,700 of which was "for the paying off on machinery bought by the company" for the sugar estate and was expected to be paid back within six months.[63]

While long-term loans were not provided by Barclays Bank (DCO), from time to time short-term loans were "rolled over" giving the appearance of being medium or long term. For example, at the beginning of 1935 the body which represented all the sugar estate owners in Jamaica went into excess on its crop advance for 1933/34 by £14,000. This loan had been due to run off at the end of September 1934.⁶⁴ In June 1935 a loan of £225,000 in overdraft was negotiated by the organization for the 1935 crop. The amount outstanding at the time stood at £141,062, and it was proposed that an increase be granted to November 30, 1935.⁶⁵ In September 1935 it was realized that by the end of the 1934/35 crop season there would be a surplus over local requirements by about 6,000 tons of sugar. Consequently, credit facilities were required to enable the sugar manufacturers' representative body to export the surplus, and the bank was asked to carry about £25,000 until the end of the following crop season when it was expected that the excess loan would be paid out of that season's sugar crop.⁶⁶

Smaller accounts were not so fortunate. The failure to settle debts to the bank when they became due often resulted in the branch being instructed to recoup the debt through the sale of the security lodged. This was the ruling made with respect to the failure of a small Jamaican retailer to reduce his loan by £750 by a certain date. The branch manager noted that the client in question had managed to repay £250 at the appointed time and asked for leniency stating that "this was absolutely all he can do and asks for . . . consideration of the fact that he has repaid £12,776 during the last two years". Though supported by the branch manager, and providing security in the form of American shares valued at £10,294, the customer was denied further accommodation, and the London Committee insisted upon a full reduction being effected by sale of the security held by the bank.⁶⁷

The repercussions of World War II on overseas trade also forced Barclays Bank (DCO) to modify its lending practices towards its clients in the West Indies. The irregularity in shipping services owing to submarine menace in the Atlantic, and the fact that fewer ships were in service because of a number of them had been requisitioned for the war effort, resulted in frequent delays in the export of colonial produce. The situation worsened by 1942. For instance, the number of vessels visiting Barbados declined by approximately 40 per cent between 1941 and 1942.⁶⁸ The export of fancy molasses and sugar from that island was particularly affected, as the carry-over from the 1941 crop amounted to approximately 65,000 puncheons or 21,450,000 wine gallons waiting to be shipped at the end of that year. At the end of 1942, as much as 50,000 puncheons of this quantity still remained on hand.⁶⁹ As a result, many of the bank's clients found it difficult to repay their loans when they became due, and faced severe loss.⁷⁰ Indeed, at the end of April 1940 a major exporting

Barbadian firm had run up an excess of £81,210 on its overdraft as a consequence of its inability to ship its produce on time. The client had only managed to reduce this excess to £60,477 at the beginning of June.[71] The circumstances of the same firm were noted at a Central Board meeting of the bank in March 1943, in which attention was called to the firm's "top-heavy" position. Nevertheless, the Board was considering advancing the firm a loan of £1,000,000, since it was expected that shipping facilities would become available in the near future.[72]

If Barclays Bank (DCO) demonstrated a fair degree of flexibility in its loan policies during this period, it was evident that it was only prepared to do so within very narrow parameters, being informed by an assessment of the general creditworthiness of the clients. This explains why the bank provided very little accommodation to Barbadian sugar plantation owners, since the relatively small size of most properties in that colony would have resulted in them being regarded as lacking sufficient creditworthiness. Barbados differed from the other West Indian territories in that British and other foreign corporate ownership was almost totally absent from this island's sugar industry.[73] This had to do with the steps taken by the planter dominated legislature to safeguard planters' interests in the face of the economic crisis of the late nineteenth century, steps that included passing legislation against the consignee lien system and voting to reject the adoption of the Encumbered Estates Act of 1854, opting instead for the English Chancery Court System.[74] Some indebted estates were kept in Chancery by their owners for years, whereas others were sold to local purchasers, some of whom were Barbadian merchants. While Barbadian merchants were in control of some property, however, the process of corporate ownership was slow in developing, and really did not get underway until after 1935,[75] so that even though major corporate firms such as R. and G. Challenor Ltd, Manning and Co., and Wilkinson and Haynes had come into possession of large tracts of land by the mid-1930s, the rationalization and centralization of production in the Barbadian industry was generally slow in coming.[76]

It is not surprising that Barclays Bank (DCO), like its Canadian counterparts in the region did not provide financial accommodation to the peasant and small farming communities in the region, since it was largely uneconomical and unprofitable to do so, even within the organizational framework of cooperative financial institutions. While Barclays Bank (DCO)'s predecessor, the Colonial Bank, had contributed towards the working capital of the cooperative banks in British Guiana, with at least $7,584.90 (£1,580) being owed to the bank at the end of 1927, no further contributions were made by Barclays Bank (DCO) in the years that followed.[77] This contrasted with the policy it had adopted towards the indigenous agricultural sector in Palestine in this same period. In 1935 the bank became involved in the formation of the Agricultural Mortgage Corporation of Palestine "in order to provide a type of finance not readily forthcoming from the banks". Barclays Bank (DCO) lent funds on overdraft to this institution, providing 45 per cent of the Cooperative Bank's working capital during 1938.[78] In Cyprus, too, Barclays Bank (DCO) supported the Central Cooperative Bank established there in 1938. In fact, the bank specialized in this area in Cyprus, having provided the initial source of funds to the cooperative bank. The funds were advanced as an overdraft on the security of British government bonds and promissory notes of member cooperative societies.[79]

The reason Barclays Bank (DCO) was unwilling to lend working capital to the cooperative banks in the West Indies, in contrast with its policy in Palestine and Cyprus, was that it was not sufficiently remunerative for it to do so. It was argued that in Palestine, peasants had been subjected to excessive interest rates charged by moneylenders and in an effort to curtail this practice, the government had encouraged Barclays Bank (DCO) to participate in the establishment of the mortgage bank. Barclays Bank (DCO) was guaranteed a return on its investment of the working capital. This was not the case in the West Indies where peasants and small farmers were in need of loans at very low rates of interest. In the essay on colonial development that he submitted to the bank in 1943, H.R. Smith of the Port of Spain branch in Trinidad, explained:

> There are agricultural credit societies in various parts of the West Indies which make loans to farmers out of funds provided by the Government and members are collectively liable for the Society's borrowing, . . . it is self-evident that the bank could play no part in this arrangement. It is true that in Palestine loans are made by the bank to bodies analogous to Agricultural Credit Societies, but the system was initiated there to enable the peasants to evade exorbitant interest rates charged by money lenders, whereas in the West Indies it is necessary to provide money at rates which could not be accepted economically by private enterprise. . .[80]

Any confidence in the stability of the cooperative banks in British Guiana which Barclays Bank (DCO) might have had would have been undermined by the decision of the colonial government to suspend its contributions of working capital in 1928. This was as a result of the worsened financial position of the colony, and it was not until 1940 that the government resumed its contributions to the cooperative banks. Until then, the cooperative banks were forced to rely solely on the previous sums granted by the colonial government along with subscribed shares by members.[81]

With the economic conditions as they stood at the time, participation by Barclays Bank (DCO) in the West Indian cooperative banks would have required a deviation from traditional banking practice which it clearly was not prepared to undertake. At least three of the cooperative banks failed to meet their repayment obligations at the end of 1927. The situation worsened in the early 1930s as the impact of the Great Depression rendered a number of borrowers unable to repay debts outstanding, which in turn meant that the cooperative banks were unable to repay loans to the government and to Barclays Bank (DCO) when they became due. In 1933, members of the cooperatives owed loans amounting to $96,406.66 and interest amounting to $8,142.62 making a total of $104,549.28 (or £21,781) outstanding. Of the total amount of loans outstanding, $80,212.85 (or £16,710) represented loans in arrears, while the entire amount of interest was overdue.[82] Barclays Bank (DCO) was forced to settle by compromise on the remaining £5,780 that was due to it in 1933.[83] Indeed, in spite of "strenuous efforts to bring about a reduction in the arrears of loans and interest which had accumulated as a result of past transactions in 1933, of the $94,541.43 (£19,696) outstanding in 1938, $60,002.47 (£12,500) represented loans in arrears".[84]

While it is clear that economic criteria was an important factor in the decision to extend or deny credit to any particular class of persons in this period in the West Indies, circumstantial evidence suggests that assessments of risk and creditworthiness were also based on assumptions about ethnicity. These assumptions were that non-whites in general lacked monetary responsibility and business acumen and therefore were unsuitable clients. Such an implication is certainly present in the explanation by R.V. Butt, manager of the Kingston branch in Jamaica, as to why an applicant's business was not desirable:

> The business was owned by a black man [who] was a clerk at ———'s garage, and bought out from the Receiver, put in by the Canadian Bank of Commerce, some of the old stock . . . He started in the garage that the firm occupied; we believe a few

friends helped him, and his wife gave a Bill of Sale over her house and furniture for £1000 . . . We do not think that [this concern has] sufficient capital to swing a motor car business here, most of which is done on credit.[85]

The reference to the race of the owner of the business and to his former position as an employee in the same business, indicates that his race and class were important factors in the bank's assessment of the garage owner's creditworthiness. It suggests that the man's racial identity was used to reinforce the view that "the business was not worth having" and that blacks generally were not accommodated by the bank, and to have done so would have been an anomaly. As well, one can assume that the bill of sale of £1000 which was offered as collateral, and the "help from a few friends", were mentioned only to reinforce the branch manager's assessment of the garage owner's lack of creditworthiness.

Such discrimination was hardly unexpected, given the context of the social and economic environment of the West Indies in this period. Having evolved out of the slave mode of production, West Indian agricultural and commercial sectors in the early twentieth century were highly stratified along racial lines. Agricultural and commercial business enterprises were predominantly in the hands of whites, and included Jews who dominated the retail and wholesale sectors. Others included Lebanese, Syrian and Chinese migrants to the region in the early twentieth century, who were able to gain a foothold in the drygoods and haberdashery trade. While considered socially inferior to whites, the forementioned groups, because of their phenotype, were considered superior to blacks, coloureds and Indians. This had spawned ethnic stereotyping, consisting of the widespread belief that people of African and Indian ancestry were intellectually and morally inferior to those of European origin or descent.[86] As Brian Moore explains, the stereotyping covered not only "social and cultural characteristics and attitudes, but also. . . economic behaviour and roles. Whites were reputedly endowed with the work ethic which made them the natural creators of wealth and leaders of industry. Blacks and coloureds by contrast were indolent and improvident, and therefore unsuited to independent economic enterprise."[87]

And even considered opinion also relegated blacks and coloureds below Indians, even if they occupied the same social and economic status. This prejudice was certainly evident in the essay that R.N. Escolme submitted to the bank's competition on the subject of postwar development in the colonies. Writing from Barbados, Escolme, who apparently worked at various branches in the region, commented that

> the East Indian and the Chinese understand the value of money and cut their cloth accordingly... But not so with the Negroe population of these islands, they are too fond of the flesh pots... they lack the opportunism of the Indian or the Chinese. The Native say, from Barbados will go to Aruba, Curacao or Maricaibo and make good money with the oil companies. He soon hankers to get back to Barbados. There he spends freely and showily until faced with no money, unemployment and the prospect of going away again.[88]

Escolme included in his indictment of the West Indian black middle class: "Negroe and Coloured lawyers, barristers, doctors and other professional men live up to their earning capacity. Good living appeals to them more than savings. They will have their wines and cigars."[89] Clearly, then, even if there was no official bank policy of discrimination on racial grounds, racial stereotyping was practised by bank employees and was apparently an important factor in determining an individual's creditworthiness.

Summary

Barclays Bank (DCO)'s customer base in the West Indies in the early twentieth century was largely determined by the nature of the society and the economy in which it operated. Its products and services were geared primarily towards providing credit facilities for agricultural production for export, and for the local commercial and retail business community who imported manufactured goods for wholesale and retail.

The bank generally adhered to conventional British banking practices, which meant that loans and advances were short term, and primarily for trade purposes, and against collateral which was considered easily convertible. At the same time, the bank exhibited a fair amount of flexibility in its lending policy in the West Indies, particularly during World War II when war-time conditions disrupted the shipping of produce, resulting in delays in the repayment of loans. In the interest of keeping the accounts of valued clients, the bank also provided loans for purposes other than the cultivation and marketing of crops and for financing trade, and on occasion was willing to provide loans on a medium-term basis.

This flexibility did not extend to providing credit facilities to the peasantry and small farming and small business communities, or to the middle classes. While the bank's assessment of the general creditworthiness of potential clients was based on economic criteria, there is evidence to suggest that race and ethnicity were also factored into the decision-making process. This is hardly unexpected, given the social and economic environment in which the bank operated. Drawing its clientele mainly from the white planter and mercantile business community meant that it catered primarily to the elite of West Indian society.

Notes

1. Chibuike Ugochukwu Uche, "Credit Discrimination Controversy in British West Africa: Evidence from Barclays (DCO)", *African Review: Money, Finance and Banking* 20 (1996): 90–91; also Chibuike Ugochukwu Uche, "Foreign Banks, Africans, and Credit in Colonial Nigeria, c. 1890–1912", *Economic History Review* 52, no. 4 (November 1999): 669; W.T. Newlyn and D.C. Rowan, *Money and Banking in British Colonial Africa: A Study of the Monetary and Banking System of Eight British African Territories* (Oxford: Clarendon Press, 1954), 72–95; M.H.Y. Kaniki, "The Colonial Economy: The Former British Zones" in *General History of Africa 7: Africa Under Colonial Domination, 1880–1935*, ed. A.H. Boahen (Paris: UNESCO, 1985), 382; P. Kennedy, *African Capitalism: The Struggle for Ascendency* (Cambridge: Cambridge University Press, 1988); G.O. Nwankwo, "The British Overseas Banks in the Developing Countries: 1 – Until 1945", part 3, *Journal of the Institute of Bankers* 93 (June 1972): 153–54.
2. Geoffrey Jones, *British Multinational Banking, 1830–1990* (Oxford: Clarendon Press, 1993), 305.
3. Ibid., 33.
4. Ibid., 32–33; R.J. Truptil, *British Banks and the London Money Market* (London: Jonathan Cape, 1936), 253; W.M. Clarke, *The City in the World Economy* (London: Institute of Economic Affairs, 1965), 8–9.
5. Jones, *British Multinational Banking*, 32–33; Truptil, *British Banks*, 251–53.
6. Deryck Brown, "The Response of the Banking Sector to the General Crisis: Trinidad, 1836–1856", *Journal of Caribbean History* 24, no. 1 (1990): 28–64, 56.

7. O. Barritt, manager, Colonial Bank Section, Barclays Bank (DCO) to Sir G.E.A. Grindle, Colonial and Dominions Office, 8 March 1930, Colonial Office (hereafter CO) 323/1113/21.
8. Phillipe Chalmin, *The Making of a Sugar Giant: Tate and Lyle, 1859–1989* (Chur, Switzerland: Harwood Academic, 1990), 309–10.
9. George L. Beckford, *Persistent Poverty: Underdevelopment in Plantation Economies of the Third World* (New York: Oxford University Press, 1972). See also Veront Satchell, *From Plots to Plantations: Land Transactions in Jamaica, 1866–1900* (Kingston: Institute of Social and Economic Research, University of the West Indies, 1990); J.H. Galloway, *The Sugar Cane Industry: An Historical Geography from Its Origins to 1914* (Cambridge: Cambridge University Press, 1989).
10. Kathleen Stahl, *The Metropolitan Organization of British Colonial Trade* (London: Faber and Faber, 1951), 39.
11. Barritt to Grindle, 8 March 1930.
12. Ibid.; Richard Lobdell, "Patterns of Investment and Sources of Credit in the British West Indian Sugar Industry", *Journal of Caribbean History* 4 (May 1972), reprinted in *Caribbean Freedom: Economy and Society From Independence to the Present*, ed. Hilary Beckles and Verene Shepherd, 322–26 (Kingston: Ian Randle, 1993); Gisela Eisner, *Jamaica 1830–1930: A Study in Economic Growth* (Manchester: Manchester University Press, 1961), 198–200; Douglas Hall, *Five of the Leewards, 1834–1870: The Major Problems of the Post- Emancipation Period in Antigua, Barbuda, Montserrat, Nevis and St Kitts* (Aylesbury: Ginn, 1977), 96–127; Michael Sleeman, "The Agri-Business Bourgeoisie of Barbados and Martinique", in *Rural Development in the Caribbean*, ed. P.I. Gomes (London: C. Hurst and Co., 1985), 15–33.
13. Eisner, *Jamaica 1830–1930*, 198–200; Hall, *Five of the Leewards*, 96–127; Sleeman, "The Agri-Business Bourgeoisie", 15–33. Beckford, *Persistent Poverty*, 102–3; M. Shahabuddeen, *From Plantocracy to Nationalism: A Profile of Sugar in Guyana* (Georgetown: University of Guyana, 1983), 90.
14. Eisner, *Jamaica 1830–1930*, 198–99. Lobdell, "Patterns of Investment", 326–27; Galloway, *The Sugar Cane Industry*, 147–48; Christine Barrow, "Ownership and Control of Resources in Barbados: 1834 to the Present", *Social and Economic Studies* 32, no. 3 (September 1983): 89; Walter Rodney, *A History of the Guyanese Working People, 1881–1905* (Baltimore: Johns Hopkins University Press, 1981), 26.
15. Norton Breton, *Henckell, Du Buisson and Co. 1697–1947* (London: Henckell, DuBuisson and Co., n.d.), 19; Michael Craton and James Walvin, *A Jamaican Plantation: A History of Worthy Park, 1670–1970* (London: W.H. Allen, 1970), 272–75.
16. S.D. Chapman, "British-based Investment Groups before 1914," *Economic History Review*, 2nd ser., 38 (1985): 231–33; Geoffrey Jones, *Merchants to Multinationals: British Trading Companies in the Nineteenth and Twentieth Centuries* (Oxford: Oxford University Press, 2000), 11.

17. R.W. Beachy, *The British West Indian Sugar Industry in the Late Nineteenth Century* (Cambridge: Cambridge University Press, 1957); also Galloway, *The Sugar Cane Industry*, 155–79; Mira Wilkins "The Free Standing Company, 1870–1914: An Important Type of British Foreign Direct Investment", *Economic History Review*, 2nd ser., 61, no. 2 (1988): 259–82; Jones, *Merchants to Multinationals*, 48–51.
18. Barritt to Grindle, 8 March 1930.
19. Beckford, *Persistent Poverty*, 102–3.
20. Ibid., 43–44.
21. Allister Macmillan, *The West Indies, Past and Present with British Guiana and Bermuda* (London: W.H. and L. Collingridge, 1938), 372–73. See also Shahabuddeen, *From Plantocracy to Nationalism*, 93
22. Bridget Brereton, *A History of Modern Trinidad, 1783–1962* (Kingston: Heinemann, 1981), 200–201; Geoffrey Jones, *The State and the Emergence of the British Oil Industry* (London: Macmillan, 1981), 105–20; Fitzroy Baptiste, "The Exploitation of Caribbean Bauxite and Petroleum, 1914–1945", *Social and Economic Studies* 37, nos. 1 and 2 (March–June 1988): 117.
23. Hall, *Five of the Leewards*, 97, 102–3, 119, 120, 132.
24. Macmillan, *The West Indies*, 259–60.
25. Ibid., 373.
26. Returns £10,000 and Over, 31 October 1929, Colonial Bank, Customers Liabilities of £10,000, Barclays Bank Archives (hereafter BBA) 11/84; Central Board Register. Colonial Advances, BBA 80/700; Barclays Bank (DCO), London Committee, Colonial Bank Section, BBA 80/698.
27. Eisner, *Jamaica 1830–1930*, 200; Sleeman, "The Agri-Business Bourgeosie", 18.
28. Sleeman, "The Agri-Business Bourgeosie", 18–19.
29. Deryck Brown, *History of Money and Banking in Trinidad and Tobago from 1789 to 1989* (Port of Spain: Paria 1989), 90; Republic Bank Ltd, *From Colonial to Republic: One Hundred and Fifty Years of Business and Banking in Trinidad and Tobago, 1837–1987* (Port of Spain: Republic Bank, n.d.), 72.
30. Chalmin, *The Making of a Sugar Giant*, 311, 327–28; *Handbook of Jamaica, 1931*; *Handbook of Jamaica, 1936*
31. Barclays Bank (Dominion Colonial and Overseas) Colonial Bank Section, 8 March 1939, Applications for limits of £20,000 and over. And Over £500,000, BBA 80/668; Allistair Macmillan, *The Red Book of the West Indies: Historical and Descriptive Commercial and Industrial Facts, Figures and Resources* (London: W.H. and L. Collingridge, 1922), 89; personal communication, Swithin Wilmot, Department of History and Archaeology, University of the West Indies, Mona, Jamaica.
32. Douglas Hall, *Grace, Kennedy and Company Ltd: A Story of Jamaican Enterprise* (Kingston: Grace, Kennedy, 1992), 6–8.
33. Sleeman, "The Agri-Business Bourgeosie", 19–20.

34. Colonial Bank Section, 6 September 1938, Central Board Register, 9 August 1938 to 22 August 1939, BBA 80/669.
35. F.E. Perry, *A Dictionary of Banking* (Plymouth: MacDonald and Evans, 1979), 75.
36. Ibid., 44.
37. Ibid., 26.
38. Ibid., 26, 27.
39. Ibid., 2.
40. Barclays Bank (DCO) Anglo-Egyptian and Colonial Bank Section. Advances. Assistant General Managers' Office, BBA 80/767.
41. G. Grindle, Short Term Advances, 8 March 1930, CO 323/1113/21.
42. S. Evelyn Thomas, *Banking and Exchange* (St Albans: Donnington Press, 1930), 208.
43. Returns of £10,000 and over. Colonial Bank Section, Customer liabilities of £10,000 and over as of 31 October 1929, BBA 11/84; Thomas, *Banking and Exchange*, 206–10.
44. Returns of £10,000 and over. Colonial Bank Section, Customer liabilities of £10,000 and over as of 31 October 1929, BBA 11/84.
45. Ibid.
46. Colonial Bank Section, December 1936, Applications for limits of £20,000 and over. Sanction for which is required in anticipation of the approval of the London Committee and or the Central Board, BBA 80/668.
47. R.K.S. Gonsalves (Port of Spain, Trinidad), essay no. 11, Bank Essay Competition 1943, BBA 38/983: 1.
48. Ibid.
49. Central Board Register, Colonial Advances, 11 July 1940, BBA 80/700.
50. Central Board Register, Colonial Advances, 11 September 1937, BBA 80/668.
51. Central Board Register, Colonial Advances, 16 September 1937, BBA 80/668.
52. Central Board Register, Colonial Advances, July 1940, BBA 80/668.
53. Hall, *Grace, Kennedy*, 10.
54. Central Board Register, Colonial Advances, 25 August 1939, BBA 80/668.
55. Central Board Register, Colonial Advances, 9 July 1937, BBA 80/668.
56. Central Board Register, Colonial Advances, 23 March 1939, BBA 80/668.
57. London Committee. Colonial Bank Section, 20 May 1941, BBA 80/698.
58. Macmillan, *The Red Book*, 86.
59. Central Board Register, Colonial Advances, 9 July 1937, BBA 80/668.
60. Macmillan, *The Red Book*, 362, 364; *The Barbados Year Book and Who's Who 1934* (Barbados: Advocate Co., 1934), 243; Sleeman, "The Agri-Business Bourgeosie", 21; Hilary Beckles, *A History of Barbados: From Amerindian Settlement to Nation-State* (Cambridge: Cambridge University Press, 1990), 149, 187.
61. Barclays Bank (DCO) Central Board, 1933, BBA 80/743.
62. Central Board Register, Colonial Advances, 25 August 1939, BBA 80/668.

63. Central Board Register, Colonial Advances, 20 April 1936, BBA 80/668.
64. Barclays Bank (DCO), 31 January 1935, Central Board Register, Colonial Bank Advances, Anglo-Egyptian Advances and East African Advances, 10 January 1935–11 July 1935, BBA 80/787.
65. Barclays Bank (DCO), Central Board Register, 13 June 1935, Colonial Bank Advances, Anglo-Egyptian Advances and East African Advances, 10 January 1935–11 July 1935, BBA 80/787.
66. Central Board Register, 26 September 1935, Anglo-Egyptian Advances, Colonial Bank Advances and East African Advances, BBA 80/783.
67. Colonial and Anglo-Egyptian Advances, 26 January 1932, Assistant General Managers' office, BBA 80/768.
68. Report for 1942. Barbados. Administration Reports, 1942–1945, CO 31/132.
69. Ibid.; Gonsalves, essay.
70. Hall, *Grace, Kennedy,* 33–34; Administration Report, 1939. Barbados Administration Reports, 1942–1945, CO 31/132; Jamaica. Administration Reports, 1942–1945, CO 140/298; Central Board Register, 13 June 1940, Colonial Advances, BBA 80/700; Sir Julian Crossley Diaries, 1942–1951, 29 December 1942, BBA 38/209.
71. Central Board Register, 13 June 1940, Colonial Advances, BBA 80/700.
72. Crossley Diaries, 29 December 1942 and 16 March 1943.
73. Sugar Commission Report, part 1, CO 318/398/1.
74. Woodville Marshall, "Nineteenth Century Crises in the Barbadian Sugar Industry", in *Emancipation II: Aspects of the Post Slavery Experience in Barbados,* ed. Woodville Marshall (Cave Hill: Department of History, University of the West Indies, 1987), 95.
75. Richard Pares, *Merchants and Planters* (Cambridge: Cambridge University Press, 1960, 1970), 33; Sleeman, "The Agri-Business Bourgeosie", 18–19.
76. Barrow, "Ownership and Control", 89–90; Sleeman, "The Agri-Business Bourgeosie", 18–19; See also *Barbados Year Book and Who's Who, 1934,* 243–48.
77. *Report of the Banks' Committee of the Local Government Board and on the Cooperative Credit Banks established in the Colony. For the Year 1927* (Georgetown: Argosy Co., 1928), 2.
78. H.R.J. Smith (Port of Spain, Trinidad), essay no. 27, Bank Essay Competition 1943, BBA 38/983.
79. Ibid.
80. Ibid.
81. *Annual Report on the Cooperative Credit Banks for the Year 1945* (Georgetown: Argosy Co., 1946), 1.
82. *Report of the Banks' Committee of the Local Government Board and on the Cooperative Credit Banks established in the Colony. For the Year 1933* (Georgetown: Argosy Co., 1934), 5.

83. Ibid., 3–4.
84. Ibid., 6; *Report of the Banks' Committee of the Local government Board on the Cooperative Credit Banks established in the Colony, 1938* (Georgetown: Argosy Co., 1938), 4.
85. R.V. Butt, Jamaica Branch to the general manager's office, Barclays Bank (DCO), London, 17 September, 1929, BBA 11/197.
86. Bridget Brereton, "Society and Culture in the Caribbean: The British and French West Indies, 1870–1980", in *The Modern Caribbean*, ed. Franklin W. Knight and Colin Palmer (Chapel Hill: University of North Carolina Press, 1989), 92.
87. Brian Moore, "Ethnicity and Economic Behaviour in Nineteenth Century Guyana", in *Working Slavery, Pricing Freedom. Perspectives from the Caribbean, Africa and the Diaspora* ed., Verene Shepherd (Kingston: Ian Randle, 2001), 378.
88. R.N. Escolme (Barbados), essay no. 34, Bank Essay Competition, 1943, BBA 38/983.
89. Ibid.

CHAPTER 8

Black Economic Empowerment in Barbados, 1937–1970

The Role of the Non-Bank Financial Intermediaries

AVISTON DOWNES

Introduction

Distinguishing between banks and non-bank financial intermediaries (NBFIs) is a challenging exercise owing to the complexity of the modern financial sector and the supposed "encroachment" of myriad NBFIs in areas once monopolized by banks. This chapter examines the challenges and achievements of a range of NBFIs in Barbados between 1937 and 1970. The majority of these NBFIs can trace their historical roots to the nineteenth century when mutual self-help was the most viable response to the laissez-faire social policy of the colonial state. The period under examination witnessed the dismantling of laissez-faire policies, the birth of the modern welfare state, the beginnings of economic diversification, political enfranchisement and political independence.

This chapter focuses on the economic empowerment of black working-class Barbadians and the contribution of NBFIs to that empowerment. Well into the twentieth century, the commercial banks in Barbados offered little assistance to Barbadians outside the agro-commercial sector and the social elites. Consequently, black working-class Barbadians resorted to the adjustment of their NBFIs such as meeting-turns and friendly societies. Regrettably, these NBFIs are relegated to the margins of academic analysis as "folk" or "traditional" benevolent arrangements which were not sufficiently "rational" to be serious economic players.

Rotating Savings and Credit Associations: Barbadian Meeting-Turns

The rotating savings and credit association (ROSCA) was a popular informal savings-credit arrangement, which Shirley Ardener defines as "an association formed upon a core of participants who agree to make regular contributions to a fund which is given in whole or in part, to each contributor in rotation".[1] These arrangements, referred to as the "box" in Antigua, "meeting-turns" in Barbados, "partner" in Jamaica and "susu" in Trinidad, have been traced to West Africa although Indo-Caribbean people also brought a similar institution called the "chitti" with them from India.[2]

In Barbados, the earliest reference to the term "turn" is in the Poor Law Commission Report of 1875. The meeting or turn, later conflated to "the meeting-turn" in the twentieth century, was very popular, with "swarms" of them observed across the island in the 1890s.[3] The 1875–77 Poor Relief Commission reported:

> There are other provident or quasi-provident associations among the working people themselves of a more questionable character. We refer to the system of class clubs or turns, which is described as being very popular among the agricultural labourers and mechanics. A number of persons, women as well as men, contribute a weekly amount not less than six pence, more commonly a shilling, and sometimes, among the better class of mechanics, as much as five shillings. Each member of the club receives in his turn the entire weekly amount.[4]

Meeting-turns possessed no written rules, did not convene formal business sessions, and were not regulated by legislation. The Poor Law Commissioners stated that "there are no means of enforcing payment of arrears, or of compelling payment on the part of those who have already reaped their advantage and consequently have nothing more to gain and every incentive to be dishonest".[5]

Dishonesty and default were extremely rare owing to the strict codes of conduct, mutual trust, social reputation and mutual accountability which underpinned their operations. "Bankers" were chosen from among the "respectable" property-holding members of the community. The *Agricultural Reporter* observed that meeting-turns organized among agricultural labourers on the plantations, were "generally under the guidance of the superintendent of the estate, or that of some leading man or woman amongst the people".[6] The meeting-turn was a very effective mechanism for pecuniary discipline and target saving, even if the critics commented that it was "a somewhat clumsy method on the part of contributors to force themselves into thriftiness and to practise compulsory saving".[7]

Unfortunately, the relative neglect of ROSCAs generally is rooted partly in some Eurocentric theoretical assumptions. For example, anthropologist Clifford Geertz, having studied the ROSCA in West Africa and South Asia, has postulated that this institution constitutes a "middle rung" of development – a transient vehicle for small-scale capital accumulation in peasant economies in their transition to more trade-oriented societies. He contends that in this transition these informal saving arrangements would eventually be "self-liquidating, being replaced ultimately by banks, co-operatives, and other economically more 'rational' types of credit institutions".[8] However, as Brent Stoffle has pointed out, such a perspective ignores culture, social norms and structures of power.[9] Superficially, Barbadian meeting-turns may have seemed irrational. For instance, how does one explain the rationale for operating a savings-credit association in which credit is in fact being offered to others without any interest being secured on such a risk? And what is there to be gained by a banker who receives no fees for his service but may be considered liable for a defaulting thrower?[10]

The "adaptation to poverty" hypothesis has been advanced as an alternative explanation for the emergence of ROSCAs. It is argued that poverty forces the impoverished to make alternative adaptations outside of the national institutional matrix in order to ensure their survival.[11] In short, an ROSCA may be the only accessible institution if the borrower is disqualified from the "established" financial or welfare avenues. Christine Barrow has lent her support to this social pathological interpretation of ROSCAs. She contends that the meeting-turns in Barbados "fit a need for those who live in hand-to-mouth circumstances".[12] Poor economic conditions *may* stimulate mutual economic activity but, clearly, "throwing" in a meeting-turn requires a regular compulsory financial commitment. Therefore, logically, one expects this savings-credit arrangement to attract participants with access to financial resources rather than those without. Trevor Purcell's research on meeting-turns in Barbados in the 1990s demonstrates that virtually all of the over one hundred participants identified in his sample were employed and were not driven by poverty.[13] In fact, participants in meeting-turns have simultaneously patronized banks, insurance companies and other formal economic institutions, not only in the nineteenth and early twentieth centuries, but even today in the diaspora of the "developed" capitalist metropoles.

Given the nature of its operation, it is difficult to quantify the contribution of the meeting-turn to business and social development in Barbados. However, we have enough anecdotal evidence and recent research to conclude that ROSCAs played an important role in small-scale business capital accumulation and social reform. Moreover, as we shall see, the meeting-turn established a pattern that was replicated in the other working-class financial intermediaries. Savings schemes were short-term and "targeted". And accumulating interest or maximizing profit was of lesser importance than fostering social capital around mutuality and brotherhood.

Friendly Societies

Friendly societies were first established by the church on the eve of emancipation but by the late nineteenth century their leadership shifted from clergymen to "respectable" leadership drawn from the black middle class. Essentially, friendly societies received regular subscriptions – usually at least 12 cents weekly – from their membership to provide specified dependent relatives and themselves with cash insurance in the event of sickness, maternity or death. The movement struggled throughout the nineteenth century, but experienced its first major wave of expansion during the first few decades of the twentieth century, coinciding with the influx of Panama remittances. Between 1906 and 1920, a total of £717,576 (or close to $3.5 million) had been declared at the port or sent through the post office. Perhaps another $2 to $3 million could have escaped the prying eyes of officialdom. "Panama money" provided working-class Barbadians with the means to acquire some land.

These remittances stimulated the explosive growth of friendly societies. The practice of returning cash pay-outs or "bonuses" to their members at Christmas time was revived and expanded. In England such a practice would render a society to be classified as a "dividing" or "terminating" one and registration would invariably be denied. Nevertheless, legislators in Barbados acquiesced to local norms and section 12 (4) of the 1891 Friendly Society Act of Barbados provided that "a society shall not be disentitled to register by reason of any rule or practice of dividing any part of the funds thereof if the rules thereof contain distinct provisions for meeting all claims upon the society existing at the time of the division before such division takes place".

In many societies the quantum of the bonus was dependent on the extent to which one claimed other benefits in the course of a year. "The advantages claimed for a bonus", the registrar was informed, "is that it has the effect in very many instances of preventing a member whose sickness is of slight nature, from sending in a claim for sick relief". He also observed: "It occurs to me that a very large number of the Friendly Societies of the present day are being worked more with the object of commending them to the favour of the public by a distribution of a bonus, than on the primary idea of relieving the sick and distressed and burying the dead, which ought to be their proper basis."[14]

"The Society that fails to distribute a Bonus," observed the registrar, "sounds its death knell."[15] So while the middle-class "secret" or affiliated friendly societies followed the actuarial standards established by their orders in England, the local independent societies seemed to be in violation of basic insurance principles. Of course, there were observers who were quick to resurrect racist explanations. For instance, Harry Franck, an American who visited the island wrote: "But they [friendly societies] are typically tropical or African in their indifference to a more distant tomorrow, for at the end of each year the remaining funds are divided among those members who have not drawn out more than they paid in, and with perhaps as much as five dollars each in their pockets the society indulges in a hilarious 'blow-out'."[16]

Table 8.1 shows that bonus payments constituted more than half of the benefits paid out by societies, and these continued to increase dramatically. While officials contended that the trend expressed an abandonment of the fundamental principles of mutual insurance, what the new trend clearly reflected was a growing preference for enhanced savings-loans schemes over mutual insurance. Indeed, it was a trend that Alan Wells and Dorothy Wells observed when they surveyed the movement in the late 1940s. They indicated that, "in fact, if members regard their Friendly Society as a Savings Club rather than an

Table 8.1: Percentages of Friendly Societies Annual Benefits, 1932–1960

Year	Burials (%)	Sick Relief (%)	Bonus (%)
1932	13.8	16.1	70.1
1936	12.4	13.2	74.4
1949	9.3	6.4	84.3
1951	8.8	6.3	84.9
1960	7.1	4.3	88.5

Source: Calculated from Half-yearly Reports of the Registrar of Friendly Societies, 1932–60.

Table 8.2: Friendly Societies in Barbados, 1937–1970

Year	Number of Societies	Membership	Contributions ($)
1937	199	54,484	333,259
1938	188	49,522	297,345
1940	176	56,601	351,492
1942	168	64,326	403,324
1944	165	80,759	511,204
1946	162	97,731	625,632
1947	159	104,734	678,431
1949	142	93,620	649,125
1951	130	101,682	732,336
1959	110	69,728	592,369
1962	106	63,539	570,815
1966	55	49,773	559,690
1970	33	42,946	514,744

Source: Reports of the Registrar of Friendly Societies, 1937–70.

insurance club, all fairly well and good; but the fact that nearly all of the annual surplus, or (as in Barbados) some two-thirds of the contribution income is returned annually to the members in cash prevents the societies from accumulating reserves to increase their benefits or expand their services".[17]

Table 8.3: Membership and Contributions of Civic Welfare Friendly Society, 1943–1970

Year	Members	Total Contributions ($)
1943	1,469	11,591
1944	4,643	33,923
1946	18,731	125,110
1948	31,416	172,988
1950	37,513	235,020
1952	44,673	281,909
1954	44,701	302,794
1956	42,793	314,204
1958	44,163	336,123
1960	40,008	329,627
1962	34,930	299,655
1964	33,021	287,306
1965	32,479	281,426
1966	31,857	313,287
1968	30,004	297,468
1970	27,001	280,602

Source: L.P. Fletcher, "The Decline of Friendly Societies in Barbados", *Caribbean Studies* 15, no. 4 (1975): 77; Auditor-General's Reports.

Bonham Richardson claims that the flood of Panama money was responsible for the dilution of the commitment to mutual insurance to that of individual indulgence. According to Richardson: "As the community-level friendly societies became more like banking institutions than mutual-help societies, the relationships between members and treasurers were altered. The community-level appeal of the local friendly society as a comfortable investment alternative to dealing with outsiders, mainly whites, had faded during the era of Panama money."[18]

The operations of the largest societies in Barbados – the Unique Progressive and the Civic Welfare Friendly Societies – indicated some changes in focus. The former was established in 1936 and by 1940 was the largest in the island with 9,102 members with contributions of $67,662.[19] The Civic Welfare, registered on 20 November 1943, soon emerged as the largest operation of its kind in the Caribbean. Its audited books for 1949 reveal a membership of 34,138 with 84,351 dependants, ten paid officials and total contributions of $219,333.[20] By the late 1960s it listed among its assets two buildings on Swan Street, Bridgetown, valued at $167,000 and rented to an associated business called the Civic Trading Company Limited.[21]

Of an overall expenditure of $201,683 in 1949, the Civic paid out a total of $179,468 on funeral, sickness and bonus benefits. Sickness payments were $14,478 (8 per cent of benefits); funerals $10,332 (6 per cent) and an incredible $154,662 or 86 per cent of expenditure on benefits redistributed as bonuses.[22] The apparent shift from mutual fraternalism to the fixation on the Christmas bonus and monetary benefits, reflected, ironically, a deep need by their membership for credit facilities. Burial and sickness relief were all well and good but were inconsequential to fostering entrepreneurship or the acquisition of land and housing.

The Barbados Savings Bank

As early as 1825, the secretary of state for the colonies had advocated the establishment of savings banks to encourage thrift among the enslaved. Government Savings Banks (or Post Office Banks) were introduced to the British Caribbean from the middle of the nineteenth century to encourage thrift and self-help among the working class, while providing a source of loans for colonial capital projects. The Barbados Savings Bank was established in 1852 and soon was heralded as a popular institution accepting deposits from individuals and from the friendly societies. In 1881 branches were established in Speightstown, St Andrew and St Philip but by 1887 those branches were closed because the rural clientele preferred the anonymity that the Bridgetown operation provided from prying neighbours, plantation owners and, above all, the magistrates who served as branch managers.[23] Although the Savings Bank was established primarily for the working class, even wealthy Barbadians were attracted to the bank not only because of its security but also because its interest rates were higher than the Colonial Bank and the other commercial banks which followed in the early twentieth century.

Table 8.4: Barbados Savings Bank, 1937–1966

Year	Depositors	Deposits ($)	Withdrawals ($)	Net Deposit ($)	Total Credit to Depositors ($)
1937–38	16,160	1,501,608	1,351,161	150,447	4,047,211
1939–40	18,533	1,736,812	1,565,515	171,297	4,493,865
1942–43	22,048	2,030,174	1,520,376	509,798	5,524,310
1944–45	28,794	3,110,323	2,375,188	735,135	1,652,595
1946	35,615	4,396,588	4,313,145	83,443	9,916,483
1948	36,969	3,375,002	3,765,127	–390,125	9,469,418
1950	41,533	4,362,333	4,022,269	340,064	10,434,882
1952	42,887	5,395,023	5,058,520	309,503	11,779,767
1954	42,490	6,042,982	5,378,982	664,006	13,179,889
1956	45,449	6,579,821	6,135,307	444,514	15,543,664
1958	45,197	7,370,099	7,053,053	317,046	19,082,236
1960	44,728	6,471,930	7,313,376	–841,446	19,754,551
1962	46,316	5,984,522	6,961,821	–977,299	17,276,494
1963	44,819	7,043,941	8,573,483	–1,529,542	16,220,415
1964	46,623	7,892,502	7,812,692	79,810	16,784,644
1966	45,270	7,125,952	8,051,232	–925,280	17,179,440

Source: Annual Barbados Savings Bank Reports.

The 1890 Savings Bank Act set a ceiling of £300 pounds ($1,440) per depositor but the governor reported in 1901 that the bank had attracted the "well to do commercial community who simply lodge their money . . . because they get better terms and better security than they get at the Colonial Bank, evading the rules of the [Savings] Bank by using the names of relatives of all degrees".[24] C.E. Stoute, manager of the bank, informed the Moyne Commission that up to 1933, limitations on deposits had been removed. But following the commercial banks' reduction of their interest from 3 to 2 per cent, a "flood of money" forced the Barbados Savings Bank to reintroduce a cap of £300 sterling per depositor. The bank's main clientele therefore continued to be working-class Barbadians. Stoute informed the commission that there were 12,000 depositors with accounts under $100, but believed most of these accounts were in the range of $50.[25] When one considers that official data from the Barbados Savings Bank indicates a total of 16,160 depositors for 1937–38, then the working class constituted no fewer than 75 per cent of all depositors. Moreover, 199 of the corporate depositors were friendly societies with a membership in 1937 of 54,484.

Not surprisingly, the short-term accumulation savings pattern of the meeting-turns and the friendly societies was replicated in the Barbados Savings Bank. Indeed, Stoute advised that the previous year (1937) some $140,000 had been withdrawn by the friendly societies to pay out bonuses. According to the official figures from the registrar of friendly societies, the total bonus payout for that year was $188,510.40 which roughly equates to $3.45 for each of the 54,484 members. Stoute himself witnessed a depositor who over a five-week period had deposited on average just over one shilling weekly and proceeded to close the account after accumulating 10 to 12 shillings to buy a pair of shoes.[26] This pattern confirms the theory that users of Government Savings Banks were " 'target savers' who are not concerned with interest but merely wish to save a certain amount, for purposes of safety, after which they consume all their income".[27]

The Barbados Cooperative Bank

Roland Edwards, president of the Leeward Workers Association, indicated to the Moyne Commission that he wished to see the substantial deposits belonging to the friendly societies in the Savings Bank freed up for more substantial benefits to their members.[28] Under sections 18 and 47 of the 1905 Friendly Societies Act, a member could hold up to £200 ($960) in a separate loan fund but few societies promoted such schemes. Wells and Wells observed that out of 161 societies in Barbados in 1946, only eight held loan funds.[29]

Nevertheless, a few friendly societies were determined to add quasi-banking services to their usual insurance functions. For instance, the Barbados "Burden Bearer" Loan and Benefit Society, which opened operations in Swan Street, Bridgetown, in 1937, claimed to be "the first and only society of its kind in the West Indies". Presumably its claim to uniqueness was based on its offer of banking services – the Burden Bearer Bank. Unlike the majority of societies, the Burden Bearer was a full-time operation, Monday to Friday from 10:00 a.m. to 4:00 p.m. and on Saturday from 10:00 a.m. to 10:00 p.m.[30] But the Burden Bearer of Barbados was not a unique prototype in the West Indies. As early as 1914, a group of black middle-class professionals established the Trinidad and Tobago Cooperative Bank. It was popularly known as the "Penny Bank" and offered loans to small entrepreneurs on very liberal terms.[31]

In 1938, Frederick MacDonald Symmonds established the Barbados Cooperative Bank (BCB) with share capital of $240,000 secured in part from a group of the black Barbadian middle class. Among the principal shareholders were Richard Bordeaux Taylor, headteacher of Roebuck Boys and president of the Unique Progressive Friendly Society; John Beckles, laundry operator; Nathaniel Stuart and Edwin Sampson, Bridgetown merchants; Frederick Carew; Gidney Ashby; and Joseph Onesimus Tudor. Symmonds himself secured 1,000 shares at $1.00 per share and the other principal investors each purchased 500 shares at $1.00 per share.[32] His parents, Algernon and Maude Symmonds, ran a wholesale and retail grocery operation on Roebuck Street, Bridgetown, and his father was secretary of the Roebuck Moravian Mutual Aid Society.[33]

Symmonds returned to his alma mater, Roebuck Boys', where he taught between 1923 and 1938, during which time he became active in the friendly society based at that school. He also served as secretary of the Unique Progressive Friendly Society whose president was R.B. Taylor, headmaster of the school. Symmonds sought to build a unique bank that would bridge the economic and welfare needs of the aspiring black middle class and the poor masses. The former would secure investment opportunities and loans for their businesses; the latter would have an avenue for small loans to meet basic welfare needs such as housing.

The BCB advertised: "No deposit too large, no loans too small. Savings-Deposit received from one penny upwards."[34] Not surprisingly, its clientele grew rapidly and by January 1943, the bank acquired prime commercial property at the corner of Marhill and Trafalgar Streets, Bridgetown. By 1947 its clientele had reached 16,912 with $287,059 to their credit. By then the BCB had made loans totalling $591,499. Loans were made to small shopkeepers and the bank undertook the risky venture of granting loans at 6 per cent interest per annum to secure modest chattel houses with up to fifteen years to repay.[35]

Table 8.5: Barbados Cooperative Bank Ltd. (Inc. 1938), 1947–1961

Year	Depositors	Balance to Credit of Depositors ($)
1947	15,869	287,059
1948	16,912	320,073
1949	17,694	353,084
1950–51	19,166	576,577
1952–53	20,684	765,446
1953–54	20,808	713,479
1954–55	21,207	741,671
1956–57	22,010	733,810
1957–58	22,252	835,591
1958–59	22,594	830,519
1960–61	22,851	848,161
1961	22,925	869,198

Source: Annual Barbados Colonial Reports, 1938–63.

The BCB set no ceiling on deposits and offered a very attractive 4 per cent interest on deposits at a time when the commercial banks offered no more than 2 per cent and the Barbados Savings Bank, 3 per cent.

Securing "a piece of the Rock" – land ownership – was the aspiration of every Barbadian in an island where control of land was the principal element of empowerment. Not surprisingly, therefore, the BCB pursued real estate sales and development as its major investment portfolio. As Kenneth Harvey, who was a long-standing clerk in the BCB, has observed, "it was more a real estate business really than a commercial bank type of business".[36] The BCB was in fact fulfilling a role that Building Societies were performing elsewhere in the British Caribbean and also responding to the chronic land and housing needs of black Barbadians. The BCB acquired substantial acres of land at Welches and Grazettes in St Michael, Canevale and Maxwell in Christ Church, and Thorpes in St James, which facilitated lower- and middle-income housing. By 1953, the BCB had over $1 million in assets and paid a 10 per cent dividend to its shareholders.[37]

The number of the BCB depositors grew steadily and by the late 1950s reached almost half of the number of those of the long-established Barbados Savings Bank. The average credit balance per depositor climbed from just under $20 in 1949 to an average of $37 from the mid-1950s. This figure was, of course, much smaller than for the Barbados Savings Bank whose average credit balance per account ranged between $256 and $334 in the same period. The Symmonds operation would not have had the range of corporate clients (including friendly societies and credit unions) which the Savings Bank enjoyed; neither did it have the range of investment options available to the Savings Bank. Nevertheless, by 1956, the BCB had advanced over $1.5 million in loans. The BCB was a unique achievement for an organization heavily dependent on black working-class patronage and totally unaided by the government. It was obviously prepared to undertake financial risks which other banks were not. In fact, Symmonds' policies ran counter to the conservative operations of the commercial banks. While those banks concentrated on highly liquid, short-term investments, Symmonds continued to concentrate principally on land acquisition. Such land was often agriculturally marginal and subdivided to meet the housing needs of mainly poor Barbadians – with a number of them being offered "chattel house mortgages".

The BCB collapsed suddenly in 1962 when there was a run on the bank by its 23,000 depositors. This followed a court judgement against the bank in favour of the Payne family of Harrow Plantation, St Philip. David Stonewall Payne, the black owner of that plantation, held 1,500 shares in the BCB along with 75 ordinary shares and 225 preferred shares in the related Joes River Sugar Estates Ltd.[38] The bank could not honour the demand of the Paynes for their money in December 1961; neither could it meet the judgement of the Supreme Court in January 1962 to pay the Paynes $75,000.[39] Concerning the demise of the BCB, Johnson and Springer noted: "It appears that it invested in illiquid assets and maintained a few very large deposits which moved at short notice."[40] Failure to diversify its investment portfolio from real-estate holdings may have been its fatal flaw.

The Cooperative Credit Union Movement

Cooperatives organized primarily to support the production and marketing of agricultural produce were established across the West Indies in the 1930s.

Table 8.6: The Cooperative Credit Union Movement in Barbados, 1953–1970

Year	Credit Unions	Cash ($)	Loans ($)	Total Current Assets ($)	Fixed Assets ($)	Total Assets ($)	Deposits ($)	Share Capital ($)
1953–54	1	1,560	1,203	2,776	–	2,776	–	2,132
1954–55	1	1,319	1,893	3,247	20	3,267	317	2,696
1955–56	1	1,212	3,826	5,095	15	5,110	641	4,150
1956–57	2	1,673	7,004	8,848	10	8,858	825	7,471
1957–58	2	2,271	10,819	13,315	8	13,323	1,197	11,146
1958–59	3	6,489	13,389	20,080	6	20,086	1,914	16,712
1959–60	6	12,287	18,681	31,125	217	31,342	2,816	26,289
1960–61	9	12,767	30,313	43,683	999	44,682	5,276	37,176
1961–62	9	17,749	31,025	53,666	878	54,546	4,261	46,750
1962–63	10	23,894	56,687	85,290	942	86,232	6,992	73,395
1963–64	12	41,006	86,304	132,902	2,428	135,330	10,685	111,241
1964–65	15	48,962	121,103	178,224	2,414	180,638	11,604	150,921
1965–66	15	66,537	127,907	209,830	2,063	211,893	13,312	176,553
1966–67	17	84,342	167,489	264,761	2,495	267,256	15,515	222,821
1967–68	17	100,839	228,789	364,536	4,739	369,277	18,880	309,596
1968–69	17	107,392	216,174	427,600	4,033	431,633	24,723	356,010
1969–70	19	121,917	280,329	437,666	2,889	440,557	26,567	359,422
1970–71	19	165,008	396,125	602,377	3,414	605,791	36,113	503,193

Source: Cooperatives Department, *Statistical Digest of Credit Union Activity from 1954 to 1994* (Barbados, 1998).

By the 1940s, cooperative credit unions, committed to the principles of thrift and democratic governance, were established primarily through the social outreach of the Roman Catholic Church. The first such union was founded in Jamaica in 1941. In August 1948, the Savings Club based at the St Patrick's Roman Catholic Church in Barbados had evolved to become the Shamrock Cooperative Credit Union Ltd with a membership of 33 and share capital of $363.[41] Most credit unions were expected to undergo a gestation period when share capital would be raised and an education programme in institutional governance and financial planning would be undertaken.

The short-lived Enterprise Credit Union in Bridgetown was the first one to register. The Shamrock, which eventually registered in 1954, remained the sole credit union in operation up to 1956. By 1954, it reported share capital of $2,132, increasing to $4,150 by 1956, and loans to its members growing from $1,203 to $3,826 in the same period.[42]

Credit unions were consciously organized around common fraternal bonds of church affiliation, place or nature of employment, and residence. The Federal Credit Union was established as the first community-based union in the large peri-urban district of Bush Hall in the parish of St Michael. In 1960, members of the police force were the first government workers to establish a credit union. Of the twelve credit unions registered between 1954 and 1964, seven were connected to churches, three to communities and two to government departments. While this kind of organization fostered social capital and facilitated payroll deductions of deposits and loan payments, this fraternal mode of operation perpetuated fractures among working people and delimited the pool of potential investors in each union.

Credit unions developed slowly in Barbados, unlike the spectacular growth reported for Trinidad and Jamaica.[43] By 1959 the entire membership of the island's six credit unions was 1,750 compared to 69,728 members in 110 friendly societies. In addition, the annual contributions from members of the friendly societies outstripped the cumulative share capital and deposits of their counterparts in the credit unions.

Both friendly societies and credit unions were regulated under the common auspices of the Office of the Registrar of Friendly Societies and Cooperatives, but by the 1960s government began to allocate more resources and training to the cooperatives division. In 1963–64, Stanton Parris, an officer in the Registrar's Office was sent to England to complete a diploma in cooperatives.

Other retired officers of that department during this period confirm that there was definitely a shift in focus from friendly societies to cooperative credit unions.[44] By 1970, the mighty Civic Friendly Society was on the verge of collapse. The credit unions, however, seemed incapable of taking advantage of these developments and hobbled along.

Credit unions struggled to shed the popular perception that they were just friendly societies or poor men's clubs in another guise, a perception that made them unattractive to the middle class. For instance, the Civil Service Association (later the National Union of Public Workers), the respected trade union for the majority of government workers launched a savings society in May 1968 as the first stage to the establishment of a credit union. However, its application for credit union status was turned down by the registrar a year later because of its obvious shortage of support. As Golwyn Edwards points out, with a potential civil service membership of 3,000 that society had attracted a mere 132 members; fewer than twenty were said to be active with a share capital of less than $15 per member.[45] After renewed efforts, the Civil Service Credit Union Ltd was eventually registered in May 1970, but up to 1974 there was little activity in that organization. But this malaise was not peculiar to the civil servants. The registrar reported in 1975 that "the Credit Union Movement has not made any significant progress in the past 23 years for the people had not taken the Credit Union into their confidence and that had slowed the growth".[46]

Frank Alleyne contends that the movement failed to attract the youth by not placing enough emphasis on loans for certain consumer durables such as vehicles.[47] It could be argued that whereas some of the larger vibrant friendly societies began to modernize their operations, credit unions were wedded to a fading culture of fraternalism. As we have noted, credit unions remained for a long time circumscribed by by-laws limiting their membership to that of specific church congregations, communities or categories of workers.

Friendly societies such as the Unique Progressive Society and the Civic in Bridgetown, Chiming Bells in St Philip, and the Buccaneer in St James had acquired their own properties, recruited agents and maintained full-time office hours. Credit unions, on the other hand, were slow to accumulate fixed assets in real estate and buildings, satisfying themselves with employing skeleton volunteer staff operating from work-based accommodation or at chapels and associated school buildings. For instance, although the Barbados Public Workers'

Cooperative Credit Union Ltd was in operation since 1974, it employed its first full-time staff member in 1980 in a small building on the compound of the National Union of Public Workers.[48] Furthermore, none of the credit unions in Barbados invested in real estate until the 1980s. In 1981–82 the United Enterprise purchased a lot valued at $37,000 and in 1985–86 the Barbados Public Workers' Cooperative Credit Union Ltd acquired real estate valued at $1.4 million dollars – land at $501,892 and buildings valued at $916,787.[49]

It was not until the turn of the 1980s that middle-class Barbadians began to warm to the cooperative credit unions. This shift reflected an awakening and disillusionment with the commercial banks. From the 1960s, possession of a bank account became something of a status symbol by an evolving middle class. This perception was soon shattered as many black Barbadians found it near impossible to secure loans from the local commercial banks. The Barbados Savings Bank did not possess a local loans portfolio; it opted for "safer" investments overseas and its depositors had to satisfy themselves with the 3 per cent interest paid on their accounts and with the peace of mind that their deposits were safely guaranteed by the government.

The three commercial banks in operation in the 1930s – Barclays Bank (Dominion, Colonial and Overseas), the Royal Bank of Canada and the Canadian Bank of Commerce held firm to the cautious conservative policies that characterized commercial banking across the region. That is, their loan portfolios were primarily of a short-term nature, ostensibly on account of the usually high demands placed on their short-term deposits. As Saunders and Worrell have observed: "Banks insisted on a high degree of liquidity in the composition of their assets, using the traditional argument that their asset portfolio should match deposits liabilities payable on demand or at short notice."[50]

Financing the Peasantry and the Sugar Business: The Role of Government

After decades of depression in the sugar industry, Britain dispatched a Royal Commission in 1897 to investigate conditions in the British West Indies and to make recommendations. The commission, under the chairmanship of Sir

Table 8.7: Sugar Industry Agricultural Bank Loans, 1930–1968

Year	No. of Loans	Loans Advanced ($000)
1930	2	2,803
1935	10	460
1940	7	18,009
1959–60	103	1,904
1967–68	58	2,401

Source: Annual Reports of the Sugar Industry Agricultural Bank.

Henry Norman, recommended, inter alia, the provision of government-supported schemes to strengthen the peasantry. The Barbadian planters had been particularly resistant to any liberal peasant policy and their terse response was: "the question of a peasant proprietorship need not trouble us in Barbados".[51] As far as they were concerned, the sugar industry held the key to the island's civilization and it was the sector that merited an imperial bailout.

It took the British government another decade before it threw the West Indian planters a lifeline. Barbadian planters secured a grant of £80,000 from the imperial exchequer along with a loan from the Colonial Bank which together capitalized a sugar industry agricultural bank. This bank continued to serve the plantations in the post-independence era, extending fifty-eight loans in the amount of some $2.4 million between 1967 and 1968.

This stubborn adherence to King Sugar rendered Barbadians especially vulnerable to the vagaries of the international sugar market. Predictably, the glut of sugar on the world market in the 1920s plunged the West Indies into another profound economic crisis exacerbated by the collapse on Wall Street and the Great Depression of 1929. The traditional outlet of emigration was severely constrained as the United States restricted immigration and demands for seasonable labour in foreign countries dried up. The resulting dramatic decline in remittances as well as an influx of returning migrants hungry for employment intensified the struggle for economic survival. The majority of estate workers were still "located" on plantation tenantries toiling for wages that had not increased since emancipation. These poor social conditions created a volatile climate which helped to catalyse the riots of July 1937.

In 1929 the British government appointed the West Indian Sugar Commission under the chairmanship of Lord Sydney Haldane Olivier, a former long-standing career colonial servant who served as the secretary to the Norman Commission of 1896–97 and authored the resulting report. Lord Olivier's commission report of 1930 echoed the fundamental recommendations that had been made by the Norman Commission some three decades before. As one of the liberal thinkers who served in the Colonial Office and as a Fabian socialist, Olivier supported state interventionism and a fundamental role for the peasantry in economic diversification and political stability in the Caribbean.

The Olivier Report was adamant that colonies such as Barbados should receive no further imperial support for their sugar industry unless and until the pro-peasant recommendations advocated by the Norman Commission were accepted as social policy. The Olivier Report stated:

> In view of the permanence of the menace of the present conditions of sugar marketing to the possibility of maintaining that industry in Barbados and the similar islands, a menace, the early materialisation of which can only be averted by means of some intervention by the Imperial Government, it appears to us that it is a matter of Imperial interest that no assistance of this character should be given by the Imperial Government to the West Indies except upon the understanding that the recommendations of the Royal Commission of 1896–97 are to be seriously taken to heart and embodied in a continuous policy: that is to say, that deliberate steps should be taken, as have been taken for many years in Jamaica, for placing many more of the populace upon a self-supporting basis.[52]

Furthermore, when Lord Moyne was appointed to chair a commission to examine the circumstances of the social disturbances of the 1930s, Lord Olivier was the first witness to appear before it in London on 20 September 1938. Again, Olivier reiterated his mantra on the importance of the peasantry for colonies such as Barbados and the Jamaica model of diversification.[53]

Up to the 1930s, there were precious few avenues for the provision of funding to the peasant or small-farming sector. The early 1930s witnessed the birth of cooperative agricultural societies in Barbados and elsewhere in the British Caribbean. In 1934–35, four such societies were established in Barbados. These societies numbered no more than four in any year and were dissolved by the early 1940s. Unfortunately, we have not yet come across any extant records detailing the resources or operations of these early agricultural credit societies. Obviously, with the exception of the Barbados Cooperative Produce Marketing Association, they catered to a small membership and might not have been very viable. Peasant farmers continued to rely heavily on the paternalism of the local plantocracy and the mercantile elite. This agro-mercantile bourgeoisie offered advances to small farmers to secure fertilizers, lumber and other supplies against the value of their growing crops. Of course, this was a business arrangement and relations of power which benefited the plantocracy. As we shall see, such advances were invariably for the cultivation and the harvesting of peasant sugar cane to aid planters in fulfilling their quotas.

The socio-political implications of this relationship can be illustrated in the case of Wynter Crawford, a black middle-class politician who sought to unseat the planter class in the constituency of St Philip in the late 1930s. While canvassing in that parish he was informed by a number of peasant farmers that they feared voting for him, lest the planters in the parish deny them credit.[54] Land possession would have been a qualification for political enfranchisement but such an achievement was hollow without economic enfranchisement. Crawford understood the connection and placed the campaign for the establishment of a government-funded peasant bank at the top of his political agenda.

In 1937 the Government of Barbados acquiesced to imperial and local political pressures and established the Peasants' Loan Bank (renamed the Agricultural Credit Bank from 1961) with initial capital of $48,000 to support the small-farming sector. This was the first time that the local legislature offered any significant tangible aid to this sector. The bank offered short-term loans to peasants who held 10 acres of land or less. For the first six years the bank issued short-term loans only on crops. From 1943 to 1944, medium-term loans were made available for livestock and long-term ones to cover mortgages and irrigation.

The majority of those loans, however, were short-term to facilitate the growing of sugar cane. In 1954 the qualifying acreage was increased to 25 and the many tenant farmers could become eligible for loans to purchase their lots or to undertake the necessary legal work to secure good titles. As a consequence, the number of peasants in receipt of loans climbed dramatically from 839 in 1953–54 to 1,534 the following year. However, the principal policy consideration

Table 8.8. Loan Portfolio of Peasants Loan Bank/Agricultural Credit Bank, 1937–1960

Year	Number of Loans Granted	Total Loans ($)
1937–38	161	3,730
1939–40	263	6,264
1941–42	286	9,941
1943–44	518	16,886
1945–46	433	19,358
1947–48	435	25,809
1949–50	515	36,603
1951–52	672	56,822
1953–54	839	105,834
1955–56	1,728	149,227
1957–58	2,352	209,179
1959–60	2,095	231,710

Source: Reports of the Peasants Loan Bank and Agricultural Credit Bank.

of the bank was to avoid the disruption of the dominant land-owning and land use configurations of the island. Although the Peasants Loan Bank did not restrict the crops or animal husbandry that it would finance, loans to support sugar production were clearly preferred. Peasants often possessed the least fertile land, thereby hindering the competitive production of vegetables. More important, though, was the impact of the bank's security of loans policy, which imposed a lien on the crop and made it mandatory for borrowers to identify specifically the contracted buyer of their produce. While it was possible to make such a firm contract to consign a sugar cane crop to a designated planter or factory owner, this was virtually impossible for the small farmer, specializing in food-crop agriculture, who catered to an amorphous market of hawkers, speculators and villagers.[55]

The Peasants Loan Bank was the first in a succession of state interventions to provide credit for the social and entrepreneurial development of Barbadians. It was a development which reflected the changing face of local politics and that of British imperialism. In the case of Barbados, the Colonial Office advocated that the local sugar industry should be required to contribute directly to government funding of workers' welfare schemes as a quid pro quo for any future favourable support for the sugar industry. This was clearly the position advocated by the Moyne Commission.[56] Following some persuasion from London, the Barbados legislature passed the Sugar Industry (Rehabilitation Price Stabilization and Labour Welfare) Act in 1947. Levies were imposed on all sugar and molasses produced in Barbados to create three funds: a rehabilitation reserve fund, a price stabilization fund and a labour welfare fund. The act stipulated that for every ton of sugar produced, $2.40 was to be paid into the labour welfare fund.[57] By the end of 1949, $817,728 had been accumulated, of which $400,000 was allocated to a sugar workers' housing loan fund, while $300,000 was provided for the establishment of community halls and playing fields.[58]

Conclusion

From emancipation through to the achievement of political independence, the working people of Barbados experienced significant difficulty in accessing credit either to finance basic social welfare needs such as housing or to establish businesses. Barbados was the quintessential plantation society and economy where the needs of that sector were paramount. The planter-mercantile ruling class ensured that the sugar plantation sector would not suffer for lack of finances. Three high-profile Royal Commissions rejected the sugar monoculture and land monopolization policies practised in Barbados. Since the eve of emancipation, the Colonial Office, Christian missionaries and the working classes themselves, identified self-help non-banking financial intermediaries such as meeting-turns, friendly societies and Government Savings Banks as potential sources of financing working-class aspirations. Migration, especially to Panama, injected millions of dollars within black working-class communities, stimulating grass roots NBFIs. Thereafter, NBFIs were consciously steered to function as savings and loans operations, unfortunately sacrificing their insurance components in the process.

With pressure from the Colonial Office and local labour politicians the barons of Bridgetown were forced to retreat from their laissez-faire approach to social issues and to place financial resources for the empowerment of

Barbadians. Thus, a series of loan schemes were developed to provide loans for peasant agriculture; housing loan schemes and assisted migration.

Notes

All references to $ currency are to colonial dollars prior to 1966 when Barbados achieved political independence from Great Britain. In 1951 an amalgamated West Indian currency (managed by the British Caribbean Currency Board with headquarters in Trinidad and Tobago) was introduced with Barbados as a participant along with British Guiana, Trinidad and Tobago, and the Windward and Leeward Islands.

1. Shirley Ardener, "The Comparative Study of Rotating Credit Associations", *Journal of the Royal Anthropological Institute of Great Britain and Ireland* 94, no. 2 (July–December, 1964): 201.
2. For a fuller discussion on rotating savings and credit associations see William R. Bascom, "The Esusu: A Credit Institution of the Yoruba", *Journal of the Royal Anthropological Institute of Great Britain and Ireland* 82, no. 1 (1952): 63–69; Margaret Katzin, "Partners: An Informal Savings Institution in Jamaica", *Social and Economic Studies* 8, no. 4 (1959): 436–40; Ardener, "Comparative Study", 201–29.
3. *Parliamentary Papers*, 1898 (c.8657) L, West India Royal Commission, app. C, pt. 3, para. 943, 194, evidence of W. Walter S. Marston.
4. Barbados, Poor Relief Commission Report (1878), 31.
5. Ibid.
6. *Barbados Agricultural Reporter*, 8 May 1888.
7. Poor Relief Commission Report, 31.
8. Clifford Geertz, "The Revolving Credit Association: A Middle Rung in Development", *Economic Development and Cultural Change* 10, no. 3 (April 1962): 263.
9. Brent William Stoffle, "'We Don't Put All Our Eggs in One Basket': An Examination of Meeting Turn, a Rotating Saving and Credit Association in Barbados" (PhD diss., Department of Anthropology, University of South Florida, 2001), 105.
10. In a few cases the "banker" receives an *ex gratia* tip from the recipient of the "turn".
11. Donald V. Kurtz, "The Rotating Credit Association: An Adaptation to Poverty", *Human Organization* 32, no. 1 (Spring 1973): 54.
12. Christine Barrow, "Meetings: A Group Savings Arrangement in Barbados", *African Studies Association of the West Indies Bulletin* 8 (December 1976): 39.
13. Trevor W. Purcell, "Local Institutions in Grassroots Development: The Rotating Savings and Credit Association", *Social and Economic Studies* 49, no. 1 (2000): 156–59.

14. Barbados Government, Minutes of the Legislative Council and House of Assembly (hereafter MCA), 1914–15, doc. 162, "Report of the Registrar of Friendly Societies for the Half-Year, January–June 1914", 4.
15. MCA 1922–23, doc. 169, "Report of the Registrar of Friendly Societies for the Half-Year January to June 1923", 2.
16. Harry A. Franck, *Roaming through the West Indies* (London: Blue Ribbon Books, 1920), 370.
17. A.F. Wells and D. Wells, *Friendly Societies in the West Indies* (London: HMSO, 1953), 53.
18. Bonham Richardson, *Panama Money in Barbados, 1900–1920* (Knoxville: University of Tennessee Press, 1985), 210–11.
19. Barbados, Auditor-General's Report, 30 January 1941.
20. Auditor-General's Report [1949–50], 13 March 1951.
21. Barbados Registrar of Cooperatives and Friendly Societies to Permanent Secretary, Ministry of Trade, Tourism, Cooperatives and Fisheries, 23 December 1968.
22. Auditor-General's Report [1949–50], 13 March 1951.
23. *Agricultural Reporter*, 7 June 1900, 2.
24. Williams to Chamberlain, 3 January 1901, Colonial Office (hereafter CO) 28/254, no. 4.
25. W.A. Beckles, comp., *The Barbados Disturbances (1937): Review – Reproduction of the Evidence and Report of the Commission* (Bridgetown: Advocate Co., 1937), 47.
26. Ibid.
27. Maurice A. Odle, *The Significance of Non-Bank Financial Intermediaries in the Caribbean* (Kingston: Institute of Social and Economic Research, University of the West Indies, 1972), 107.
28. *West Indies Royal Commission: Proceedings of Investigations in Barbados* (Bridgetown: Advocate Co., 1937), 153
29. Wells and Wells, *Friendly Societies*, 48.
30. See Barbados Department of Archives (hereafter BDA), *Rules of the Barbados "Burden Bearer" Loan and Benefit Society*, no. 80 [1937].
31. Michael F. Toussaint, "The Evolution of the Credit Union Movement in Trinidad and Tobago in the Early Nineteenth Century: Ideology and Romance in the Gestation Period" (paper presented at thirty-ninth annual conference of the Association of Caribbean Historians, 6–11 May 2007, Kingston, Jamaica), 14–15.
32. Prospectus of the Barbados Progressive and Co-operative Bank, Ltd, 10 March 1946 (personal papers of Leila Salazar).
33. [Leila Salazar], "Personal Notes on the Occasion of the Granting of the Barbados [Gold] Medal of Merit, Frederick MacDonald Symmonds" [paper prepared for the Cabinet, Government of Barbados, 1983]; BDA, *Rules of the Roebuck Moravian Mutual Aid Society* [Barbados 1928], 24.

34. *The British Caribbean: Who, What, Why, 1955–56* (Glasgow: Lloyd Sydney Smith, [1956–57]), 49.
35. "Why That Co-op Bank Failed", *Weekend Nation*, 13 April 1984, 27.
36. CHOH-BCB-002, transcript of Kenneth Harvey interviewed by Aviston Downes, 11 September 2004, 4.
37. *The British Caribbean*, 774.
38. BDA, Inland Revenue encl. in Will of David Stonewall Payne; "Why That Co-op Bank Failed", 27.
39. See Henderson Carter, *Business in Bim: A Business History of Barbados, 1900–2000* (Kingston: Ian Randle, 2008), 62–63.
40. See J.M. Cave, "Notes on Cooperation", Bulletin no. 17, new ser. (Department of Science and Agriculture, Barbados, November, 1951).
41. Gloria Selby, "Shamrock Co-operative Credit Union Ltd", *Golden Anniversary of Shamrock Co-operative Credit Union Ltd, 29th July 1947 to 29th July 1997* (Bridgetown: n.p., 1997).
42. Data from Cooperatives Department, *Statistical Digest of Credit Union Activity from 1954 to 1994* (Bridgetown: n.p., 1998).
43. Sean NgWai, "Credit Unions in Trinidad and Tobago, 1942–1994" (seminar paper, Department of History, University of the West Indies, St Augustine, 30 September 2004); Claremont Kirton, "Credit Unions in Jamaica: Performance, Problems and Prospects", in *Financing Development in the Commonwealth Caribbean*, ed. Delisle Worrell, Compton Bourne and Dinesh Dodhia (London and Basingstoke: Macmillan Caribbean, 1991), 111–28.
44. CHOH-FS-001–003, transcripts of Stanton Parris, interviewed by Aviston Downes, 6 November 2003; Myrtle Jones, interviewed by Aviston Downes, 14 June 2002; Everton Browne interviewed by Aviston Downes, 14 June 2002.
45. Golwyn Edwards, "Barbados Public Workers' Co-operative Credit Union Limited: Historical Perspective and Data" (n.p., n.d.), 4.
46. Ibid., 3.
47. Frank Alleyne, "A Critical Evaluation of the Impact of Credit Union Activity Upon the Social and Economic Development of Barbados 1961–83", *Bulletin of Eastern Caribbean Affairs* 11, nos. 4 and 5 (1985): 41–47.
48. "Members Pleased with Headquarters", *Thrift: A Quarterly Publication of the BPW-CCUL*, no. 5 (1990), 6.
49. "Credit Union Owns Property", *Thrift: A Quarterly Publication of the BPWCCUL*, no. 1 (1986), 1; *Statistical Digest of Credit Union Activity from 1954 to 1994* (n.p., 1998), 36, 38.
50. See Muriel Saunders and Delisle Worrell, "Commercial Bank Credit in Barbados, 1946–1977", *Central Bank of Barbados, Quarterly Report* 5, no. 4 (December 1978): 31

51. *Parliamentary Papers*, 1899 (c.9046–30), LXI, Barbados Blue Book Report for 1898, 27.
52. Great Britain, *West Indian Sugar Commission Report, 1929–1930* (London: HMSO, 1930), para. 163, 58–59.
53. See Great Britain, *Report of the West India Royal Commission* (Cmd. 6607, 1945), Appendix A; Paul Rich, "Sydney Olivier, Jamaica and the Debate on British Colonial Policy in the West Indies", in *Labour in the Caribbean from Emancipation to Independence,* ed. Malcolm Cross and Gad Heuman (London and Basingstoke: Macmillan, 1988), 208–33; Richard Lobdell, "British Officials and the West Indian Peasantry, 1842–1938", in *Labour in the Caribbean from Emancipation to Independence,* ed. Malcolm Cross and Gad Heuman (London and Basingstoke: Macmillan, 1988), 195–207; Richard Lobdell, "Repression Is Not a Policy: Sydney Olivier on the West Indies and Africa", in *West Indies Accounts: Essays on the History of the British Caribbean and the Atlantic Economy In Honour of Richard Sheridan,* ed. Roderick A. McDonald (Kingston: University of the West Indies Press, 1996), 344–46.
54. CHOH-BNB-004G, transcript of A. Wynter Crawford interviewed by W.K. Marshall, 24 March 1985, 22; Woodville K. Marshall, ed., *I Speak for the People: The Memoirs of Wynter Crawford* (Kingston: Ian Randle, 2003), 46.
55. Anthony D. Griffith, "The Diversification of Peasant Agriculture in Barbados" (MA thesis, Department of Geography, McGill University, 1972), 86.
56. Great Britain, *Report of the West India Royal Commission* (Cmd. 6607, 1945), paras. 66–70.
57. Cleviston Haynes, "Sugar and the Barbadian Economy 1946–1980", in *The Economy of Barbados 1946–1980,* ed. DeLisle Worrell (Bridgetown: Central Bank of Barbados, 1982), 90–91.
58. Colonial Office. *Report on Barbados for the Year 1949* (London: HMSO, 1950), 36.

SECTION 3

Traders, Transporters and Retailers

CHAPTER 9

Joseph Rachell and Rachael Pringle-Polgreen

*Petty Entrepreneurs**

JEROME S. HANDLER

By the end of the seventeenth century, the tiny south-eastern Caribbean island of Barbados had become England's richest colony in the New World. Barbados' wealth derived from the production of sugar, which was primarily cultivated on large-scale plantations by African slaves. In addition to slaves, the island contained a minority population of European descent or birth, which included an even smaller plantocratic group that controlled the island's means of production, internal legislative apparatus, and other society-wide institutions. Gradually, over the years, a third group emerged comprised of persons whose racial ancestry was mixed or solely African but who were legally free. Whether free born or manumitted from slavery, these free blacks and free "coloreds" were accorded a variety of privileges and rights not extended to slaves. But because of their racial ancestry they were denied other privileges and rights that white society reserved for itself.

---

*Originally published in *Struggle and Survival in Colonial America*, edited by David G. Sweet and Gary B. Nash (Berkeley and Los Angeles: University of California Press, 1981), 376–91. Reprinted by permission of the University of California Press.

There were very few freedmen during the seventeenth century, but the group increased slowly until there were some two thousand (about half or more being women) at the close of the eighteenth century. At that time freedmen were overshadowed by close to 16,000 whites and over 64,000 slaves.

Despite their small numbers and the fact that they were free subjects of the British crown, by 1721 the Barbadian legislature had legally denied freedmen the right to vote, hold elective office, serve on juries, and testify in court cases or other legal proceedings involving whites. As the years progressed, some other legal constraints were placed on freedmen, but regardless of their legal status at any given time they were always held in a subordinate position and subjected to a variety of discriminatory practices. Some of these practices derived their strength from the legal code, others from social conventions based on the premise of racial supremacy, which permeated all segments of white society. As in other New World slave societies, however, the system allowed some flexibility: although no one in Barbados of known African ancestry could be considered white with respect to social or legal status, some freedmen were able to succeed economically within the occupations to which they were relegated by custom.

Freedmen shunned plantation wage labor. They did not own plantations during the eighteenth century, and few of them were independent small-scale agriculturalists. They were largely an urban group concentrated in Bridgetown, the island's political and commercial center and largest town. There they engaged in a variety of skilled trades and participated actively in the internal marketing system as hawkers or higglers and small shopkeepers. By the end of the eighteenth century, a few women also kept hotels or taverns.

None of these people led dramatic lives in the conventional sense, and most simply coped under very trying circumstances. However, the lives of some of them are worthy of note, because they reveal the possibility of achieving relative economic success by creatively adapting to and strategically exploiting the limited opportunities that Barbados' circumscribed social order provided.

Two of these economically successful freedmen, a black man and a "colored" woman, are the subjects of this essay. Both were born in slavery, and their combined lives spanned the eighteenth century. Although neither was a typical freedman, their very atypicality testifies to remarkable personal characteristics and also reflects various dimensions of the socioeconomic environment in which they lived.

Joseph Rachell: Shopkeeper

The proceeds that freedmen saved from marketing activities, as well as monies they earned in trades, permitted some to acquire the capital to open small shops that sold foodstuffs and hard goods to other freedmen, poor whites, and slaves. As with white-owned shops of comparable scale, the shops owned by freedmen traded in various types of goods that slaves stole from their masters' or others' properties. With low profit margins, a heavy dependence on credit from merchant suppliers and importers, and the burden of the extension of credit to their often impoverished customers, relatively few of these freedmen were able to develop their businesses into mercantile establishments that could compete with the larger enterprises of wealthier whites. For all intents and purposes, freedmen were excluded from larger businesses, not only because whites consciously strove to maintain their dominance in enterprises that traded abroad and supplied the needs of local planters, but also because freedmen largely lacked the capital and credit, and the internal and overseas business and social connections within whose framework such large-scale enterprises operated.

Although some freedmen were able to achieve mercantile establishments by the first few decades of the nineteenth century, during the eighteenth century economically successful freedmen were largely relegated to very small businesses. An outstanding early exception was Joseph Rachell.

Born around 1716, Rachell was manumitted before the age of ten, and by the time of his death in October 1766 he had become a Bridgetown merchant with extensive business interests. Nothing is known of his childhood, the circumstances surrounding his manumission, or his early life, and little information is available on his family and social life. At about the age of twenty-five he married Elizabeth Cleaver, a "free mulatto" woman two years his senior, by whom he had at least three children.

The process by which Rachell established and developed his business interests is also unknown, but by his mature years he was a well-known figure in Bridgetown. A contemporary observed that he "dealt chiefly in the retail way, and was so fair and complaisant in business, that in a town filled with little peddling shops, his doors were thronged with customers . . . his character was so fair, his manners so generous, that the best [white] people showed him a regard, which they often deny men of their own colour".[1] Rachell was considered "an ingenious, industrious, and upright tradesman". Younger businessmen solicited his advice, and his opinion was often deferred to when the selling price of imported goods was established, and "whenever . . . vessels arrived with a cargo, J.R. was one of the first persons . . . to whom the cargo was offered".[2]

Rachell's trading activities did not extend to England but were largely confined to British colonies in the Caribbean, including Guiana. He also maintained fishing boats and used a group of his slaves as fishermen. In what was an extremely unusual situation for the period, Rachell employed some whites, and they "always spoke of him in a very respectful manner, and particularly revered him for his humanity and tenderness".[3] He was also "extremely kind in lending out money to poor, industrious men" so that they could establish their own businesses or extricate themselves from financial difficulties. Moreover, when a planter or merchant was forced to sell his property for reasons of financial duress or debt, Rachell would often attend the auction, purchase the property at a "fair market price", and then return it to the owner at the same price – frequently having cleared the debt himself before bidding. "By these humane and judicious means", Rachell was able to save "many families from ruin".

Whether the "benevolence of this excellent Negro" was motivated by altruistic sentiments, as the above comments would have us believe, or by a shrewd perception of white society and a practical understanding of the value of building and maintaining a network of allies within it, Rachell certainly could not have afforded to alienate or threaten whites.

In his relationship with an unnamed white man, a wealthy, propertied person who was a colonel in the Barbados militia and who had the reputation of being a "penurious miser", Rachell might have risked such alienation; presumably, however, he would not have undertaken the actions reported in the following episode unless he felt comfortable in his position and had the support of the wider white community. The colonel "used to call frequently at Joseph's shop, on pretence of cheapening cocoa; he was always sure to carry away as much for a taste as his pocket would hold, but never bought any".[4] Rachell was in a quandary, for although he objected to his continued losses he knew that, as a black, he could not bring legal charges against a white man. Finally he struck upon the idea of hiring a white clerk. He ordered the clerk to weigh out a bag of cocoa and to keep that bag under his particular care; whenever the colonel appeared he was only supplied with cocoa from the bag. When the bag was emptied, Rachell claimed payment for the cocoa, notifying the colonel that if payment was not made charges would be brought by the clerk. Although the colonel "stormed, swore, and threatened", he wanted to avoid the expense of a lawsuit "and suggested that being so fairly taken in, there was nothing to be done . . . but to pay the money peaceably. By this innocent stratagem Joseph got rid of the colonel's tasting visits."

Rachell's "charitable" endeavors extended in various directions, and years after his death poor whites talked about the "blessed man, for no poor thing ever went away hungry from his house; and some, who had seen better days, were shewn into a back room, and had victuals set before them".[5] In the early 1750s, the vestry of the parish in which Rachell lived even took the unusual step of providing him an annuity to support the illegitimate daughter of a married or widowed white woman who had died, and Rachell also supported a few impoverished elderly whites who received a modest bequest after his death. When Rachell's fishing boats returned with their daily catch, he would take a portion of the fish to the prisoners in the Bridgetown jail. We are told that he regularly visited the jail, "enquired into the circumstances of the prisoners, and gave them relief, in proportion to their distress and good behavior". Whites often considered freedmen slaveowners as "generally more severe, because [they] are less enlightened owners", but Rachell was viewed as "remarkable [because] he was extremely kind to his Negroes".[6]

Freedmen who were Christians belonged to the Anglican church, the island's official or state church. Rachell was baptized when he was about ten years old and was also married in an Anglican ceremony (a church marriage being an uncommon event among freedmen); as an adult he regularly attended Sunday services at the cathedral in Bridgetown. Although the rector considered him "a very attentive and devout hearer", and although Rachell "was so much esteemed for his honesty that he was commonly admitted to the company and conversation of merchants and planters",[7] along with other nonwhites he was relegated to a segregated seating area in the cathedral. When he died he was buried in a segregated churchyard in Bridgetown, the social distinctions of Barbadian society being enforced to the last. His funeral was attended by a "prodigious concourse of blacks" and a large number of white people as well.[8] A stone was erected over his grave but without any inscription or memorial. In his will Rachell bequeathed all his real and personal property to his widow "and her heirs forever". Although "possessed of a good deal of property" at his death, the extent and nature of this property is unknown.

The few biographical details that are available on Rachell reveal a man enjoying a certain lifestyle, served by domestic slaves with quality wines at a table lit by spermaceti candles, that was comparable to the lifestyle of whites of similar means. Rachell was clearly a success in Barbadian society and had achieved the maximum status allowed to free black men of his generation. One can only speculate on how he viewed his own behavior and on the extent to which circumstances forced him to demean or compromise himself with whites. Certainly in his outward behavior he had to appear to acquiesce in the norms of compliance and accommodation white society considered appropriate to the behavior of nonwhites. Rachell was not perceived as threatening to the social order and to the maintenance of white supremacy; and he also met certain economic needs of the white community.

Rachael Pringle-Polgreen also met the needs of white society, but in a different way.

Rachael Pringle-Polgreen: Tavern Keeper

Women were much less visible than men in the social and political life of the freedman community, but some women nevertheless accumulated property and achieved a standard of living that rivaled or even exceeded that of many of the males. Shopkeeping was the major vehicle by which freedwomen might become economically successful; and as among men they usually acquired shops by saving monies gained through huckstering activities. Freedwomen also established themselves in shopkeeping by profiting from their sexual relationships with whites.

White males in Barbados – creoles, migrants from Britain, and British naval and military personnel – were regularly involved in interracial sexual relations, which, as elsewhere in New World slave societies, were the major social area exempt from a system that was designed to maintain a distance between whites and nonwhites. The social conventions of the colony neither condemned nor inhibited these relations, and although some freedwomen may not have liked them, they were apparently perceived as devices for social mobility and material security. Just as the slave mistress of a white man could sometimes achieve freedom for herself and her children and acquire material rewards or removal from the more onerous aspects of slavery, such as plantation field labor, so a freedwoman could materially benefit from a sexual alliance with a white man. He could provide her with decent clothes, a house and furnishings, and other goods and property, such as land, a horse and carriage, and even slaves. Also she might inherit from him the goods or money with which she could establish some type of business.

Aside from small shops, by the last quarter of the eighteenth century various hotels or taverns in Bridgetown were owned by women who usually had been the favored mistress of a white man from whom they had gained manumission, or who had worked in the taverns as slaves and were then manumitted by their freedwomen owners.

There were apparently no more than two or three hotel-taverns owned by freedwomen at any one period, but these establishments provided important services in the form of meals, lodging, and washing to island visitors and ship passengers in transit. The taverns were also popular rendezvous for white creoles and British military and naval personnel. Their owners sponsored "dignity balls", formally organized supper dances requiring an admission fee, which were largely attended by "colored" females and which only admitted white men. Another major attraction of the taverns was that they were "houses of debauchery, a number of young women of colour being always procurable in them for the purposes of prostitution".[9]

Understandably, given the services they provided, these hotel-taverns were usually successful businesses; their owners became relatively wealthy and frequently amassed a significant amount of property in the form of houses and slaves. Visitors to Barbados often commented on the resourcefulness of the proprietresses in their business dealings, as well as on their independent spirits, assertiveness, and managerial abilities.

Legendary among these women, and immortalized in a 1796 print by Thomas Rowlandson, was Rachael Pringle-Polgreen; in the late 1770s she became one of the earliest, if not the first, freedwomen to own a hotel-tavern.

Born around 1753, Rachael was the daughter and slave of William Lauder, a Scottish schoolmaster, and an African woman whom he had purchased not long after emigrating to Barbados in about 1750. He first took a position in a Bridgetown "grammer school", a job from which he was dismissed for incompetence in 1762. He then opened a small shop in Bridgetown, which he ran with the assistance of Rachael's mother and presumably Rachael herself – an experience that would serve the daughter well in later years.

By her "juvenile days", Rachael "was a remarkably well-made, good-looking girl, possessing altogether charms that . . . awakened the libidinous desires of her [father] who made many . . . unsuccessful attempts on her chastity".[10] Angered by her failure to respond to these advances, one day the father ordered her whipped. But we are told that just as she was being prepared for the whipping, Thomas Pringle, a British naval officer who was witnessing the scene, "seized the whip . . . and rescuing his panting victim, carried her off in triumph amidst the cheers of a thronging multitude". Lauder was infuriated by Pringle's action; and since his daughter was also his slave, he brought charges against Pringle under a law that prohibited the harboring of a runaway slave. The case was then settled out of court, when Lauder sold Rachael to Pringle "at an extortionate price".

"Not then eighteen", Rachael was established by Pringle in a "small house" in Bridgetown, and soon afterward he manumitted her; she in turn dropped the name of Lauder and adopted that of Pringle. At one point during their relationship, the story goes, Rachael became "anxious to strengthen her influence over her benefactor [and] contrived to deceive him". She feigned pregnancy, and when Pringle returned from a tour of duty presented him with a child "as the offspring of their loves". The child's real mother ruined the deception, however, by demanding that her infant be returned; and when Pringle discovered that he had been fooled he not only returned the child but also severed his ties with Rachael. Soon after, his ship sailed for Jamaica and he left Barbados for good. "Rachael, however, was not long without a 'protector'; a gentleman of the name of Polgreen succeeded to the possession of her charms", and she added his name to that of Pringle.

"By her industry" Rachael managed to enlarge the house that Thomas Pringle had obtained for her, and sometime in the late 1770s, when she was in her twenties, she opened her tavern and hotel. Around 1780 her house carried a tax assessment of six pounds per annum, which suggests that it was a modest wooden structure such as many others in Bridgetown. Within a year, however, she also owned a "large house" in another section of the city, which was assessed at fifty pounds. Had she been a white male, the ownership of this house alone would have placed her among the small group of people, probably numbering no more than several hundred, whose lands or houses had the ten-pound minimum taxable value that qualified them to vote, hold elective office, and serve on juries. This large house became her major enterprise – the celebrated Royal Naval Hotel.

The hotel was given its distinctive name after Prince William Henry (later King William IV) visited there in 1786, when the naval vessel he commanded docked in Barbados for a week. Half a century later, the editor of a Barbadian newspaper recalled how Rachael walked "with the Prince, actually leaning on the Royal Arm and accompanied by other naval officers and a host of mulatto women as His Highness promenaded the crowded streets".[11]

One legendary episode in the hotel's life took place during the prince's second brief visit to the island. On the night of February 2, 1789, after he and several resident British army officers had dined, they went to the Royal Naval Hotel where, during the course of the evening, the prince "commenced a royal frolic by breaking the furniture, etc.". Joined by his fellow officers, they "carried on the sport with such activity, that in a couple of hours every article was completely demolished". While this drunken spree and wanton destruction was going on, Rachael, by now a heavy-set woman of around thirty-six years, was reported to have "sat quite passive in her great arm chair at the entrance door of the hotel" claiming that, as the king's son, the prince had license to do as he pleased. When the prince left, he bid Rachael good night, but "to crown his sport, upset her and chair together, leaving her unwieldy body sprawling in the street, to the ineffable amusement of the laughing crowd". Rachael, we are told, was calm and displayed no anger; but the following morning she sent the prince an itemized bill for seven hundred pounds sterling in damages, which was duly paid and which allowed "Miss Rachael" to refurbish her hotel with more splendor than before.

During the years between the start of her business and July 23, 1791, when she died at around the age of thirty-eight, Rachael Pringle-Polgreen acquired property that was considerable by Barbadian standards for persons of any sex or racial group. In addition to her hotel, she owned at least ten other properties in the same Bridgetown neighbourhood. Freedmen and whites of means commonly owned multiple rental properties, but the number of houses that Rachael owned was unusually high. She also possessed a large amount of movable property, and her hotel was elaborately furnished even before its destruction by Prince William Henry. He and his fellow officers destroyed, for example, beds, feather mattresses, "pier glasses", pictures, chandeliers and lamps, decanters, goblets, wine glasses, porcelain, and crockery. The day after the rampage, Rachael placed a newspaper advertisement offering a reward for other missing property, which presumably had been thrown out of the windows: "a small filigree waiter, scolloped around the edge . . . seven silver table spoons, seven teaspoons, two desert spoons marked R.P. in a cypher".[12]

Like Joseph Rachell and many other freedmen, whether free-born or manumitted, Rachael's property included slaves who were employed in various capacities relating to the running of her business. There is no suggestion that she, or most other members of her group, had any compunction against owning slaves; indeed, she probably shared the view of many other freedmen that slaveownership was a fundamental property right that they possessed as free persons. Rachael's last will, made two days before her death, shows that she owned at least nineteen slaves, a substantial number for a person of any racial group living in an urban area. Following a property transmission pattern that was also characteristic of whites, she bequeathed most of her slaves; eleven were inherited by five white legatees, Bridgetown merchants with whom she had close business dealings, and two daughters of one of these merchants; two other slaves were bequeathed to a slave woman who won her freedom under the terms of Rachael's will.

In all, Rachael's will provided for the manumission of six slaves. Although they constituted a minority of the total number of slaves she owned, in terms of islandwide manumission practices for white and nonwhite slaveowners, they represented a disproportionately large percentage of manumissions by one owner at the time of death. Rachael, despite her apparent commitment to and acceptance of slaveownership, seems to have been moved by a sense of loyalty to those who had served her well and with whom she had particularly close ties. Her "charity", however, did not extend to the provision of other property or monies to most of those manumitted; only one manumitted slave received the house and land on which she resided. Rachael ordered her executors, two of the merchant legatees, to use the money raised from the sale of all her other property to pay the required manumission fees as well as her funeral expenses and outstanding debts. All the residual proceeds left from the sale of her property were to be divided equally between two "good friends", the Bridgetown merchants, who between them had also received eight of the slaves Rachael bequeathed, and Thomas Pringle, whose actions had resulted in her freedom many years before.

Aside from the manumitted slaves, all Rachael's legatees were white. She never married and apparently had no children – at least none who were alive at the time of her death; it is not known if she recognized any family connections through her mother. It is one of those anomalies of the slave society that the social relationships to which she attached the greatest importance, as reflected at any rate by the property bequests in her will, were with white people. The greatest homage that white creole society ever bestowed on her, however, was that she was called "Miss Rachael . . . the prefix being then rarely given to black or coloured women".

In their own ways Joseph Rachell and Rachael Pringle-Polgreen were unique individuals in eighteenth-century Barbados. Both had risen from slavery and had succeeded under extremely difficult conditions because of their industry, resourcefulness, and shrewdness. These attributes enabled them to manipulate a circumscribed system to their own advantage. They learned effectively to conduct, and even to enrich, themselves and were able to fill a niche in the socioeconomic order by meeting various needs of white society. They were able to maintain this niche because of their acumen and because their behavior was acceptable by the white-defined standards for the behavior of nonwhites; moreover, they never openly challenged or defied the racial underpinnings of the slave society that confined all freedmen, regardless of education, wealth, and lifestyle, to an inferior and subordinate social status.

We shall never know how Rachell and Pringle-Polgreen really felt about themselves and the society in which they lived. Inwardly they may have rejected many dimensions of the racist ideology that governed white perceptions of nonwhites. There is every indication, however, that their creative adaptation to Barbadian society was facilitated not only because they shared a general lifestyle with white creoles of comparable economic means but also because they identified with white creole values. These values involved a commitment to the concept of private property and slaveownership, and an acceptance of a class system with its concomitant ideology of privilege. By identifying with these values Rachell and Pringle-Polgreen found a measure of security for themselves while abetting the exploitative foundations of Barbadian society.

Notes

1. James Ramsay, *An Essay on the Treatment and Conversion of African Slaves in the British Sugar Colonies* (London: James Phillips, 1784), 254.
2. William Dickson, *Letters on Slavery* (London: J. Phillips, 1789), 180.
3. All quotations in this paragraph are from Dickson, *Letters*, 180–81.
4. Quotations in this paragraph are from Ramsay, *Essay*, 258–59.
5. Dickson, *Letters*, 181.
6. Dickson, *Letters*, 182.
7. Robert B. Nicholls, testimony in *Parliamentary Papers* (London, 1790), 30: 333.
8. Dickson, *Letters*, 182.
9. John A. Waller, *A Voyage in the West Indies* (London: Sir R. Phillips, 1820), 6.
10. Unless otherwise noted, all quotations in this section on Rachael Pringle-Polgreen are taken from J.W. Orderson, *Creoleana: Or, Social and Domestic Scenes and Incidents in Barbados in Days of Yore* (London: Saunders and Otley, 1842), 94–102.
11. "Extracts from the Barbadian Newspaper", *Journal of the Barbados Museum and Historical Society* 10 (1943): 143.
12. Quoted in Neville Connell, "Prince William Henry's Visits to Barbados in 1786 and 1789", *Journal of the Barbados Museum and Historical Society* 25 (1958): 163.

Sources

The principal source on Joseph Rachell is William Dickson's *Letters on Slavery* (London: J. Phillips, 1789). Dickson's account (180–81) is mainly from a "private journal" whose unnamed author resided in Barbados in 1769 and who derived his information on Rachell from hearsay accounts. James Ramsay's *An Essay on the Treatment and Conversion of African Slaves in the British Sugar Colonies* (London: James Phillips, 1784) has a brief account of Rachell (254–59) which is based on the oral report of someone who had personally known him. In his testimony before a House of Commons committee investigating the slave trade (*Parliamentary Papers*, London, 1790, 30: 325–60), the Barbadian-born Reverend Robert B. Nicholls provides a few corroborative details which he apparently obtained through hearsay. The dates of Rachell's birth, baptism, marriage, and death, and similar materials on various members of his family, come from the St Michael parish registers, located in the Barbados Department of Archives (RL 1/2, 270; RL 1/3, 19, 24, 90, 257; RL 1/4, 326); the Archives also contain Rachell's will (RB 6/21, 42–43) and that of his wife (RB 6/33, 336–37). The annuity Rachell received from the St Michael vestry is reported in "Records of the Vestry of St Michael", *Journal of the Barbados Museum and Historical Society* 24 (1957): 145, 196.

The major source on Pringle-Polgreen's life is J.W. Orderson's novel *Creoleana: Or, Social and Domestic Scenes and Incidents in Barbados in Days of Yore* (London: Saunders and Otley, 1842). Written in the late 1830s, when its author, a prominent white Barbadian creole, was in his seventies, the novel is set in the last quarter of the eighteenth century. The general social conditions and ambience of the period, as depicted by Orderson, are consistent with many other primary sources; moreover, key personages in the sketch of Pringle-Polgreen (94–102), such as William Lauder (her father), Thomas Pringle, and, of course, Prince William Henry, actually lived. One cannot be certain, however, that various biographical details, such as Lauder's incestuous advances, the circumstances under which Rachael met Thomas Pringle and events in their life together, have not been distorted or even invented.

Information on Pringle-Polgreen's house ownership is contained in the St Michael parish levy book, located in the Barbados Department of Archives. This information was published by Warren Alleyne in his "Rachael Pringle Polgreen" (Barbados, 1977), a three-page brochure written to accompany the Barbados Museum and Historical Society's full-scale color reprint of Thomas Rowlandson's 1796 caricature. The Barbados Department of Archives contains Pringle-Polgreen's will (RB 6/19, 435–37) and the St Michael parish register (RL 1/5, 538), which carries the notice of her burial. Minor sources, all published in the *Journal of the Barbados Museum and Historical Society*, were used to round out various details in Pringle-Polgreen's life: an anonymously authored article, "Rachael of Barbados", *Journal* 9 (1942): 109–111; Neville Connell, "Prince William Henry's Visits to Barbados in 1786 and 1789", *Journal* 25 (1958): 157–64; "Extracts from the Barbadian Newspaper", *Journal* 10 (1943): 139–45; and Neville Connell, "Eighteenth-Century Furniture and Its Background in Barbados", *Journal* 26 (1959): 162–90.

Suggestions for Further Reading

For Barbadian social history during the period of slavery, see Jerome S. Handler, *The Unappropriated People: Freedmen in the Slave Society of Barbados* (Baltimore, MD: Johns Hopkins University Press, 1974); Jerome S. Handler and Frederick W. Lange, *Plantation Slavery in Barbados: An Archaeological and Historical Investigation* (Cambridge, Mass.: Harvard University Press, 1978); and Richard S. Dunn, *Sugar and Slaves: The Rise of the Planter Class in the English West Indies, 1624–1713* (Chapel Hill, NC: University of North Carolina Press, 1972).

There is a small body of literature on freedmen (free "colored" and free black) populations in the British West Indies. Aside from my *Unappropriated People*, other useful works include: Arnold A. Sio, "Race, Colour, and Miscegenation: The Free Coloured of Jamaica and Barbados", *Caribbean Studies* 16 (1976): 5–21; Sheila Duncker, "The Free Coloured and Their Fight for Civil Rights in Jamaica, 1800–1830" (MA thesis, University of London,

1960); Mavis C. Campbell, *The Dynamics of Change in a Slave Society: A Sociopolitical History of the Free Colored in Jamaica, 1800–1865* (Rutherford, NJ: Fairleigh Dickinson University Press, 1976); and Edward L. Cox, "Shadow of Freedom: Freedmen in the Slave Societies of Grenada and St Kitts, 1763–1833" (PhD diss., Johns Hopkins University, 1977).

The position of freedmen in other areas of the Caribbean is explored in essays on the French Antilles, Cuba, Haiti, and Curaçao and Surinam in David W. Cohen and Jack P. Greene, eds, *Neither Slave Nor Free: The Freedmen of African Descent in the Slave Societies of the New World* (Baltimore, MD: Johns Hopkins University Press, 1972). In their introduction to this volume, Cohen and Greene offer a useful comparative perspective on various problems relating to freedmen.

CHAPTER 10

The Economic Role of the Chinese in Jamaica
*The Grocery Retail Trade**

JACQUELINE LEVY

The research for this paper was originally undertaken during the period 1965–1966 and designed for presentation at a seminar organized by the Department of History of the University of the West Indies in January 1967. At that time the only published works which dealt in any detail with Chinese participation in the grocery trade were those of Andrew Lind and Lee Tom Yin.[1] Subsequent to the preparation and presentation of this work, nearly two decades have elapsed, and despite an initial response which seemed to indicate a significant interest in the subject, little further investigation of the issues then discussed has materialized. Howard Johnson has published an article which as its title indicates, is mainly concerned with the Anti-Chinese riots in Jamaica in 1918, but which includes as one of its objectives a "review of the economic role of the Chinese in Jamaica".[2] James Carnegie in his book has included several penetrating and relevant observations concerning the antagonism directed against the Chinese during this period, partially as a result of their success in the grocery retail trade and other affiliated business enterprises.[3]

---

*Originally published in the *Jamaican Historical Review* 15 (1986): 31–49. Reprinted by permission of the Jamaica Historical Society.

Basically, this study endeavours to explore the factors which permitted or facilitated Chinese domination of the grocery retail trade in Jamaica by the early decades of the twentieth century. This took place in the face of overt hostility by at least some segments of the host community. While these attacks were for the most part verbal – demonstrated by frequent denunciation in the press – there were several instances where physical attack was not excluded, involving sporadic outbreaks of violence, generally confined to property rather than to persons.

Another central concern of this work is to examine the accuracy of the assertion that the Chinese monopolized the grocery retail trade in Jamaica. Information, statistical as well as impressionistic, indicates that whereas the Chinese dominated or controlled the trade, this predominance never at any time constituted a technical monopoly.

In a wider context some allusions have been made to the history and socio-economic background of the Chinese in Kwangtung province, as these provide a perspective for the examination of the economic goals of the Chinese who migrated to Jamaica. In addition, some reference has been made to Chinese Philosophy, particularly as it relates to ancestral veneration and kinship obligation, as these considerations influenced the economic role of the Chinese in Jamaica – specifically in connection with the grocery retail trade.

The segmental nature of the roles of an individual in society can facilitate assimilation in one particular sphere of human activity, while at the same time, sharp cultural divergencies continue to exist in several other areas.[4] By the close of the nineteenth century there were definite indications that Chinese immigrants to Jamaica had already accomplished a significant degree of economic integration, but this was not accompanied by a similar rate of cultural assimilation into the Jamaican pattern of life and they remained a "highly visible" minority group. Henceforth, they became an increasingly important element in the entrepreneurial and commercial sectors of the community, while agricultural pursuits commanded the attention of only a small proportion of their expected representation.[5] Incursions into the ranks of the professions and participation in other non-commercial livelihood activities have been comparatively recent developments.

This marked preference for trade on the part of the Chinese who migrated to Jamaica, was in some ways an unorthodox selection by traditional Chinese standards. Many of the original immigrants were "farmers or the sons of farmers"[6] and had been recruited from village communities in Kwangtung province[7] where farming was the basic livelihood activity, in order to provide agricultural labour in Jamaica. However, Chinese participation in commercial pursuits is seen to be a natural development when considered against the background of employment opportunities in south-east China, and in conjunction with the economic role of the overseas Chinese in general. There is little doubt that local conditions also contributed to their success as traders, and this could, in fact, have been the decisive determinant in the occupational pattern which evolved in connection with Chinese migrants to Jamaica.

In many areas of south-east China, the situation appears to have been that whereas the majority of Chinese were attached to small family farms, it was quite usual for these farmers to have some craft or trade whereby they were able to supplement their uncertain agricultural incomes.[8] Also, surplus agricultural produce was often disposed of in nearby market towns,[9] and the procedures involved in such transactions must have provided the villagers with an introduction to the intricacies of commercial bargaining.

There are other socio-economic factors relating to the history of the Chinese in Jamaica which could have prepared them for their role as traders who were members of a minority immigrant community. The Chinese in Jamaica are almost exclusively Hakka.[10] The Hakka or "guest people" were originally from northern China, but over the course of sixteen centuries they had participated in several inter-regional migrations, the last of which took place during the eighteenth and nineteenth centuries and brought them into the central and lowland areas of Kwangtung province. Here they were able through frugality and hard work, to acquire a considerable amount of property, and this led to serious clashes with the native inhabitants of the province.[11]

It appears therefore, that some familiarity with the processes of trade was provided by the environment of the Chinese who migrated from south-east China to Jamaica, and that their decisive rejection of agricultural occupations in favour of retail trading may not have been as innovatory as it first appears. Firm precedents for this same combination of migration followed by occupational change had long been established in their native land. The recognition of participation in trade as economically desirable is seen to be a particularly important objective, when the motivation for Chinese migration overseas is taken into consideration. Emigration was disapproved of socially and until 1894 carried legal penalties.[12] Those who migrated did so mainly because of the expectation that a financially successful return would advance them and their families. Thus, most Chinese migrants viewed their residence abroad as a temporary arrangement to be discontinued as soon as circumstances permitted. Early immigrants to Jamaica were advised by friends and relatives in China not to acquire property in the island as this could lead to permanent residence away from their homeland.[13] In order to eradicate the stigma of having migrated in the first place, it was essential to acquire some amount of wealth. Failure to achieve this could amount to a sentence of perpetual exile.

In general, the quickest monetary return abroad could be obtained from commerce and the least from agriculture.[14] Occupational choice, however, was obviously limited by the particular circumstances in which the overseas Chinese found himself. In Jamaica, social and economic conditions made it possible for the Chinese immigrant to forsake the certain toil and uncertain remuneration of both sugar estate and independent small holding for the more congenial and potentially more lucrative occupation of retail trader.

Given an inclination towards trade combined with an unpleasant introduction to agricultural work,[15] and reinforced by the determination to accumulate money as quickly as possible, Chinese penetration into the grocery trade is, from their own point of view, a readily understandable development. Far more complex are the social and economic circumstances which made it possible for them to infiltrate this area of the island's economic life so rapidly that by 1910 it was stated by an official source that the Chinese controlled practically all the small retail trade of the country.[16]

It would appear that there are three possible explanations of this penetration into the provisioning trades on the part of Chinese immigrants to Jamaica. It is possible that they supplied services the need for which existed prior to their arrival, but which had not been satisfied hitherto;[17] that they successfully challenged and eliminated at least some of their local competitors already established in the retail trade; or that their arrival coincided with a period of significant expansion in the consumer market, upon which circumstance they capitalized with more alacrity, greater efficiency and from a position of greater advantage than did potential traders within the local community. These considerations are not, of course, mutually exclusive.

The relative merits of these hypotheses can best be measured by an examination of how the consumer market in Jamaica developed after emancipation. During slavery the bulk of the island's export and import trade had been conducted through the coastal towns of the island. The slaves, who represented a large majority of the inhabitants of the country, did not, at this time, form a consumer market, as their needs were met by the estate.[18] Important dietary supplements were provided by the ground provisions which the slaves were permitted to grow on the steep slopes of the hills or in the deep hollows which were not suitable for sugar cultivation. Surplus produce was sold in the public markets.[19]

After emancipation the situation changed considerably as the drift away from the plantations resulted in a dispersal of the peasant population. Many of the estates declined and the decrease in the volume of trade conducted by the estates was accompanied by an increase in commercial activity within those areas where towns and villages were rapidly springing into existence. Here was an expanding market for consumer goods from which the creole population seemed in an ideal position to benefit. And, in fact, retail trading was one of the avenues in which the emancipated labouring classes sought occupation. But shops were being opened not only by labourers and craftsmen, but also by merchants in the large towns who seized the opportunity to extend their interests, as well as by the managers of some sugar estates.[20] However, subsequent developments seem to indicate that the creole peasant's predominant concern was the production and marketing of traditional food crops, rather than the distribution of imported goods.

The socio-economic structure of the Jamaican peasant family facilitated this type of trading, for while the heavy cultivation was done by the males, the women did the marketing and buying, and in general supervised the various business transactions involved in the produce business.[21] These were activities for which their African heritage had provided the necessary training and experience, and which had been fostered by the slave system in Jamaica, which allowed for the allocation of provision grounds to slave families. The pattern of women as hucksters and men as cultivators remained consistent both before and after slavery and persists in modified form up to the present.[22]

The Jamaican pattern of small-farm cultivation and marketing was wedded not only historically, but functionally and psychologically as well, and it is probable that, "had it not been for the pattern of subsistence-plot cultivation under slavery, and the perpetuation of subsistence cultivation by the growth of a rural peasantry after emancipation, the Jamaican economy would have taken on a very different character".[23] These facts lead to the conclusion that though some of the ex-slaves and their descendants engaged in retail trading, the main preoccupation of this group was to establish themselves as independent peasant proprietors. "It is to the possession of provision grounds that the industrious negro turns with greatest liking."[24]

There was another class in Jamaican society, the "free coloured" group, which appeared to have the best possible opportunities for establishing themselves as the commercial sector in the post-emancipation period. For some time before emancipation the free coloured members of the society had been favourably poised to enter a wide variety of occupations and to acquire property.[25] They were also in a better position to benefit from such educational opportunities as existed locally.[26] In trade many appeared to have achieved some success in the earlier period, but subsequent developments show that they were not completely satisfied with or committed to a predominantly economic role in the society.[27] Perhaps the main reason for this was that their talents and ambitions were directed towards other achievements, particularly after the removal of civic and political disabilities in the 1830s, when they became free to engage in public life.[28]

This preoccupation with prestige occupations could have been the result of the intermediate social position of the free coloured group. In order to remove the positive restrictions on their opportunities it had been necessary to demonstrate equality, which involved the attainment of living standards equivalent to the white members of the society. The most direct way of achieving these ends was by the acquisition of advanced educational qualifications, entering the professions and through the prestige and power conferred by public service.[29]

These circumstances suggest that neither of the two main groups in Jamaican society regarded trade as the best way in which to fulfil their social and economic goals. And this was in marked contrast to the Chinese where compelling motives for purely economic success existed, and who concentrated almost exclusively on the grocery retail trade for a livelihood. In fact, it would be true to say that most of the Chinese immigrants to Jamaica, in the post-indenture period, came to the island for the express purpose of engaging in the retail trade. This almost total commitment to commercial activity is illustrated by the fact that a series of failures in various trading ventures did not deter the Chinese immigrant or suggest that he should transfer his efforts to other occupational fields.[30]

In this connection it is relevant to note that the other main ethnic group introduced into the island as indentured labourers also achieved a limited success as shopkeepers, and that the incursions of the Indians preceded those of the Chinese. As early as 1883, a significant number of Indians had begun to engage in shopkeeping. During that year 56 time-expired Indian immigrants were occupied as shopkeepers.[31] By 1910, their numbers had increased considerably as 359 Trade Licences were granted to them as well as 103 Spirit Licences.[32] During the next two decades the numerical position of the Indian retailers remained relatively static.

The position was that while shopkeeping attracted some Indians, this was not, as was the case with the Chinese, virtually the only form of livelihood activity that commanded their attention. The system whereby time-expired Indian immigrants might be granted a small freehold proprietorship, encouraged many to continue to engage in agriculture. The total acreage of land held by Indian immigrants increased steadily during the early decades of the twentieth century.[33] The contracts offered to the Chinese indentured immigrants who had arrived in 1884 did not contain any similar incentives in the form of grants of land.[34]

Both creole and Indian shopkeepers were engaged in the retail trade when the alleged "Chinese Invasion" took place. Their situation was such that it offered, at any rate superficially, good opportunities for extended participation. The subsequent emergence of the Chinese as the dominant group engaged in this occupation, cannot therefore be simply explained by saying that they fulfilled certain needs which existed in the society, but for which there had been no previous provision. What may be noticed, however, is that such consumer outlets as did exist in the penultimate decade of the nineteenth century probably did not exploit the entire potential of the existing market.

For half a century after emancipation, the great majority of the island's population depended principally on locally produced provisions for their subsistence. "Imported foods are not the staple foods of the labouring population, nor are they likely to become so", was the opinion expressed by the Collector of Taxes in 1883.[35] The main articles of foodstuffs imported into Jamaica during the period 1879–1884 were breadstuffs, rice, saltfish and saltmeat. Breadstuffs included flour and cornmeal which were to some extent consumed by the peasant population in the towns and villages, but in some country districts, bread was rarely if ever seen, and "as a general article of food may be regarded rather as a luxury than as a necessity".[36] It was also stated that "the island as regards foodstuffs is virtually independent of foreign supplies".[37]

These comments suggest that in the 1880s it was the opinion, at least in some official circles, and the relevant statistics support this conclusion, that a large consumer market for imported foodstuffs did not exist among the labouring population. However, it could have been that a market did exist, but that there was at the time no organized system of introducing potential customers to imported goods and of facilitating the distribution of such items.

At this same period it was observed "that competition, in Kingston at least, especially among the Jews, was very keen" and also that "the monopoly of supply has been taken out of the hands of a few large houses, and the increased number of importing firms consequent on the growth of the steamer traffic must induce keener competition and so have the effect of reducing prices to the retailer".[38] By the turn of the century internal trade was characterized by a noticeable increase in the number of retail shops, accompanied by the failure on the part of the big merchants to retain control of import trade. The smallest traders who at one time had made their purchases from the local merchants and storekeepers realized that it was to their advantage to import on their own account. Vociferous protests from the merchants could not prevent the dispersal of the trade among a larger number.[39]

Thus the decade and a half between 1885 and 1900 was a period of general expansion for most sectors of the commercial classes. There was an overall increase in the number of traders from 252 in 1883 to 591 in 1897. Between 1882 and 1893 the increase was visible in all categories listed, but the interval between 1893 and 1897 saw a decrease in the number of merchants, storekeepers and 1st class retailers, while the categories 2nd class retailer and, in particular, 3rd class retailer, show a very definite increase.[40]

It has not been possible to determine how many of the small retail traders were Chinese, but it is significant that their incursions into the grocery trade coincided in point of time with a period of accelerated activity in this field. This increase in the number of retail traders was accompanied by the breaking down of merchant control over the import trade. The closing years of the nineteenth century were therefore a particularly opportune period for investment in the provisioning trades.

Chinese participation in the grocery retail trade in Jamaica is believed by older members of their community to have dated back to the post-1854 period,[41] but there is no official confirmation of this. It is not until the final decade of the nineteenth century that official publications begin to indicate the extent of Chinese participation in the island's trade by means of lists of applicants for Spirit Licences during the year 1897. It is possible to identify these because, in addition to the characteristic form of many Chinese family names, the official practice was to indicate the members of this particular ethnic group by inserting the term "Chinaman" after their names. Indians were identified by means of the designation "cooly" similarly appended.[42]

By 1908 official interest in the commercial activities of the Chinese had become more positive. This manifested itself in an attempt on the part of government officials to ascertain, through the compilation of relevant statistics, the extent to which this immigrant group had supplanted other ethic groups engaged in the retail trade of the island. The following table was produced by the Collector General's Department.[43]

Chinamen	834 or 13.2 per cent
Coolies	444 or 7.0 per cent
Syrians	88 or 1.4 per cent
All Others	4,933 or 78.4 per cent

An examination of these figures discloses that while the Chinese had by 1908 accomplished a considerable degree of penetration into the retail trade of the island, and had in fact outstripped the Indians in this respect, their participation could not in any real sense be said to constitute a "monopoly". The main significance of this report is to be adduced by comparison with certain demographic figures. In 1911, the Chinese in Jamaica numbered 2,111, and constituted 0.3 per cent of the total population.[44] This means that their participation in the retail trade was extremely high in proportion to their total numerical strength within the population, and that in fact, more than one out of every three Chinese persons in the island was engaged in the retail trade. Perhaps it was not entirely true to assume that one Chinese person meant one grocery shop, but the indications are that it was reasonable to equate one Chinese household with one grocery shop.

By 1910 the general impression had been created that the Chinese were a serious threat to creole shopkeepers. Public resentment was soon expressed in the press: "Can the authorities do nothing to let Jamaicans feel that Jamaica is still their home, and strangers will not be allowed to elbow them out of what is theirs by right?"⁴⁵ The indications were that there would be widespread resistance to the continuation of unrestricted Chinese immigration into the island. By March 1925, the number of Trade Licences held by the Chinese had increased to 1,805 or 28.2 per cent of the total number of such licences issued during the previous financial year.⁴⁶ The Chinese population had increased to approximately 3,696 persons.⁴⁷ This means that there had been an increase of roughly 75.1 per cent in the Chinese population since 1911 and that this had been accompanied by an increase of about 116.0 per cent in the number of trade licences granted to Chinese residents. The position then, was that nearly one out of every two persons belonging to the Chinese ethnic group was engaged in the grocery retail trade.

This was the period when Chinese participation in the retail trade reached its zenith, in relation to the total numerical strength of the group within the population. It is little wonder then that by the 1930s the terms "Chinese" and "shopkeeper" became synonymous in local thought. One observer commented in the press that, "today, throughout the entire length of Jamaica, we find one grocer who is an Irishman, one an Englishman, and perhaps half a dozen native shopkeepers, while there are as many 'Chinese shops' in the island as there are Chinese men".⁴⁸

Despite this sort of pronouncement, the extent of Chinese activity in the grocery retail trade still could not, in the generally accepted sense, be said to constitute a monopoly. The total number of Trade Licences issued during the year ending 31 March 1925 was 6,405.⁴⁹ Since the Chinese accounted for only 1,805 of these, the remainder must have been issued to traders belonging to other ethnic groups. In fact, by the middle of the ensuing decade the number of Chinese residents engaged in the grocery trade had actually decreased,⁵⁰ although it is apparent that the Chinese population had continued to increase, since the 1943 Census classification shows 12,394 persons of pure Chinese and partial Chinese descent resident in the island.⁵¹

The total number of licences issued for the financial year ending 31 March 1936 was 2,158 Spirit Licences and 9,265 Trade Licences.⁵² The number of Chinese engaged in these occupations were 1,543 who were holders of Dry Goods and Grocery Retail Licences, while the number holding Spirit Licences were 865.⁵³ Therefore the large majority of such licensees were non-Chinese. During the mid-1950s only one-eighth of the business licences issued were held by Chinese proprietors. A survey undertaken by the *Daily Gleaner* during the latter part of 1962 showed that many shops were operated by creole proprietors and not persons of Chinese descent.[54]

Despite the contrary indications provided by both official and impressionistic sources, popular belief that the Chinese had ousted all other ethnic groups from any significant role in the provisioning trades had persisted until the mid-1960s. But disturbances in the city during September 1965 had the effect of revealing that the Chinese were not the only group engaged as proprietors of grocery shops in the parish of St Andrew, although this is the parish with the heaviest concentration of Chinese residents.[55] "Out of the city close-down came the revelation that in some rural St Andrew villages there are no Chinese shops. All such retail provision shops are operated by Jamaicans of local origin, either because Chinese have shunned these areas or that they are kept out."[56]

This divergence between the facts as revealed by official data as well as public observation, and the persistent local myth regarding Chinese monopoly of the grocery retail trade, does not actually involve two irreconcilable positions. A probable explanation is that the so-called monopoly of the grocery trade in Jamaica by the Chinese, is constituted not so much in the proprietorship of the numerical majority of such businesses in the island, but rather in the volume of trade enjoyed by the Chinese shopkeepers in comparison with retailers belonging to other ethnic groups. There is a definite tendency for Chinese pre-eminence in the trade to be particularly apparent in the urban and suburban areas, where their business activities are more easily observed by a larger number of people, and where trading is far more lucrative than in the remote and thinly populated village communities where many creole traders operate their retail shops. It is probable for this reason that the impression has been created that the majority of persons engaged in the grocery retail trade are Chinese.

But even when these explanations are made, and the possibility of a true monopoly is discarded, the predominance of the Chinese in the grocery retail trade remains, particularly in the more profitable areas of operation. Consequently, the issue that becomes most relevant to the analysis is not so much which circumstances enabled the Chinese traders to supersede the creole and Indian retailers "throughout the length and breadth of the island", but rather what factors made it possible for them to capture the consumer market in those areas where there was the greatest volume of trade and thus where the operation of a grocery retail shop would prove economically beneficial.

As has already been observed, large numbers of the creole population were committed to the ownership of small freeholds and to the production and marketing of ground provisions and other crops. This meant that where they sought to combine this with shopkeeping, they were inhibited in their choice of location. In any event, their mobility was curtailed by domestic ties. The Chinese immigrant, with no local commitments or prestige goals, was free to move about in search of a profitable "spot" and frequently did so.

Like the creole traders,[57] the Chinese did not make their initial ventures into the provisioning trades from a position of economic advantage. The first shops operated by them were extremely humble concerns and " . . . it is hard to visualize the heart-rending struggles that the first settlers had to endure. They worked long, hard hours, clothed themselves in flour-bag suits" and "fed themselves on cod fish fritters".[58] One Chinese trader described his position thus, "I came here with empty fists."[59]

Despite the initial shortage of capital on the part of Chinese immigrants, the way in which the migration was unofficially organized facilitated a modest amount of capital accumulation. Male immigrants often arrived alone and were consequently relieved of the economic and social responsibilities which dependent families would have imposed. In these circumstances, it was possible for the Chinese immigrant to Jamaica to work for a number of years, accumulate some savings and then from a position of relative economic stability arrange for the establishment of a shop and then for the importation of other members of his family. Also, the close-knit character of the minority immigrant community involving as it did relationships within the same agnatic groups, provided opportunities for obtaining credit. In fact, borrowed capital could have played an important part in the setting up of new businesses.

On the other hand, creole entrepreneurs or would-be entrepreneurs were limited in their attempts to accumulate capital by the demands of domestic commitments, and the restrictions imposed by social conventions. As Lind observes, "the black or coloured populations of Jamaica were handicapped as tradesmen by the personal claims of relatives and friends while the immigrant Chinese (and Syrians) found in trade the one field of economic endeavour in which their alienism was an asset rather than a liability".[60]

Nor did the Chinese in Jamaica enter into economic competition from a socially advantageous position similar to that which seems to have been enjoyed by the Portuguese traders in British Guiana.[61] Press references to the Chinese during the early decades of the twentieth century were nearly always characterized by derogatory terminology. The most widely used references were "celestial" and "John Chinaman", while the immigration itself was alluded to as the "Chinese Invasion", and the members of the Chinese community were regarded as constituting the "Yellow Peril".[62] Conflict was involved in the relations between the Chinese and most other sections of the Jamaican society and although they found some initial support in British government's representative,[63] this attitude was later modified.

But in order to offset this, the Chinese possessed the special advantage which is common to minority groups who make their way into a society which is undergoing a process of modernization and change. In such a situation an immigrant group may capitalize on the need for middlemen to funnel imported consumer goods through wholesale and retail outlets to the mass of the population. This is so because the social goals of the resident groups continue to be realized within the framework of the traditional class and occupational structure.[64]

In addition, the traditional structure of Chinese family life and the discipline and responsibilities imposed thereby upon individual members of the community, constituted an invaluable business asset. According to Confucian concepts the interest of the family is given priority over the interest of its individual members. When a business was founded, all members of the family were under obligation to expend labour in it, without the payment of a formal wage. It was labour for subsistence, but had the advantage of keeping overhead expenditure low and eliminating labour problems. Thus a substantial portion of what appeared to be profit in a family business is really value for labour from all members of the family. The importance of the Chinese family structure to the economic success of the small grocery store has been clearly defined by one member of the community in the following terms: "The reason for the apparent discrimination is not racial but economic, because these small concerns are profitable only when operated on a family basis. These concerns pay no salaries and money is withdrawn only for the necessities of operation and living expenses. Consequently, the meagre profits accumulate and the capital grows until it is sufficiently large to provide a good standard of living for the operators."[65]

In any discussion of the success of the Chinese retailer in Jamaica the part played by superior business acumen is important. There have been two schools of thought on this subject, the one attributing great credit to the Chinese shopkeepers, who "give their customers better service, including free delivery and buying on credit", and the other attributing Chinese prosperity to sharp and even illegal business practices.

The assertion that the Chinese provide better service to their customers is one which has received considerable support. One member of the Jamaican purchasing public, basing his observations on the situation in the 1920s, narrated an anecdote to illustrate the attitude of the Chinese in connection with the extending of credit facilities to customers. This was based on personal experience. When he entered a particular shop and "fruitlessly searched" his pockets for money, the young Chinaman in charge immediately offered credit without this being solicited. "I will trust you if you have no money." This, despite the fact that he was not even familiar with the name of the would-be customer, merely having observed his presence in the shop on a number of occasions.[66]

The same writer continued to state, "I should not have been his only debtor. He had many customers in the neighbourhood – any Chinaman has – and these drift into the habit of taking goods from him and paying at the end of the week or month."[67]

This willingness to extend credit has persisted until the contemporary period. In the survey undertaken by the *Daily Gleaner* in 1962 to determine the extent to which the grocery shop was being threatened by the modern self-service supermarket, and to examine the reasons for the relative positions of each, it emerged quite clearly that one of the main factors which contributed to the continued popularity of the grocery shop was the willingness of the proprietors to extend credit to their customers, while the supermarkets did not provide this facility.[68] The extension of credit was in the past, and continues to be, an important way in which the Chinese grocer develops a steady and even a dependent clientele.

Available evidence also suggests that it was the Chinese grocer who popularized the notion of selling the smallest quantities of goods for correspondingly small denominations of coin. In informal evidence presented before the 1883 Commission of Enquiry, it was remarked that restrictions had been imposed on trade by too great a reliance on the "quattie". "A bad effect is derived from the idea that the 'quattie' is the only coin. A man may have stuff worth 3½d which he must sell for 4½d because to the negro there is nothing between 3d and 4½d."[69] As a corollary to this, goods worth less than 1½d could not become the subject of a trading transaction.

By the 1920s the farthing had become an important medium of exchange and at least one observer attributed its popularity to the Chinese traders: "A farthing was once a coin not held in any regard. The ordinary unit of purchase was 1½d (quattie) some 40 years ago, and there were silver coins of this denomination in common use. John made the farthing of importance."[70]

Another comment made in the 1940s also makes reference to the willingness of the Chinese to sell very small quantities of goods. They sell "believe it or not, half a packet of cigarettes, and ha'penny's saltfish, and a gill's (¾d) worth of butter". Pennies really contained four farthings and so a farthing's worth of goods could be bought. Wrapping paper was, without asking, forthcoming for putting up even small and inexpensive purchases.

A very different point of view was held by those who sought to explain Chinese success in terms of unfair business practices. Charges of duplicity, craftiness, unfair competition; of depressing the plane of living, gambling and incorrect weights and measures were all levelled against the "Celestials". A comprehensive description of the Chinese businessman as conceived of by those sections of the Jamaican society who perceived him to be a threat has been included in Howard Johnson's article.[71] One of the most frequent allegations was that the Chinese prostituted the bankruptcy laws in order to avoid paying their creditors.[72]

There was a disproportionate number of Chinese traders involved in bankruptcy proceedings during the decade 1925–1935.[73] With this, members of the Chinese community are ready to concur.[74] However, it is difficult to decide whether this indicates deliberate manipulation of the law for purposes of economic advantage, or whether they were the result of circumstances beyond the control of the particular persons affected. In any event, it is difficult to apply any general conclusion to accusations of this nature, given the premise that a man is innocent until he is proven guilty.

One possible explanation for the excessively high percentage of Chinese bankruptcies during the period 1925–1929, and the diminution which marked the early 1930s could be the pattern of Chinese migration into Jamaica, as it developed during the decade 1925–1935. During the late 1920s the highest annual rate of Chinese migration into the island occurred.[75] It was at this period also that immigrant ships arrived bearing comparatively large numbers of Chinese.[76] These newcomers had not all been sponsored by relatives, and so for some there was no immediate introduction into an established household, although some assistance was usually given by the Chinese Benevolent Association.[77] If we use the number of applications for retail licences as a guide it would appear that many of the new arrivals sought to enter into the retail trade of the island. It is probable that expansion in this field was taking place too rapidly, and that a market saturation point had been reached. There are indications of serious competition within the Chinese community itself.[78] After 1930 the annual Chinese immigration to Jamaica fell dramatically, the number of applications for retail licences decreased, and the amount of Chinese bankruptcies declined. It is likely that these circumstances were interrelated.

However, it must be noted that there were individual cases where convictions were secured in the courts. For example, "a Chinese shopkeeper doing business at Montego Bay, will spend the next three months in jail for not keeping proper books of accounts as required by law. The debtor went into bankruptcy a short time ago, and it is said that his liabilities amounted to an enormous sum. The only books that were produced were some small pass books written in Chinese."[79] Some of these newspaper accounts suggest that unfamiliarity with Western law and custom could have been the cause of the Chinaman's predicament, but a converse argument could just as readily be advanced.

Arson was another legal offense of which the Chinese were frequently accused in the early 1920s.[80] This was said to have reached "epidemic" proportions by 1923. But in the matter of the Chinese conspiring to burn their own business places for profit, those accused were acquitted and since public opinion was once again sharply divided on the "burning" question it is not possible to advance any argument that would be anything but conjecture.

The Chinese had numerous charges levelled at them, some involving serious allegations and others distinctly frivolous. The early 1930s saw the formation of the Native Defender Committee under the leadership of Leonard Wilson.[81] This added a new perspective to the hostility which had hitherto been felt towards the "Celestials" and eventually resulted in the official recognition of a Chinese "problem". A Government Committee was subsequently appointed to enquire into the whole question of Chinese immigration and into the effects that their presence was having on the community. The Immigration Laws were eventually revised but the Chinese in Jamaica continued to maintain their position of dominance in the grocery retail trade. This dominance, although it never acquired the proportions of a monopoly, in the sense of exclusive control of the grocery retail trade, remained highly visible and therefore susceptible to attack.

Chinese predominance in the grocery retail trade of Jamaica was the result of several ponderables in juxtaposition at a particular point in time. Some of the factors were positive, while others were negative – default, disinterest and lack of adequate motivation. Existing economic circumstances were an important determinant. Local conditions contributed much to the success of the Chinese in the grocery retail trade, as their arrival coincided with a period of expanding market forces and thus of increased opportunities in trade. There was no group in the host society specifically committed to this type of economic endeavour, especially if this meant that their predetermined goals and life style would be disrupted.

As a minority trading group, the Chinese capitalized on the market forces in existence when they arrived in Jamaica. They had migrated to this country with the express design of improving their economic circumstances; and when it became apparent, soon after their arrival in the island as agricultural labourers, that this occupation would not fulfil their expectations, they deserted the field for the shops. This compelling urge to succeed gave them a certain psychological advantage over their creole competitors. In these endeavours they were assisted by the traditional structure of Chinese family life, based on a philosophy of group survival. In the post-indenture period the immigration was unofficially organized in such a way as to facilitate capital accumulation and minimize expenditure. Social pressures were slight.

On the other hand, their creole and Indian counterparts were traditionally attached to agricultural pursuits and did not approach the grocery retail trade with the same single-mindedness that characterized the Chinese determination to achieve economic independence. They were also handicapped by family ties and social conventions, as well as by lack of capital within a system that did not assist in capital accumulation.

Commitment, common goals and, to be fair, competence, contributed much to the Chinese dominance of the grocery retail trade; while diversity of interest, demands on limited resources, and a certain lack of sophistication in dealing with their clientele had an adverse effect on creole endeavours. Customers, who were their social and cultural peers, were probably not regarded by the proprietors of creole-operated shops as a group to be courted, and furthermore, to be courted by such small favours as selling them goods "for a farthing less".

But however the facts be interpreted, and whatever the possibilities that may be adduced from them, there is one essential conclusion concerning which there can be no controversy. The Chinese grocery retail store or "Chiney shop" became an integral part of Jamaican life, and as such a Jamaican institution.

Notes

1. Andrew Lind, "Adjustment Patterns among the Jamaican Chinese", *Social and Economic Studies* 7 (1958): 144–64. This article, although relatively brief, remains an important and comprehensive study of the cultural and economic conflicts that developed between the Chinese and the creole population of Jamaica. Its time span extends from the indenture period to more recent manifestations of anti-Chinese sentiment in the early twentieth century. Lee Tom Yin, *The Chinese in Jamaica* (Kingston: Chung San News, 1963). This publication, written partly in Chinese and partly in English, represents the first and only effort to record a comprehensive history of the Chinese in Jamaica. Mr Lee, in addition to his scholarship, assisted in this research by providing introductions to many of the older Chinese immigrants in Jamaica, and by extending unfailing courtesy and encouragement to the author of this paper.
2. Howard Johnson, "The Anti-Chinese Riots of 1918 in Jamaica", *Caribbean Quarterly* 28 (1982): 19–32.
3. James Carnegie, *Some Aspects of Jamaica's Politics 1918–1938* (Kingston: Institute of Jamaica, 1973).
4. G.H. Weightman, "The Chinese in the Philippines" (PhD thesis, Cornell University, 1960), introduction.
5. *Eighth Census of Jamaica* (1943), 179–82.
6. Lee, *Chinese in Jamaica*, 55.
7. Ship's Papers, SS *Prinz Alexander*, Jamaica Archives, File 1B/9/Ref. 33.
8. Richard Coughlin, *Double Identity: The Chinese in Modern Thailand* (Hong Kong: Hong Kong University Press, 1960), 21.

9. Hsiao-Jung-Ch'uan, *Rural China: Imperial Control in the Nineteenth Century* (Seattle: University of Washington Press, 1960), 11.
10. Interviews with twenty-five members of the Chinese community. Interview with the editor of the *Chinese Public News*. Interview with Father Cormac Shannahan, Passionist priest resident in south China for many years and then a parish priest in western Kingston. The Hakka people may be identified by the "speech-group" to which they belong. All Chinese write the same script, but the differences in the spoken language are such that many dialects are mutually incomprehensible. Scientifically there appears to be no label suitable for these entities other than "speech-group" or "dialect-group". See Maurice Freedman, *Chinese Family and Marriage in Singapore* (London: HMSO, 1957), 12.
11. Cecil Clementi, *The Chinese in British Guiana* (Georgetown: Argosy Co., 1915), 14.
12. Harley McNair, *The Chinese Abroad, Their Position and Protection: A Study in International Law and Relations* (Shanghai: Commercial Press, 1924), 2.
13. Interviews.
14. Weightman, "Chinese in the Philippines", chapter 3.
15. Jacqueline Levy, "Chinese Indentured Immigration to Jamaica during the Latter Part of the Nineteenth Century" (paper presented at the conference of the Association of Caribbean Historians, Jamaica, 1972).
16. Annual General Report, Protector of Immigrants, 1910–1911, Departmental Reports, 162.
17. Johnson, "Anti-Chinese Riots", 23.
18. Douglas Hall, *Free Jamaica, 1838–1865* (New Haven: Yale University Press, 1959), 207.
19. Amy K. Lopez, "Land and Labour to 1900", *Jamaican Historical Review* 1 (1948): 290.
20. Hall, *Free Jamaica*, 219.
21. Lord [Sydney] Olivier, *Jamaica: The Blessed Isle* (London: Faber and Faber, 1936), 158–59.
22. Sidney W. Mintz, "The Jamaican Internal Marketing Pattern: Some Notes and Hypotheses", *Social and Economic Studies* 4 (1955): 96–99.
23. Ibid., 99.
24. *Jamaica Gazette*, 1884, supplement, 152.
25. C.H. Wesley, "The Emancipation of the Free Coloured Population in the British Empire", *Journal of Negro History* 19 (1934): 157–70.
26. Shirley Gordon, *A Century of West Indian Education* (London: Longmans, 1963), 13, 46.
27. Gisela Eisner, *Jamaica, 1830–1930* (Manchester: Manchester University Press, 1961), 314–15.
28. Clinton V. Black, *The Story of Jamaica* (London: Collins, 1965), 166–67.
29. Eisner, *Jamaica*, 315.

30. Interviews. One Chinese shopkeeper, who subsequently became very prosperous, explained that the reason he had removed his business so frequently was that he was in search of a good "spot". When one location did not offer good opportunities in the retail trade he changed the location, but not his occupation.
31. Annual Report, Protector of Immigrants, 1883.
32. Annual Report, Protector of Immigrants, 1910–1911.
33. Jamaica, Annual General Reports with Departmental Reports, 1911–12.
34. Immigrant's contract, Ship's Papers, SS *Prinz Alexander*.
35. Annual General Report, Collector of Taxes, *Jamaica Gazette*, 1884, supplement, 168.
36. Ibid.
37. Ibid.
38. Evidence of Mr Marescaux, Manager, Colonial Bank, before Royal Commission, *Jamaica Gazette*, 1883, supplement.
39. Annual Report, Collector of Taxes, 1897.
40. Ibid.
41. Lee, *Chinese in Jamaica*.
42. *Jamaica Gazette*, 1897.
43. Annual General Report, Collector General, year ending 31 March 1908.
44. *Eighth Census*, table 48, 93.
45. *Daily Gleaner*, 23 May 1913.
46. *Legislative Council, Jamaica, Minutes*, 18 March 1925; Annual General Report on Customs and Revenue, year ending 31 March 1925.
47. *Eighth Census*, 93.
48. *Daily Gleaner*, 9 September 1932 (Father Leo Butler).
49. Annual General Report, Customs and Revenue, year ending 31 March 1925.
50. Legislative Council, Jamaica, Minutes, 1935, Appendix 58.
51. *Eighth Census*, table 48, 93.
52. Annual Report, Customs and Internal Revenue, year ending 31 March 1936.
53. Legislative Council, Jamaica, Minutes, 1935, Appendix 58.
54. *Daily Gleaner*, December 1962 and January 1963 (consecutive Thursdays).
55. O.C. Francis, *The People of Modern Jamaica* (Kingston: Department of Statistics, 1963).
56. *The Star* (Kingston), 23 September 1965.
57. For an in-depth analysis of the difficulties encountered by post-emancipation retail traders, see Hall, *Free Jamaica*, 222–23.
58. For emphasis on hardships suffered by early immigrants to Jamaica, see Lee, *Chinese in Jamaica*.
59. Interview. "I came here with empty fists", means of course, "I came here without any money."
60. Lind, "Adjustment Patterns", 154.

61. K.O. Laurence, The Establishment of the Portuguese Community in British Guiana", *Jamaican Historical Review* 5 (1965): 50–74.
62. *Planter's Punch* (Kingston), 1, no. 4 (1923): 9.
63. Johnson, "Anti-Chinese Riots", 22.
64. Coughlin, *Double Identity*, 12.
65. *Star*, 9 August 1963, 13.
66. "John Chinaman", *Planter's Punch* (1927): 9.
67. Ibid.
68. *Daily Gleaner*, December 1962 and January 1963 (consecutive Thursdays).
69. Informal evidence to Commission of Enquiry, 1883, *Jamaica Gazette*, 1884, supplement, 230.
70. *Planter's Punch* (1927): 9.
71. Johnson, "Anti-Chinese Riots", 24.
72. Legislative Council, Proceedings, 6 December 1938.
73. Annual Departmental Reports, 1925–35.
74. Lee, *Chinese in Jamaica*, 45.
75. Report, Committee to Enquire into the Question of Alien Immigration, Legislative Council, Minutes, 1931, Appendix 16, section 10.
76. Ibid., section 8.
77. Legislative Council debates on alien immigration, in *Daily Gleaner*, 31 November 1930.
78. *Daily Gleaner*, 20 November 1930, editorial.
79. *Daily Gleaner*, 4 July 1923.
80. *Daily Gleaner*, 15 January 1923.
81. Carnegie, *Some Aspects of Jamaica's Politics*, 120.

CHAPTER 11

The Rise of Black Businesses in Barbados, 1900–1966*

HENDERSON CARTER

In 1900, one of the immediate scenes to salute the visitor to Barbados was the bustling trade of Bridgetown's black hucksters and hawkers.[1] For the first half of the twentieth century, however, such a scene only conveyed a partial view of the black business experience. Oral accounts indicate that blacks established hotels, manufacturing establishments, retail stores, pharmacies and transport companies, rivalling some of the white-owned businesses. But little is known of the circumstances that led these entrepreneurs to establish enterprises. What motivated them to enter business? Where did they obtain their capital and what alliances did they make to secure a solid footing for their enterprises? Using newspaper articles, commission reports and interviews with the entrepreneurs themselves or family members, this article attempts to analyse the reasons for their participation in business in the period 1900 to about 1966, when the island acquired independence from Britain. In doing this, these business triumphs are located within the social, economic and political life of the country, which allows for a brief discussion of the reasons that many black businesses did not survive to the second generation.

Two main arguments emerge in the discussion of the rise of black businesses. First, blacks were enterprising entrepreneurs, who in the face of severe

---

*Extracted from *Business in Bim: A Business History of Barbados 1900–2000* (Kingston: Ian Randle, 2008).

obstacles, and the lack of government support, sought to create viable enterprises in a range of business sectors. It is also noteworthy that individual entrepreneurs were involved in more than one sector of the economy, giving a measure of diversity to their operations. Second, the black entrepreneurs who graced the business stage were, to some extent, circumscribed by the planter/merchant elite's domination of the economy, which, along with other factors, challenged the longevity of their businesses.

Any discussion therefore on the rise of black entrepreneurs in Barbados must invariably begin with a brief survey of the socio-economic and political conditions in the first half of the twentieth century. From an economic perspective, the Barbadian business scene was dominated by two sectors: the plantation economy and the merchant trade. In 1930, the plantation economy, based on heavy manual labour producing sugar, molasses and rum for export, had been in existence for nearly three hundred years. In the first half of the twentieth century sugar was still king, controlling most of the arable land and employing the majority of Barbadian workers. At the same time, approximately forty thousand Barbadians remained unemployed because of the economy's inability to provide gainful opportunities.

Moreover, the plantation economy produced the planter elite, who by their ownership of land and racial background dominated the local institutions such as parliament, the judiciary and the vestry. This political power allowed local whites to pass legislation to create a system of tenancy and continue a regime of child labour, which limited business opportunities for blacks. Their control of both land and labour were hindrances to aspiring black entrepreneurs who wished to establish enterprises.

The second sector, the merchant establishment, had for a long time played second fiddle to the sugar planters, but they emerged as a force to be reckoned with in the middle decades of the nineteenth century when the planters were affected by falling sugar prices. The merchants exported the planters' produce and imported foreign goods, not only to support the plantation economy but the entire population. In so doing, they controlled prices of commodities, leading to the charge of price fixing in the 1920s and 1930s.[2] As leading importers and representatives of British and US manufacturers, the Barbadian commission merchants sold goods on credit to provisions merchants (many of them black) and, in so doing, controlled the growth and development of these provision establishments.

When planters and merchants formed combinations in 1917 and 1920, respectively, emerging black businesses had a difficult task competing with these large conglomerates.³ Indeed, planter-merchant control over key aspects of the economy continued throughout much of the twentieth century, attracting investigations by sociologists and historians. For instance, Christine Barrow and J.E. Greene, in their analysis of the small business sector in the 1970s, have singled out inter-marriage and interlocking directorships as factors responsible for the continuation of the planter-merchant establishment.⁴ Hilary Beckles, also alluding to the interlocking directorships, places emphasis on the power and influence wielded by the large corporations such as the Barbados Mutual Life Assurance Society and Barbados Shipping and Trading. Indeed, there is a school of thought which suggests that the influence of these conglomerates played a critical role in retarding the development of black-run establishments.⁵

However, the evidence suggests that all blacks did not resign themselves to be workers or supervisors in white-owned firms. Rather, they sought to establish themselves in a variety of business sectors, including those areas thought to be the special preserve of whites. As they launched themselves on to the business landscape, they explored new areas in the economy, received help from both whites and other blacks, relied on family support and used strong overseas connections to "kick-start" their enterprises.

In the first half of the twentieth century, the majority of the black entrepreneurs exploited new niche areas in the slowly expanding economy. One of the popular areas occupied by blacks was the transport sector. This became possible by the cessation of the tramway and train service in 1925 and 1937, respectively. With the disappearance of these modes of transport, some black entrepreneurs, following the lead of a few whites, used savings acquired as artisans to buy buses and established companies to fill the void. In 1937 six black entrepreneurs owned omnibus companies in Barbados and by 1953 the number had risen to fourteen. Together they had 162 omnibuses on Barbadian roads.⁶

Before 1955, they filled most of the Barbadian routes, transporting commuters from all parts of the country to Bridgetown. They also ran a late-night theatre service, as well as a Sunday service. Between 1930 and 1955 these buses were the main mode of transport used by Barbadians for excursions. However, black control over this part of the transport industry came to an end in 1955 when government acquired all but two of the private concessions, thereby expanding the government-run Transport Board. Even so, one noted black entrepreneur, Mrs Erma Rock, kept her Rocklyn Transport Company afloat, servicing the northern parishes of St Joseph and St Andrew well into the 1970s. In Mrs Rock's case, ownership of a bus company allowed her to expand into the ownership of three sugar plantations: Seniors, Cambridge and Parks. She also operated a limestone quarry, a canteen at Belleplaine and was the joint owner of Hinkson Funeral Home.[7] This business diversity, also seen in other black-run businesses, points to the quest for expansion and indicates that blacks made intelligent decisions to sustain their enterprises.

Mrs Rock was only one of the black entrepreneurs to enter the lucrative funeral business. This was an area of economic activity dominated by white-owned establishments up until the 1950s. However, Harold A. Tudor, a black entrepreneur, started a funeral business in 1896, making his business the oldest black-run establishment currently operating in Barbados. In the late 1940s and 1950s, he was joined by companies such as Clyde B. Jones Funeral Home, and Downes and Wilson Funeral Home. Black entrepreneurs established such enterprises to meet a growing need for deceased persons of the lower classes to have what Barbadians called "a decent turn-out". Indeed, Barbadians were now demanding a hearse and not a donkey cart to transport the deceased, and a finely finished coffin, rather than a rough wooden box. The funeral directors, many of them black, understood this need and worked hard to satisfy it.

Other new areas in the expanding economy, particularly after 1945, were the hotel business and light manufacturing. Barbadians had always welcomed visitors, and blacks such as Rachel Pringle had established hotels during the slavery period. But with the advent of commercial air travel to Barbados in 1938 and jet travel in the 1950s, the number of visitors to the island increased rapidly. However, the hotel and guest house stock did not increase proportionately.[8] This burgeoning tourism created opportunities for business, which blacks and whites exploited. In 1945, when many blacks were setting up provision stores in Roebuck Street, a black entrepreneur, William Maxwell, bought a fifteen-room hotel in Bathsheba, St Joseph, which he called Atlantis. He would have felt that, with the war at an end, visitors would soon vacation in large numbers. He ran the hotel until 1969, when his daughter, Enid Maxwell, took over the helm.

Another entrepreneur, N.E. Wilson, who had built a name for himself as a leading Bridgetown retailer, also exploited the opportunity to diversify into tourism when he bought a fifty-room property at Fontabelle, St Michael, in 1945. While his sojourn in this area was short-lived (his property was gutted by fire in 1948), it can be argued that black entrepreneurs were mindful of the emerging opportunities for business activity, as evidenced by the many more who built or acquired guest houses or small hotels in the 1960s and 1970s.

Even before manufacturing took off in the 1950s in Barbados, black entrepreneurs had ventured into this area. In 1937, James Roberts started a soap manufacturing plant in his backyard employing five persons with the intention of supplying soap to Barbadians. The venture was a success, leading to the establishment of a larger entity called Roberts Manufacturing Company. Although Roberts sold his shares in the company to a white entrepreneur, K.R. Hunte, he saw new business opportunities and was willing to take the risk.

James A. Martineau was another black businessman to exploit the opportunities offered in manufacturing, creating a soft drink company just outside Bridgetown in 1920. For over thirty years his products enjoyed pride of place in the Barbadian marketplace, until lack of succession and failure to innovate caused the demise of his company.

The need to supply concrete bricks for home construction was partly met by another black entrepreneur, Keith Rayside, who commenced block construction in the 1940s. At the same time, the black craftsman Lionel E. Daniel started a small woodwork operation at Culloden Road, St Michael, with the intention of supplying quality furniture to home owners. These early manufacturers launched into business even before the Barbados industrialization plan, Operation Beehive, was formally launched in 1951. Also significant is that with government not yet wholly supportive of these early industrial efforts, the entrepreneurs were required to find the support wherever they could.

Interestingly, blacks made strategic alliances with whites who had already established themselves. This is an important finding, because the impression is usually given that the domination of the whites did not offer much hope to black entrepreneurs and that whites had set themselves against black businesses from the inception. We now know, for example, that the black entrepreneur William Maughan, in setting up this pharmacy, borrowed $5,000 from his former white employer, Noel Roach. Along with some savings he had amassed, he opened a pharmacy on the Pier Head in Bridgetown, providing a service to the many stevedores and waterfront men who worked in the busy Carlisle Bay up until 1961. Unfortunately, when the Deep Water Harbour opened in 1961, much of his business dwindled, but his establishment was wound up mainly because of the lack of succession.

There is also evidence of deeper partnerships with white businessmen in the 1950s. Archibald Rollock, who established a large department store known as the Five and Ten Model Store on Broad Street in November 1959, got a start in 1937 when he agreed to a partnership with the Jewish merchant, Kriendler. Operating first from a small Swan Street shop, the arrangement was for Kriendler to supply the building and stock, while Rollock managed the business. This was the start he needed to establish himself. The businesses quickly expanded and Rollock was secure enough in his own operation. By 1959, Rollock had acquired his three-storey building on Bridgetown's main business street, Broad Street.[9]

The black-white association reached another level when white-owned companies sold out to outstanding black employees. The case of a commission agency, C.L. Pitt and Co., selling out to its black employee Lionel Richards deserves special mention. The Englishman Pitt arrived in Barbados after World War II and immediately established a commission agency. Richards, who started his career in the commission business of John D. Taylor, moved over to C.L. Pitt and Co., first as an office assistant and then as a sales representative. From there he moved to company secretary and in 1954 was made a director of the company. C.L. Pitt retired in 1959, and Richards bought the company from his employer. On Richards' retirement in the 1980s, C.L. Pitt and Co. was taken over by another black Barbadian, Berkley Blades.[10] While partnerships with whites did launch some blacks into business, securing capital, stock, property and advice, some black businessmen did not always find this strategy a smooth option, leading to conflict and eventual closure or take over. This has led to the charge that whites conspired to dash the dreams of black businessmen by placing pressure on their enterprises the moment they became too large or influential. Nevertheless, white support for black businesses indicates that the prevailing race/class structure of the age still allowed for business linkages.

Some blacks, however, well aware of the complications of white partnerships, used capital from their families or other black entrepreneurs to establish themselves. One of the leading provision merchants between 1930 and 1955,

James A. Tudor, started his one-door shop in 1912 with $50 and borrowed another $100 from his mother-in law. By 1952, in addition to his main property on Roebuck Street, in Bridgetown, he had established approximately thirty-five shops throughout Barbados. He also started a soft drink and a soap factory in 1929. Tudor, however, as a provision merchant, was always at the mercy of the large commission merchants who advanced goods to him on credit. When the merchants demanded sums in outstanding credit, Tudor had no choice but to sell some of his properties to save himself from financial embarrassment.[11]

Before his "empire" closed, however, he was able to launch other blacks into the retail business by placing them in managerial positions within the local village shops. The supermarket owner Norman Howard, who currently owns a large supermarket in Bush Hall, St Michael, owes his rise to this relationship with Tudor. Tudor also laid the foundation for another shop owner, Devere Jordan, giving him the responsibility of marketing one of his rums "King James Rum". Later, Jordan acquired his own retail shop on Martindale's Road, St Michael.[12]

Perhaps the largest black collaborative effort before independence was the establishment of the Barbados Cooperative Bank Ltd in 1938. Managed by Frederick MacDonald Symmonds, this bank was started with a capital of BWI$240,000 and by 1960, had pulled in 22,851 depositors, with total deposits of £84,166.36. In 1946, its main shareholders were black businessmen who had made a name for themselves in the provision business. One of the directors, also black, was a planter from Harrow estate, David Stonewall Payne, who had invested over BWI $50,000 in the bank. Although the bank collapsed in 1962 as the Paynes withdrew their capital, these types of partnerships indicate that blacks did try to form partnerships to strengthen their enterprises, especially in a hostile financial environment surrounded by about four international banks.[13] However, black mergers and partnerships were more the exception than the rule. Probably, had it been done more often more blacks would have been able to sustain their enterprises in the long run.

The rise of blacks in business was not solely as a result of capital earned in Barbados. Blacks, for a long time, had complained of difficulty accessing capital from the local banks for business development. Some of them relied on money earned in other locations to finance their Barbadian business ventures. Bonham Richardson has pioneered research into Barbadian/Panama migration between 1904 and 1914, arguing that this migration resulted in the injection of large sums of money into the Barbadian economy. He notes that some Barbadians bought land and established shops with what he calls "Panama money".[14] But the full impact of this "Panama money" was felt in 1941 when an organization known as the Barbados Progressive Society in Colón, Panama, bought five sugar estates for £52,000 with a total land area of 1,475 acres. These estates (Colleton, Trents, Lascelles, Mount Prospect and Four Hills), located in the north of the island, were placed under the management of black Barbadians, but internal conflict and lack of working capital led to their demise in 1952.[15] However, this was a prime case of capital earned by Barbadians overseas being used to finance the purchase of plantations, an area of economic activity dominated by whites.

Even before this, the Grenadian-born James A. Martineau's entry into the soft-drink industry in Barbados was partly financed by his earnings made in countries such as Venezuela, Panama, Cuba and Brazil. Another Grenadian, N.E. Wilson, worked at T.E. Noble and Smith in Grenada and Carriacou before he came to Barbados at the age of nineteen. He used savings earned in Grenada to rent a building at 31 Swan Street and purchase his stock. This evidence of blacks using capital accumulated from their migration experience explains why black businesses continued to emerge in a climate where finance was difficult to obtain from the commercial banks.

However, Wilson's success for over fifty years raises another factor which must be brought into the equation in the examination of the rise of black businesses. It is that blacks showed courage to leave secure jobs to establish their own enterprises. In addition, they exhibited good managerial skills to take their enterprises to positions of strength and respectability.

In Wilson's case, he met several obstacles in obtaining stock for his store and had to meet with the manufacturers' representatives by night for fear of being seen by local whites. More important, Wilson decided to go in person to Europe and the Far East to source his stock, thereby bypassing the local commission merchants altogether. This worked admirably, and by 1965, he was in a position to construct a three-storey building with 14,000 square feet of space, making his enterprise a fully fledged department store comparable with any on Broad Street.

Archibald Rollock's experience was also similar. He left a secure job at the Barbados Foundry after a white supervisor kept stepping on his feet with heavy boots in what he felt was a deliberate act of provocation. Rollock left his job, established a partnership with a Jewish merchant and, like Wilson, travelled to the Far East and Germany to acquire stock for the store. Not only was he able to undersell his competitors, but he was the first businessman in Barbados to introduce the escalator and use rotated displays in his show window.[16]

This courage to leave the employ of another and create employment for others, was seen again in 1961 when Everson Elcock left a steady job at Manning and Co. in 1962. As a senior electrician whose upward movement in the company seemed stunted, he decided to set up his own electrical contracting firm, Everson R. Elcock and Co. The company acquired several government and private contracts for schools and office buildings, and it is now one of the leading contracting firms in Barbados.[17]

These individuals started out as workers in white-owned businesses, and they were clearly not prepared to retain the status of "worker" throughout their careers. They were not daunted by the presence of well-established whites operating in areas they hoped to venture into. In displaying such courage, they became path-breakers to many others who established their own enterprises and, in so doing, added vitality to the country's economy.

A discussion on the rise of black businessmen in Barbados, however, naturally invites one of the most contentious questions in West Indian business history: Why did most of these enterprises fail to enter the second generation? A full discussion on this issue would require another chapter, but suffice it to say, four main reasons have been identified. First, some black entrepreneurs, such as Rollock, Tudor and Wilson, were excellent managers of their businesses but they failed to establish a second or even a third tier of management responsibility to offer advice and managerial support, especially in the event of sickness or death of the founder/manager.[18] Second, even if they had not restructured their enterprises, they might have survived had enough attention been given to succession planning. In many of the black businesses (with the notable exception being Tudor's Funeral Home), the succession plan came too late or did not come at all, so that the businesses died with their founder. Third, research has also shown, in the case of Martineau and the Guilers, that their products needed to be repackaged to meet the changing tastes of Barbadians. Born Bay Rum produced by the Guilers in the 1940s fell to stiff competition offered by products such as Limacol and Alcolad Glacial, while Martineau's drinks could have been enhanced by more sophisticated production machinery and transport services.[19] Fourth, lack of attention to product offerings was compounded by the fact that the Barbadian business environment was extremely competitive. Some white-owned companies, which had been established towards the end of the nineteenth century and in the early twentieth century, had first-mover advantage on the business landscape and were therefore in a position to challenge emerging black businesses. Where such companies controlled stock or credit offered to black enterprises, they always held the upper hand. It is not surprising, therefore, that provision merchants and dry good retailers experienced difficulty coping with the competition. Only those black entrepreneurs (Wilson and Rollock) who had loosened their dependence on the commission merchants could exist with some degree of independence.

Conclusion

It is interesting that in the 1920s and 1930s, when conditions of extreme poverty pervaded the society and white-owned businesses held centrestage, black entrepreneurs, using capital from various sources, launched themselves into substantial business enterprises. Exploiting a range of opportunities offered in the slowly expanding economy, black business persons effectively created avenues of social mobility for their families and business associates. Like the white-owned businesses, their businesses also employed persons and supported families and, in some cases, led to the availability of cheaper products for customers. Where these businessmen established light manufacturing operations, they reduced the country's dependence on foreign goods.

The black contribution to the development of Barbados must now be understood, not only as labourers but as intelligent organizers of capital and labour to produce a range of products and services. As such, therefore, the active participation of black entrepreneurs helped to shape the Barbadian business environment, setting the tone and laying the foundation for many others to follow in the post-independence era.

Notes

1. Hawkers are small traders who display ground provisions for sale, while hucksters sell cakes, nuts and confectionery.
2. See W.A. Beckles, comp., *The Barbados Disturbances (1937): Review – Reproduction of the Evidence and Report of the Commission* (Bridgetown: Advocate Co., 1937).
3. Ronald Hughes, *A History of the Barbados Shipping and Trading Co. Ltd, 1920–1995* (Bridgetown: Barbados Shipping and Trading Co., n.d.).
4. Christine Barrow and J.E. Greene, *Small Business in Barbados: A Case of Survival* (Cave Hill: Institute of Social and Economic Research, University of the West Indies, 1979), 16–39.
5. Hilary Beckles, *Corporate Power in Barbados, Economic Injustice in a Political Democracy* (Bridgetown: Lighthouse Communications, 1989).
6. Henderson Carter, *Business in Bim: A Business History of Barbados, 1900–2000* (Kingston: Ian Randle, 2008) 55.
7. Ibid.
8. See the comments of Ronald Tree, *A History of Barbados* (London: Rupert Hart Davis, 1973) 1–8.
9. Interview with John Rollock, son of Archibald Rollock, 2007.
10. Carter, *Business*, 143.
11. Charles Harding, "James A. Tudor: Coming in from the Cotton Fields", *Nation*, 1 June 1982, 10.
12. Carter, *Business*, 76.
13. See story in the *Advocate*, 30 January 1962.
14. Bonham Richardson, *Panama Money in Barbados, 1900–1920* (Knoxville: University of Tennessee Press, 1985), 206. The organization, made up by Barbadians who ventured to Panama and stayed, dedicated itself to raising funds in Panama. See Carter, *Business*, 64–65.
15. Interview with John Rollock, 2007.
16. Interview with Everson R. Elcock, 2007.
17. Interview with John Rollock, 2007.
18. Charles Harding, "Where Some May Have Gone Wrong", *Advocate*, 28 October 2001, 16.
19. Ibid.

Suggested Further Readings

For recent comprehensive surveys of the field of business history generally, see *The Oxford Handbook of Business History*, edited by Geoffrey Jones and Jonathan Zeitlin (Oxford: Oxford University Press, 2008). Readers interested in the ways in which the business history of the West Indies fits with the larger economies of the British Empire and the Atlantic World may consult John J. McCusker and Russell R. Menard, *The Economy of British America, 1607–1789* (Chapel Hill: University of North Carolina Press, 1985); Kenneth Morgan, *Slavery, Atlantic Trade and the British Economy, 1660–1800* (Cambridge: Cambridge University Press, 2000), for the period to the end of the eighteenth century. There is also Trevor Burnard's, "'The Grand Mart of the Island': The Economic Function of Kingston in the Mid Eighteenth Century", in *Jamaica in Slavery and Freedom: History, Heritage and Culture*, edited by Kathleen E.A. Monteith and Glen Richards, 225–41 (Kingston: University of the West Indies Press, 2002). A more recent study is David Beck Ryden's, *West Indian Slavery and British Abolition, 1783–1807* (Cambridge: Cambridge University Press, 2009).

Large-scale economic models of West Indian business history are discussed in Lloyd Best, "Outlines of a Model of Pure Plantation Economy", *Social and Economic Studies* 17 (1968): 283–326; and George L. Beckford, *Persistent Poverty: Underdevelopment in Plantation Economies of the Third World* (New York: Oxford University Press, 1972).

A great deal has been written on the organization of plantations during slavery. General works include Richard B. Sheridan, *Sugar and Slavery: An Economic History of the British West Indies, 1623–1775* (Barbados: Caribbean Universities Press, 1974); J.R. Ward, *British West Indian Slavery, 1750–1834: The Process of Amelioration* (Oxford: Clarendon Press, 1988). Older texts that still have some value are Frank Wesley Pitman, *The Development of the British West Indies 1700–1763* (New Haven: Yale University Press, 1917); Lowell Joseph Ragatz, *The Fall of the Planter Class in the British Caribbean, 1763–1833* (New York: American Historical Association, 1928); and Eric Williams, *Capitalism and Slavery* (Chapel Hill: University of North Carolina, 1944). A recent assessment of the role of West Indian slavery in the development of metropolitan mercantile wealth is N. Draper, "The City of London and Slavery: Evidence from the First Dock Companies, 1795–1800", *Economic History Review* 61 (2008): 432–66.

For the history of particular sugar plantations, see Michael Craton and James Walvin, *A Jamaican Plantation: The History of Worthy Park 1670–1970* (London: W.H. Allen, 1970); B.W. Higman, *Plantation Jamaica: Capital and Control in a Colonial Economy, 1750–1850* (Kingston: University of the West Indies Press, 2005).

Livestock production is discussed in Verene A. Shepherd, "Livestock and Sugar: Aspects of Jamaica's Agricultural Development from the Late Seventeenth to the Early Nineteenth Century", *Historical Journal* 34 (1991): 627–42; and her recent book *Livestock, Sugar and Slavery: Contested Terrain in Colonial Jamaica* (Kingston: Ian Randle, 2009). There is also Philip D. Morgan's, "Slaves and Livestock in Eighteenth-Century Jamaica: Vineyard Pen, 1750–1751", *William and Mary Quarterly* 52 (1992): 47–76. Coffee is covered in S.D. Smith, "Sugar's Poor Relation: Coffee Planting in the British West Indies, 1720–1833", *Slavery and Abolition* 19 (1988): 68–89; and Kathleen E.A. Monteith, "Planting and Processing Techniques on Jamaican Coffee Plantations during Slavery", in *Working Slavery, Pricing Freedom: Perspectives from the Caribbean, Africa and the Diaspora*, edited by Verene A. Shepherd, 112–29 (Kingston: Ian Randle Publishers, 2002), and "Labour Regimen on Jamaican Coffee Plantations During Slavery", in *Jamaica in Slavery and Freedom*, 259–73. Some of these economic activities were the province of free coloured people during slavery, as described in Carl Campbell, "The Rise of a Free Coloured Plantocracy in Trinidad 1783–1813", *Boletín de Estudios Latinoamericanos y del Caribe* 29 (1980): 33–53.

The management of land resources on a range of enterprises is considered in B.W. Higman, *Jamaica Surveyed: Plantation Maps and Plans of the Eighteenth and Nineteenth Centuries* (Kingston: Institute of Jamaica Publications, 1988). Higman discusses trade between units in "Patterns of Exchange within a Plantation Economy: Jamaica at the Time of Emancipation", in *West Indies Accounts*, edited by Roderick A. McDonald, 211–31 (Kingston: The Press, University of the West Indies, 1996). Early works on internal marketing include John H. Parry, "Plantation and Provision Ground: An Historical Sketch of the Introduction of Food Crops into Jamaica", *Revista de Historia de America* 39 (1955): 1–20; Sidney W. Mintz and Douglas G. Hall, *The Origins of the Jamaican Internal Marketing System* (New Haven: Yale University Publications in Anthropology 57, 1960), 3–26. There is also Lorna Elaine Simmonds', "The Afro-Jamaican and the Internal Marketing System: Kingston, 1780–1834", in *Jamaica in Slavery and Freedom*, 274–90.

Another popular topic in West Indian business history is the efficiency of plantation management during slavery. Recent examples of this approach include Selwyn H.H. Carrington, "Management of Sugar Estates in the British West Indies at the End of the Eighteenth Century", *Journal of Caribbean History* 33 (1999): 27–53; and Heather Cateau, "Conservatism and Change Implementation in the British West Indian Sugar Industry 1750–1810", *Journal of Caribbean History* 29 (1995): 1–36. Older studies that remain useful include R. Keith Aufhauser, "Slavery and Scientific Management", *Journal of Economic History* 33 (1973): 811–24; W.A. Green, "The Planter Class and British West Indian Sugar Production, before and after Emancipation", *Economic History Review* 26 (1973): 448–63; Douglas Hall, "Slaves and Slavery in the British West Indies", *Social and Economic Studies* 11 (1962): 305–18. Within this theme, the question of absenteeism has worried many students: Douglas Hall, "Absentee-Proprietorship in the British West Indies, to about 1850", *Jamaican Historical Review* 4 (1964): 15–35; Christopher J. Cowton and Andrew J. O'Shaughnessy, "Absentee Control of Sugar Plantations in the British West Indies", *Accounting and Business Research* 22 (1991): 33–45.

Studies of individual managers during slavery shed light on general patterns. Richard B. Sheridan published "Samuel Martin, Innovating Sugar Planter of Antigua 1750–1776", *Agricultural History* 24 (1960): 126–39; and "Simon Taylor, Sugar Tycoon of Jamaica, 1740–1813", *Agricultural History* 45 (1971): 285–96. Taylor's letters are available in *The Letters of Simon Taylor of Jamaica to Chaloner Arcedekne, 1765–1775* (London: Cambridge University Press, for the Royal Historical Society, Camden Miscellany, vol. 35, 2002), edited by Betty Wood. See also Mark Quintanilla, "The World of Alexander Campbell: An Eighteenth-Century Grenadian Planter", *Albion* 35 (2003): 229–56; and Alan Karras, "The World of Alexander Johnston: The Creolization of Ambition, 1762–1787", *Historical Journal* 30 (1987): 53–76.

The extent of the wealth accumulated by slaveowners in the West Indies has been a matter of some debate. Sheridan's estimate in "The Wealth of Jamaica in the Eighteenth Century", *Economic History Review* 18 (1965): 292–311, was criticized by Robert Paul Thomas, "The Sugar Colonies of the Old Empire: Profit or Loss for Great Britain?" *Economic History Review* 21 (1968): 30–45. More recent contributions include J.R. Ward, "The Profitability of Sugar Planting in the British West Indies, 1650–1834", *Economic History Review* 31 (1978): 197–213, his *British West Indian Slavery, 1750–1834: The Process of Amelioration* (Oxford: Clarendon Press, 1988), and T.G. Burnard, "'Prodigious Riches': The Wealth of Jamaica before the American Revolution", *Economic History Review* 54 (2001): 506–24.

The metropolitan merchant class during slavery came under close scrutiny from Richard Pares in his pioneering essay on the Lascelles family, "A London West-India Merchant House, 1740–1769", in *Essays Presented to Sir Lewis Namier*, edited by Richard Pares and A.J.P. Taylor, 75–107 (London: Macmillan, 1956); and gave it greater scope in *Merchants and Planters* (Economic History Review Supplement no. 4, 1960). Work on the Lascelles is expanded substantially by S.D. Smith in his article, "*Merchants and Planters* Revisited", *Economic History Review* 55 (2002): 434–65; and his book, *Slavery, Family and Gentry Capitalism in the British Atlantic: The World of the Lascelles, 1648–1834* (Cambridge: Cambridge University Press, 2006). See also David Thoms, "The Mills Family: London Sugar Merchants in the Eighteenth Century", *Business History* 11 (1969): 3–10. The role of slave traders is emphasized in David W. Galenson, *Traders, Planters, and Slaves: Market Behavior in*

Early English America (Cambridge: Cambridge University Press, 1986); and Trevor Burnard and Kenneth Morgan, "The Dynamics of the Slave Market and Slave Purchasing Patterns in Jamaica, 1655–1788", *William and Mary Quarterly* 58 (2001): 205–28. Local merchant business activity during the period of slavery is the focus of Stephen Alexander Fortune's *Merchants and Jews: The Struggle for British West Indian Commerce, 1650–1750* (Gainesville: University of Florida Press, 1984), and Glen O. Phillips' "The Stirrings of the Mercantile Community in the British West Indies after Emancipation", *Journal of Caribbean History* 23 (1989): 62–95, focuses on its expansion in the period immediately following the abolition of slavery.

The use of capital derived from Compensation is the subject of work by Kathleen Mary Butler, *The Economics of Emancipation: Jamaica and Barbados, 1823–1843* (Chapel Hill: University of North Carolina Press, 1995), and Nicholas Draper, *The Price of Emancipation: Slave-Ownership, Compensation and British Society at the End of Slavery* (Cambridge: Cambridge: Cambridge University Press, 2010).

Alternative modes of managing sugar enterprises adopted in the twentieth century are discussed in Carl Stone, "The Sugar Co-operatives in Jamaica: 1974–80", in *Plantation Economy, Land Reform and the Peasantry in a Historical Perspective: Jamaica 1838–1980* edited by Claus Stolberg and Swithin Wilmot, 85–104 (Kingston: Friedrich Ebert Stiftung, 1992); Clem Seecharan, *Sweetening Bitter Sugar: Jock Campbell, the Booker Reformer in British Guiana, 1934–1966* (Kingston: Ian Randle, 2005); and Philippe Chalmin, *The Making of a Sugar Giant: Tate and Lyle 1859–1989* (Chur, Switzerland: Harwood Academic, 1990).

Money and banking has had a good deal of attention. Deryck R. Brown has written a *History of Money and Banking in Trinidad and Tobago from 1789 to 1989* (Port of Spain: Paria, 1989), commissioned by the Central Bank of Trinidad and Tobago; and "The Response of the Banking Sector to the General Crisis: Trinidad, 1838–56", *Journal of Caribbean History* 24 (1990): 28–64. Kathleen E.A. Monteith has published "Competitive Advantages through Colonialism: Barclays Bank (DCO) and the West Indian Sugar Depression, 1926–1939", *Journal of Caribbean History* 31 (1997): 119–48; "Local Pressure vs Metropolitan Policy: The Clash over Banking Policy in the West Indies, 1939–1943", in *Before and After 1865: Education, Politics and Regionalism in the Caribbean*, edited by Brian Moore and Swithin Wilmot, 226–35 (Kingston: Ian Randle Publishers, 1998); "Competition between Barclays Bank (DCO) and the Canadian Banks in the West Indies, 1926–45", *Financial History Review* 7 (2000): 67–87; "Regulation of the Commercial Banking Sector in the British West Indies, 1837–1961", *Journal of Caribbean History* 37 (2003): 204–32; and her book *Depression to Decolonization: Barclays Bank (DCO) in the West Indies, 1926–1962* (Kingston: University of the West Indies Press, 2008).

The important topics of financial accounting and insurance have been relatively neglected, but Marcia Annisette has published "Importing Accounting: The Case of Trinidad and Tobago", *Accounting, Business and Financial History* 9 (1999): 103–33; and there is Cecilia Karch and Henderson Carter, *The Rise of the Phoenix: The Barbados Mutual Life*

Assurance Society in the Caribbean Economy and Society, 1840–1990 (Kingston: Ian Randle, 1997).

Small business in its modern forms is taken up by Howard Johnson, "The Chinese in Trinidad in the Late Nineteenth Century", *Ethnic and Racial Studies* 10 (1987): 82–95; and Gina A. Ulysse, *Down Town Ladies: Informal Commercial Importers, A Haitian Anthropologist, and Self-Making in Jamaica* (Chicago: University of Chicago Press, 2007). Large-scale wholesaling and manufacturing is studied, for example, in Douglas Hall, *Grace, Kennedy and Company Limited: A Story of Jamaican Enterprise* (Kingston: Grace, Kennedy, 1992), and Cecilia Karch, *Corporate Culture in the Caribbean: A History of Goddard Enterprises Ltd* (Barbados: Cole's Printery, 2008). Henderson Carter's recent *Business in Bim: A Business History of Barbados 1900–2000* (Kingston: Ian Randle Publishers, 2008), a privately commissioned work, offers a general treatment of the development of the business outside of the agricultural sector in twentieth-century Barbados.

Index

Absenteeism, 25, 44, 47, 49, 52, 59, 90, 103, 113, 227

Accountability, 70, 152

Accounting: and auditing, 138, 158; and banks, 128–39, 144; capital, 56, 64, 70, 105–6; of commission agents, 46–47, 50; financial, 228; of planters, 59–72, 102; of privateers, 18–19, 21; of shopkeepers, 208

Advances; by banks, 107, 119, 126–29, 134–38, 141, 144, 163, 168; by merchants, 59, 61–62, 106, 113–14, 170, 220; by shopkeepers, 93

Agricultural credit societies, 87, 141, 170–71

Agriculture: and banks, 141, 144, 168; and Chinese, 195–96; and land use, 163; and marketing, 163; and merchants, 131–32; plantation, 127; and race, 143; small-scale, 171, 173, 180, 199; techniques of, 69, 114; and women, 73–74, 83, 88, 95

Alleyne, Frank, 166

Antigua, 4, 42–53, 68, 102–3, 105, 112, 127, 152

Apprenticeship, 102–3

Ardener, Shirley, 152

Bananas, 87, 117, 119, 137

Bankruptcy, 112–13, 207–8

Banks: 1, 4–5, 228; and agriculture, 87, 125–45, 168; British, 125–45; commercial, 151–54, 157, 163, 167, 220–21; cooperative, 141–42, 160–62, 220; deposits in, 46, 107, 158–67, 220; local, 106–8, 114, 118–20, 220; and merchants, 46, 49; peasant, 170–71; savings, 88, 158–63, 167, 172

Barbados, 32, 42, 68, 104–5, 110–19, 124, 127, 131–33, 136–40, 144, 151–90, 214–23, 229

Bargaining, 86, 195

Barrow, Christine, 153, 216

Beckles, Hilary, 216

Benevolent associations, 152, 208

Best, Lloyd, 5, 225

Bills: documentary, 133–34; credit, 133–34; of exchange, 46, 49–52, 59, 106, 126, 133–34

Biography, 3–4, 184, 191

British companies, 127, 131, 136

British Guiana, 4, 104, 107–20, 127, 130, 136, 141, 182, 205

Buccaneers, 19, 23, 25–26, 35

Building societies, 128, 162

Bullion, 12, 20, 23–24, 28, 49

Business: big, 1, 6; case studies of, 4, 52; defined, 2; enterprise, 2–3, 5–6, 64, 143, 193, 223; groups, 130; history, 1–7, 22, 225–56; schools, 1; small, 3, 145, 181, 216, 229; studies, 2–3; as a system, 3, 5

Calculability, 56, 64–65, 69
Canada, 140, 142, 167

Capital: accounting, 56, 64, 70; accumulation, 44, 153–54, 181, 204–5, 209, 221; and banks, 5, 170, 220; British, 130; colonial, 22, 44, 158, 220; equipment, 66; finance, 104, 120; investment, 22, 66, 101, 104–8, 110–11, 113–14, 117, 119–20; markets, 130; of merchants, 46, 121, 137; and privateering, 6, 12–15, 22; risk, 69, 105; share, 130, 161, 164–66; shortage, 105, 143, 181, 204, 209; sources of, 6, 103–8, 118, 120, 130, 204, 214, 219, 221, 223; stock, 111; and sugar, 3, 55, 130, 132; working, 114, 140–42, 221

Capitalism, 1, 6–7, 56, 64, 70, 118, 154

Carnegie, James, 193

Cash, 20–21, 84, 86, 93, 154, 156, 164

Chandler, Alfred, 5

Children, 46, 75–80, 84, 86, 91, 96, 185, 215

Chinese, 93, 95, 143–44, 193–210

Churches, 154, 165–66, 172, 183

Class: 4, 189, 205, 217; and gender, 91–95; middle, 144–45, 154–55, 161, 166–67, 170; and race, 94–95, 143, 198, 219; working, 151, 154, 158, 160, 163, 172, 197

Cocoa, 18, 20, 22, 73–96, 111, 117, 119, 131, 135, 182–83

Coin, 49, 68, 206–7

Commission agents, 43, 46, 48–51, 59, 64, 130–31, 137, 215, 219–23

Companies, 1–5, 25, 44–45, 47, 52, 60–63, 67, 110, 112, 117, 137–38, 158, 219, 222–23; British, 127, 130, 136; funeral, 217; insurance, 5, 154; joint stock, 2, 111; limited liability, 132; manufacturing, 4, 111, 136, 218; merchant, 117, 120, 126, 129, 131; multinational, 121, 130; non-resident, 112–13, 121; oil, 87, 144; public, 4, 114; trading, 136; transport, 214, 216–27; vertically integrated, 121

Compensation, 66, 106, 228

Competition, 67, 129, 137, 144, 171, 196, 200, 204, 207–9, 222–23

Consignee merchants, 43, 46–52, 59–60, 106, 108, 113, 118, 120, 129, 140, 171

Consumers, 2, 66, 196–205

Consumption, 20, 32, 46, 49, 64, 66, 78, 85

Contraband, 22, 25, 27–28

Cooperative agricultural societies, 87, 169–70

Cooperative banks, 88, 128, 140–42, 160–62, 220

Cooperative credit unions, 163–67

Correspondence, 29, 44, 46–52

Costs of production, 55, 61, 64, 69, 87, 102–5, 110, 112–17, 120

Courts, 15, 17–19, 21, 25, 30, 34, 112–13, 140, 163, 180, 208

Craton, Michael, 4, 226

Credit: 64, 93, 153, 207; bank, 5, 107, 114, 118, 126, 133–36, 139, 144–45, 159, 161–63; consignee, 108, 113–14, 118, 220, 223; government, 114, 119–20, 170–71; and overdrafts, 136; in privateering, 15, 20, 23; and risk, 49, 111, 142; rotating, 152; savings, 152–53, 158; shortage, 117, 129, 172, 181; societies, 87, 141, 152–53, 170; sources of, 5, 20, 59, 101, 106, 113, 118, 121, 204; trade, 46, 86, 106, 181, 206, 215; unions, 163–67

Creditworthiness, 106, 113, 125, 130, 140, 142–45

Cuba, 15, 20, 23–24, 28, 106, 109, 192, 221

Currencies, 58–59, 68–69, 126, 173

Customers, 127, 130–31, 134, 137–39, 144, 181–82, 200, 206, 210, 223

Customs duties, 29, 42, 46, 62, 66, 115

Davis, Ralph, 15

Debt, 20, 45, 48–52, 55–56, 60–61, 64, 67, 84–87, 92, 106–8, 112, 129, 139–42, 182, 188, 206, 208

Depressions, 56, 131, 142, 167–68

Directorships, 107, 216–20

Discounting, 107, 133–34

Discrimination, 125, 143–44, 180, 205, 208

Diversification, 24, 119, 151, 163, 169, 217

Dominica, 117

Dry goods, 202, 223

Earle, Peter, 17–18

East Indians. *See* Indians

Education, 46, 76–78, 84, 95, 161, 165, 185–86, 189, 198, 206, 222
Edwards, Golwyn, 166
Efficiency, 65, 121, 132, 196, 226
Emancipation, 66, 69, 71, 74–75, 88, 101–6, 154, 169, 172, 196–99, 228
Embezzlement, 21
Emigration, 154, 168, 172, 220–21
Encumbered estates, 55–56, 59, 64, 68–69, 90, 112–13, 120, 140
Entrepreneurs, 1–5, 52, 158, 161, 171, 194, 204, 214–19, 222–23
Ethnicity, 6, 92, 125, 142–45, 199, 201–3

Factories, 94, 103–5, 111–20, 132, 135, 137, 171, 220
Factors, sugar, 42–53
Failure, 3–4, 6, 45, 48, 56, 94–95, 129, 139, 142, 163, 166, 196, 198, 200, 218, 222
Families, 3–6, 42–53, 65–68, 75–76, 82–90, 96, 113, 121, 181, 189, 196–97, 204–5, 209, 216, 219, 223
Finance: 5, 42, 84, 105, 126, 128–29, 136, 140, 151–53; capital, 104, 113, 117, 120; and colonization, 11–12; corporate, 69, 119; cost of, 118, 171; and gender, 92; and London, 51; sources of, 61, 105–7, 114, 118–19, 126, 131, 141–42, 153–54, 163, 172, 220–21; trade, 126, 129, 145
Fishing, 12, 23, 182–83
Food: crops, 83–84, 87–88, 171, 197; and gender, 73, 76; preparation, 78–79; prices, 84–86; of privateers, 16, 20; supplies, 76, 86; trade, 59–60, 136, 181, 199–200
Fraternalism, 158, 165–66
Free coloured and black people, 179–89, 192, 198, 226
Friendly societies, 88, 151, 154–66, 172
Funerals, 158, 183, 188, 217, 222

Government: banks, 88, 118, 158, 160, 165, 170; bonds, 135, 141; British, 115, 141, 168–70, 205; and business, 6, 216–17; colonial, 114, 119–20, 142, 163, 165, 170, 172, 215, 218; credit, 114; as employer, 61, 165–66; 222; instability of, 68–69; and regulation, 2, 6, 27, 108–9; securities, 107; taxes, 59, 108;
Geertz, Clifford, 153
Gender, 74–75, 79–84, 88, 95–96
Greene, J.E., 216
Grenada, 44–46, 56–64, 68, 103–5, 117, 131, 221
Grocery retail trade, 5, 49, 161, 193–210
Ground provisions, 76, 84, 96, 197, 204
Guyana. See British Guiana

Hawkers, 171, 180, 214, 224
Health, 76–77, 84, 154, 155, 158
Higglers, 2, 180
Housing, 75–76, 82, 158, 161–63, 172–73
Hucksters, 94, 184, 197, 214, 224

Immigrant communities, 74, 76, 79, 82, 88, 194–201, 204–5
Immigration, 82, 110, 168, 194–95, 202, 205, 208–9
Imports, 66, 71, 111, 132–33
Incalculability, 67–69
Indentureship, 2, 20, 46, 49, 75–82, 88, 91, 110, 114, 119–20, 198–99, 209–10
Indians, 88, 92, 94–95, 143, 199, 201
Inheritance, 43, 56, 62–64, 89–92, 184–85, 188
Insurance, 5, 50, 69, 82, 134, 137, 154–57, 160, 172, 228
Interest: 21, 55, 61, 154, 160; bank, 107, 141–42, 158–59, 160, 162, 167; charged by merchants, 50–51, 59, 61, 118; charged by moneylenders, 141; compound, 87; on debts, 64, 87; on loans, 87, 107, 118, 142, 161; on mortgages, 55; rates, 46, 50, 87, 118, 141, 153, 158–59, 161–62, 167
Interlocking directorships, 216
Investment: 110, 118, 129; absentee, 25; accounting, 69; in agriculture, 22, 70, 83, 101, 110–11, 116; and banks, 107, 114, 118, 141, 163, 167, 220; capital, 66, 101, 104–8, 110–11, 113–14, 117, 119–21; in credit unions, 165, 167; foreign direct, 130; in

friendly societies, 157, 161–63; groups, 130; by merchants, 46, 106, 118; portfolios, 162–63; in privateering, 13, 22, 32; in public funds, 46; in retail trade, 200; scale of, 13, 32, 64, 83, 110, 116; and slavery, 66, 106

Jamaica, 11–32, 42, 48, 68, 70, 104–5, 107–8, 113, 117, 130–39, 142, 152, 165, 169, 193–210
Jews, 143, 200, 219, 221
Johnson, Howard, 193, 207, 229
Jones, Geoffrey, 125

Kinship, 6, 194, 204–5, 216

Labour: 3, 65–66; agricultural, 75–80, 82–86, 92, 152–53, 195, 209, 215; child, 215; cost, 66, 102–3, 105, 110, 117, 120, 134; defined, 66; domestic, 88; efficiency, 110; female, 74–75, 77–80, 83–84, 95–96; free, 61, 65–66; history, 2; indentured, 75, 77, 88, 199; plantation, 88, 185; problem, 104–5; productivity, 66; regulation, 172; seasonal, 168; slave, 59–61, 65–67, 71, 108, 197; supply, 111, 119, 205; task work, 81; wage, 66, 74–75, 78, 80, 83–84, 88, 95, 180
Land: clearing, 20, 22, 27, 70, 84, 92, 95; Crown, 77, 83–84, 87–89, 91; grants, 88, 199; leased, 87, 92; ownership, 26, 83, 90, 112, 162, 171; purchase of, 49–51, 83–84, 88–90, 111–12, 136, 140, 154, 158, 162–63, 167, 221; rented, 59–60; sale of, 112, 117, 140; as security, 107, 114, 118, 170; tenure, 83–84, 171–72, 199, 215; use, 20, 22, 27, 70, 75, 84, 89, 92, 111, 117, 127, 163, 171–72, 215; and women, 88–90, 92, 185, 187–88
Law: accounting, 64, 94, 208; and arson, 208; bankruptcy, 112, 207; British, 66; and credit unions, 166; and debt, 112, 208; immigration, 82, 91, 209; labour, 79, 82, 91; Poor, 152; and privateering, 6, 27, 29; and slavery, 186; and theft, 93–94; trade, 93; and uncertainty, 64, 67; and women, 92

Lebanese, 143, 201
Letters, 24, 29, 47–48, 50–51, 53, 227
Liens, 67, 135, 137, 140, 171
Lind, Andrew, 193, 204, 210
Liquidations, 61, 66, 87, 112, 126, 132, 153
Liquidity, 163, 167
Loans: bank, 87, 107, 114, 120, 128–29, 131, 133, 136–44, 161, 163, 167–68, 170–71; credit union, 164–66; crop, 135, 137–39; friendly society, 160–61, 163, 172; housing, 158, 161–63, 172–73; long-term, 138; medium-term, 137–38, 145, 170; merchant, 46, 49–50, 61–62; mortgage, 52, 118; as overdrafts, 133, 136; personal, 114, 131; portfolios of, 138, 167, 171; repayment of, 139, 142, 144, 165; short-term, 138, 144, 170; sources of, 118–19, 141, 158; unsecured, 136–37; and women, 87

Machinery, 58, 66, 87, 104–5, 109–11, 113, 116–17, 120, 138, 222
Management: and absentees, 90, 103; by attorneys, 51; of banks, 135–43, 158–59, 220; hierarchies, 5, 220, 222; internal, 4; plantation, 42, 52, 56, 59, 63, 65, 90, 111–12, 130, 197, 221, 226; structures of, 5–6, 64–65; studies, 3–4; systems, 2, 6;
Manufacturing, 69, 92–94, 105, 114–15, 214, 217–18, 223, 229
Manumission, 179, 181, 185–89
Marketing: by agents, 65, 106; associations, 170; collective, 87; costs, 59, 62, 64–65, 69, 111, 134, 136, 144; of crops, 49, 51, 55, 63, 65, 74, 86–87, 92–93, 115, 163; firms, 4; internal, 3, 180–81, 197, 204, 226; regulation of, 65–67, 70, 102, 108–10, 113, 115, 129, 168–69
Marriage, 48–51, 91, 95, 183, 216
Marshall, Alfred, 11
Meeting-turns, 151–55, 161, 172
Mercantilism, 65, 67
Merchants: 59, 126; as bankers, 5, 49, 106, 114, 118; business houses of, 1, 59–60, 67, 112–13, 118, 129–30; colonial, 43, 45, 51, 59, 117, 131–32, 140, 161, 188–89, 215; commis-

sion, 63–64, 133, 215, 220–23; consignee, 106, 113, 118; metropolitan, 42, 44, 52, 55, 59, 106, 113, 120–21, 126, 129, 227; and planters, 3–4, 43–44, 52, 66–67, 106, 108, 127, 129, 183, 215–16; provision, 219–20, 223; retail, 126, 181, 197, 200, 215, 219; ships of, 17, 29, 46; as traders, 22, 28, 200, 215; wealth of, 52, 132; wholesale, 126, 181, 200, 215
Money: 20–21, 27, 84, 107, 126, 144, 188, 196; and banks, 159, 163, 228; borrowed, 50, 61, 87, 107, 114, 119, 182; compensation, 106; exchanges, 68; grants, 88; lenders, 141; market, 46; Panama, 154, 157, 220–21; and privateers, 21; public, 114
Monopoly, 13, 108, 112, 117–18, 151, 172, 194, 200–3, 209
Montserrat, 46, 117
Moore, Brian, 143
Mortgages, 46, 49–52, 55, 61, 118, 129, 134–35, 137, 141, 163, 170
Multinational corporations, 2, 121, 125–26, 130
Muscovado, 48, 63, 108–15

Nevis, 4, 46, 68
Non-bank financial intermediaries, 5, 151–52, 172

Oliver, Vere Langford, 43
Overdrafts, 133, 136, 139, 140–41

Panama, 15–16, 20–27, 154, 157, 172, 220–21
Pares, Richard, 4, 42, 227
Partnerships, 2, 43–45, 52, 132, 219–21
Peasantry, 145, 167–70, 197
Pharmacies, 214, 218
Piracy, 6, 11, 13, 16–17, 25–31
Plantation economy, 5, 12, 42, 172, 215, 225
Plantations: 5, 17, 168; banana, 137; cocoa, 74, 83; histories of 1, 4, 226; income from, 46, 106, 113, 117, 129; and privateers, 17, 20; management of, 42, 51–52, 102, 121, 225; mortgaged, 50; purchase of, 49–50, 112–13, 221; and slavery, 53, 185; sugar, 3–4, 45, 48, 75, 83, 127, 131, 137, 140, 153, 172, 179, 217, 221

Planters: absentee, 44; associations, 87; debts of, 49–50, 52, 105–6, 114, 119–20, 129, 182; families of, 43, 50; and merchants, 4, 42–50, 52, 66, 126–27, 172, 215–16; origins of, 27; and privateers, 21, 27–28, 31; wealth of, 53, 55, 67, 102, 114, 215
Police, 94, 165
Ports, 12, 20–23, 26, 50–51
Portuguese, 95, 205
Post offices, 88, 154, 158
Poverty, 78, 153–54, 183, 223
Prices: cocoa, 76, 82, 85–87, 92–93; fluctuation of, 69–70, 129; food, 84–86, 200; of imports, 182; indigo, 27; logwood, 20; of prize goods, 21; rum, 60; of ships, 15; stabilization of, 172, 215; sugar, 48, 51, 64–69, 102–3, 106–10, 115, 118–19, 129, 133, 135, 172, 215;
Privateering, 6, 11–32
Productivity, 66, 86, 106
Profitability, 2, 18, 25, 65, 68, 86, 109, 120, 140, 203–5
Profits: 2, 21, 64–65, 70, 92, 120, 181; in cocoa, 90–93; distribution of, 16, 18; marginal, 24; in privateering, 13, 16–17, 20, 24–25, 29, 32; in shipping, 17; in sugar, 55, 68–70, 90, 102, 110, 114–17, 130–31; in trade, 51, 203–5
Property rights, 11, 32, 74, 88, 188
Protectionism, 67, 70, 129
Provision grounds, 76, 79, 82, 197–98
Provisioning trades, 86, 131, 196, 200, 203–4, 215, 217, 219–20, 223
Purcell, Trevor, 154

Race, 92, 94, 143, 145, 155, 179, 189, 219
Rationality, 56, 64–65, 68, 106, 152–53
Regulation, 2, 7, 18, 59, 64–66, 82, 165
Remittances, 49, 51, 154, 168
Rent, 42, 59–60, 63, 75–76, 78, 158, 187, 221
Respectability, 91, 114, 153–54, 221
Retailers, 86, 94, 126–31, 137–39, 143–44, 161, 181, 193–210, 214, 217, 220, 223
Richardson, Bonham, 157, 220
Risk, 17–19, 23–24, 48–49, 69, 87, 105, 125, 135, 142, 152–53, 161, 163, 218

Rotating savings and credit associations, 88, 152–54

Salaries, 5, 17, 29, 59–60, 205
Savings, 83, 88, 106, 108, 111–16, 120, 144, 152–67, 172, 184, 204, 216–18, 221
Securities, 17, 27, 31, 46, 107, 114, 118–19, 126, 134–37, 139, 141, 171
Seecharan, Clem, 4
Shares, 134, 139, 142, 161, 163, 218
Sheridan, Richard, 4
Shipping, 17, 29, 42, 46, 49, 59, 69, 126, 129, 131, 139–40, 144, 216
Shops, 79, 84, 86, 181–85, 197, 200, 202–4, 209–10, 220–21
Shopkeepers, 86–87, 92–95, 161, 180–81, 184, 199, 201–6, 208
Slavery, 2, 4–6, 53, 65, 73, 76, 88, 102–3, 179–80, 185, 188–89, 196–97, 217, 225
Smallholders, 83–87, 90, 92–93, 127, 141, 169, 170–71
Speculation, 129, 171
Spirit licences, 199, 201–2
St Kitts, 42, 68, 103–5, 112, 116–17
St Lucia, 68, 112, 114, 119
Stoffle, Brent, 153
St Vincent, 46, 112, 117, 127
Success: assessment of, 6, 56; of black entrepreneurs, 184–85, 218, 221; business, 7, 180; of Chinese, 193–99, 205–9; in cocoa, 75, 94; of companies, 121; of free coloured people, 180–81, 184; of merchants, 132; of planters, 50, 105, 120; in privateering, 18, 20, 24; sources of, 4; and wealth, 4; of women, 184–85
Succession, 218–19, 222
Sugar: bakers, 47; beet, 101, 114–15; colonies, 32, 52, 59; duties, 108–9; exports, 24, 45, 48–49, 52, 127, 139; industry, 101–21, 167–72; merchants, 42–47, 50–52; mills, 48, 104–5, 110–11, 114, 137; plantations, 3–4, 22, 45, 48, 55–70, 75, 83, 126–40, 217, 221; prices, 47–48, 102, 108, 129, 215; refining, 49, 51, 109–10, 130; yields, 49
Supermarkets, 206, 220

Syrians, 143, 201, 204

Taxes, 59–60, 66, 84, 93, 109, 186–87, 199
Thoms, D.W., 42
Thrift, 20, 52, 153, 158, 165
Tourism, 217–18
Trade: contraband, 22, 25–28; credit, 46; dry goods, 143; export, 131–33, 139, 196; free, 101, 108, 115; financing, 126, 129, 131, 144–45; grocery, 5, 193–210; import, 132–33, 139, 196, 200; licences, 93, 199, 202, 208; monopolies, 13; orientation, 153, 194–96, 209; plantation, 42–45, 49, 129, 131, 136, 197, 215; privateering, 11–13, 16, 21–32; provisioning, 196, 200, 203–4; retail, 86, 94, 126–31, 137–39, 143–44, 161, 181, 193–210; routes, 12, 129; shuttle, 49; Spanish American, 12–13, 23–25, 28–29
Trade unions, 70, 166–67
Transport, 63, 86, 104, 111, 120, 214, 216–17, 222
Trinidad, 5, 73–96, 103–5, 110–12, 114, 117–20, 127, 130–31, 135–36, 141, 152, 161, 165, 173; and Tobago, 103, 127, 133, 161, 173

Uncertainty, 67, 69, 109, 135

Vertical integration, 121

Wages, 17, 62, 74, 78, 80–82, 84, 102, 168
Walvin, James, 4
War, 13, 24–25, 45–48, 51, 62–66, 69, 73, 81, 84, 102, 106, 139, 144, 217, 219
Warehousing, 46, 63
Wealth, 7, 12–13, 53, 143, 179, 187–89, 196, 227
Weber, Max, 56, 64–65, 67–70
Wholesalers, 126, 128–32, 137–38, 143–44, 161, 205
Wills, 43–44, 46, 60, 184, 189
Women, 5, 58, 73–96, 152, 180, 184–89, 197
Workers, 64, 70, 76–82, 110, 160, 165–68, 172, 215–16, 222

Yin, Lee Tom, 193, 210

www.ingramcontent.com/pod-product-compliance
Lightning Source LLC
Chambersburg PA
CBHW020647300426
44112CB00007B/271